From the celebrated Portrait of the Discoverer painted from Life by Bronzino — always preserved by the Vespucci Family and by them committed to C. Edwards Lester Esq U.S. Consul to Genoa.

THE

LIFE AND VOYAGES

OF

AMERICUS VESPUCIUS;

WITH

Illustrations concerning the Navigator,

AND

THE DISCOVERY OF THE NEW WORLD.

Agit grates, peregrinæque oscula terræ
Figit, et ignotos montes agrosque salutat.
OVID, Met. iii. v. 14.

BY C. EDWARDS LESTER,
U. S. CONSUL FOR SIX YEARS TO GENOA; AUTHOR OF "THE GLORY AND SHAME OF ENGLAND;" "MY CONSULSHIP," ETC.

ASSISTED BY

ANDREW FOSTER

FIFTH EDITION.

NEW HAVEN:
PUBLISHED BY HORACE MANSFIELD.

1854.

DEDICATION

TO THE

REV. T. WOODBRIDGE,

OF AUSTERLITZ, N. Y.

MY DEAR UNCLE,

I should long ago have inscribed to you some one of my books, if I had written one worthy of being dedicated to my earliest and latest Teacher, and my truest Friend. Long study and calm reflection have made you familiar with almost every department of learning: and I am happy in the thought that, while you read this volume as a scholar, you will judge it as a friend.

One of my earliest recollections is of leading you through the gardens, and maple groves, and green fields of the home of my childhood; when I looked up and saw serene cheerfulness always beaming from your face, and heard you talk about all my little sports, I could not then solve the mystery that one whose eyes the holy light of heaven never visited, could sympathize so warmly with everything around him.

Since then the lights and shadows of more than twenty-five years have fallen upon our path—nor have I ever, in all my wanderings, found a fellow-man, to whom you could not say,

> "I see a hand you cannot see;
> I hear a voice you cannot hear."

If I have accomplished any thing in life worthy of your approbation, I owe it chiefly to your sage counsels and generous encouragement. I have never fled from the crowded city to breathe the calm, pure country air without a kind greeting to your hospitable dwelling, and I never left it without your benediction. I never returned from my wanderings in other lands without your generous welcome. My children, too, who now lead you round your own green fields, hear your kind voice, and kneel before your household altar to receive your blessing.

Around that altar may the richest blessings of Heaven cluster, for many years.

Now, as always, your
Affectionate nephew,
C. EDWARDS LESTER.

New York.

PREFACE.

Residing for some years in the land which gave birth to the two great men who have divided the honour of discovering America, my attention was frequently turned to the subject of this volume. Without any fixed purpose of writing about Americus or his times, I devoted the leisure I had, to the study of the era of Discovery, and collected those books, charts, and MSS., which throw light over the subject.

A superficial survey of my materials begat a feeling of surprise, that no English or American historian had ever been attracted towards so fine a theme, while a more diligent investigation at last kindled a desire to possess my countrymen generally of information which could not be found in the literature of our language.

But I was beset with uncommon difficulties in the very beginning of my labours. Various accounts of Americus and his Voyages had appeared in Italian, Spanish, and German books, but no writer of research or celebrity had thrown much light over the Life and Voyages of the Discoverer. A careful review of Canovai, Bandini, and Bartolozzi, who are almost the only Italians that have written much about Americus, with a minute examination of other authors, convinced me it would be no easy task to recon cile their conflicting opinions, and separate history from fiction. But the very obstacles I found in my way only served to show the claims of the subject upon the historian. I wished to publish the result of my studies before my return to Europe. but this would have been impossible without essential aid from some one familiar with the subject. For this purpose, I applied last autumn to my friend, Mr. Andrew Foster, of Boston, whose acquaintance with the languages and literature of Modern Europe rendered his assistance invaluable. He kindly complied with my request, and for several months has devoted himself entirely to this work. It was but an act of simple justice to insist that his name should appear on the title-page, and to make this grateful acknowledgment, which I do with unmixed pleasure.

It has been remarked of Petrarch, that "his verses and his let ters, when read together, furnished a sort of running history of the man." Though this remark cannot be applied in its fullest force to Americus, yet it may be said to be partially true with regard to him. His letters carry us through the scenes which he visited during the most interesting part of his life, and though seldom alluding to himself personally, it is easy to place him in the imagination in every position he describes. I thought it advisable to adopt a new arrangement of these documents, or rather to follow the arrangement partially laid out by Canovai, and to divide the letter to Soderini into four parts, placing the different accounts of each voyage together.

In preparing the translation of the letters many different editions in Italian, Latin, and Spanish, have been consulted and compared. The letter to Soderini follows principally the text of the Gruniger edition, translated into Spanish by Navarrête, with some alterations and corrections of manifest errors. The letters to De Medici were taken from the Italian of Bandini and Canovai, with the exception of the second letter, giving an account of the third voyage, which was translated from the work of Bartolozzi. The Latin copy of the letter contained in the Novus Orbis of Grinæus was compared with the Italian.

The works of Mr. Irving, "The Life of Columbus" and "The Companions of Columbus," have been carefully consulted. The Paris edition has been used, and is the one referred to. It is the last edition, and published under Mr. Irving's own eye, and therefore in all probability the most correct. The Collection of Señor Navarrête has been invaluable, and has brought to light many facts of which all previous biographers of Americus were ignorant.

Before concluding these prefatory sentences, I wish to express my warm sense of obligation to Mr. Moore, the Librarian of the New York Historical Society, for his uniformly courteous treatment and his kind aid in facilitating the researches necessary in the preparation of this work. The Library itself is a fine collection of valuable historical works, and I doubt whether any one, with the exception perhaps of the Ehbeling collection, in the Harvard University Library, is more rich in matter relating to the early history of America. Indeed, there are some rare works found in the N. Y. H. S. Library which are not readily met with in Europe.

I cannot close this account of my labours without petitioning the reader to lay aside the prejudice so common in this country against the very name of Americus. The learned have said that he "usurped the name of the continent," and the vulgar have repeated it. How poorly the great Navigator has merited this charge the following pages will show. The work is now given to the Public, with the hope that the labours of the authors will not be in vain.

C. EDWARDS LESTER.

New York.

CONTENTS.

PART I.

CHAPTER I.

PAGE

CHAPTER II.

CHAPTER III.

CHAPTER IV.

CHAPTER V.

CHAPTER VI.

CHAPTER VII.

CHAPTER VIII.

CHAPTER IX.

FIRST LETTER OF AMERICUS TO LORENZO DI PIER-FRANCESCO DE' MEDICI, GIVING AN ACCOUNT OF HIS SECOND VOYAGE.

CHAPTER X.

CONTINUATION OF THE LETTER OF AMERICUS TO PIERO SODERINI, GIVING AN ACCOUNT OF HIS SECOND VOYAGE.

CHAPTER XI

CHAPTER XII.

SECOND LETTER OF AMERICUS TO LORENZO DI PIER-FRANCESCO DE MEDICI, GIVING A BRIEF ACCOUNT OF HIS THIRD VOYAGE, MADE FOR THE KING OF PORTUGAL.

CHAPTER XIII.

SECOND LETTER OF AMERICUS TO LORENZO DI PIER-FRANCESCO DE' MEDICI, GIVING A FULLER ACCOUNT OF HIS THIRD VOYAGE, MADE FOR THE KING OF PORTUGAL.

CHAPTER XIV.

CHAPTER XV.

CHAPTER XVI.

CHAPTER XVII.

CHAPTER XVIII.

PART II.

EULOGIUM OF AMERICUS VESPUCIUS, WHICH OBTAINED THE PREMIUM FROM THE NOBLE ETRUSCAN ACADEMY OF CORTONA, ON THE 15TH OF OCTOBER, IN THE YEAR 1788.

II.

A NARRATIVE ADDRESSED TO LORENZO DI PIER-FRANCESCO DE' MEDICI;

III.

LETTERS OF PAOLO TOSCANELLI TO COLUMBUS.

IV.

MARCO POLO AND HIS TRAVELS.

V.

FELLOW-VOYAGERS OF AMERICUS.

VI.

DOCUMENTS RELATING TO AMERICUS VESPUCIUS: PRESENTED IN THE COLLECTION OF NAVARRÊTE.

VII.

LETTER OF M. RANKE TO M. DE HUMBOLDT, RESPECTING THE CORRESPONDENCE OF AMERICUS WITH SODERINI AND DE' MEDICI.

VIII.

PART I

BIOGRAPHY.

LIFE AND VOYAGES

OF

AMERICUS VESPUCIUS.

CHAPTER I.

Introductory Remarks.—General View of the State of the Commerce of the World previous to the Discovery of America.—Merchants necessarily Travellers.—High Rates of Interest of Money.—Evidence of approaching Change.—Italian Manufactories.—State of Civilization, 1400.—Effects of the Conquest of the Eastern Empire.—Marco Polo.—Mandeville.—Invention of the Compass and Astrolabe.—Prince Henry of Portugal.—Robertson's Character of him.—His Zeal for the Cause of Discovery.—Vasco De Gama—Doubles the Cape of Good Hope, 1497.—Progress of Discovery.—Portuguese expeditions to the Coast of Africa.—Papal Grants of Dominion.—Death of Prince Henry.—Discoveries by Columbus.—What moved him to attempt them.—Islands of St. Brandan and of the Seven Cities.—Paolo Toscanelli.—Discoveries of the Scandinavians.—Italian Navigators.—Verazzani.—Sebastian Cabot.—Pre-eminence of particular ideas at particular Epochs.—Cotemporary Authors.—Fernando Columbus.—Bartolomeo de las Casas.—Gonzalo Fernandez de Oviedo.—Andrez Bernal.—Antonio Herrera de Tordesillas.—Francisco Lopez de Gomara.—Peter Martyr.—Concluding Remarks.

Commerce of the fifteenth century.

THE commerce of the world until nearly the close of the fifteenth century was carried on chiefly by means of land transportation. Voyages of much extent were almost unknown, and the mariner confined himself to inland waters, or hovered along the shores of the great Western Ocean, without venturing out of sight of land. The principal marts of Europe were the Hanseatic cities—a league of mercantile

CHAPTER I.

towns, which was formed for the purpose of security and mutual protection.

The thriving Republics of Italy were the carriers of the world. For many centuries their citizens were almost the only agents for commercial communication with the countries of the East. Venice and Genoa maintained establishments on the farthest shores of the Mediterranean and Black Seas. Immense caravans crossed the deserts of Arabia and Egypt, their camels laden with the costly fabrics of the Indies, which were received by the Italian traders from the hands of the Mahometans, and distributed over Europe. Here and there upon the deserts, a green oasis with its bubbling spring or fresh rivulet, served these mighty trains for a resting-place, where man and beast halted to recover from the fatigues of their weary journeys.

Olden cities of the East.

Occasionally, on these spots, where the soil was of sufficient fertility to sustain a population, villages grew up. In rarer instances and in earlier ages, large cities had been built upon these stopping-places, and were for the time the centres of traffic. Their warehouses, cumbered with the fruits, the treasures, and the fabrics of India, tempted the traders of all nations to their gates, and their market-places resounded with the busy hum of a crowded population. While the current of business flowed in that direction, all within their walls evinced life and activity, but as soon as a new channel was adopted by merchants, they fell into insignificance, and were once more abandoned to the solitude of the desert. Travellers of the present day occasionally visit their sites, and tell tales of wonder of the gigantic ruins of some Balbec or Palmyra of the wilderness.

System of business in the Middle Ages.

In the fifteenth century merchants were, of necessity, travellers. They could not, as in the present day, sit quietly in their counting-rooms, and transact business with all parts of the known world, receiving by each day's post communications from distant agents, and issuing orders for future operations, with the certainty of their receipt and prompt execution. The stranger was regarded as an enemy by the laws of most countries, and the foreign merchant was looked upon with distrust and apprehension. There existed little confidence in mercantile honor, and bills of exchange were rarely resorted to, except in cases of emergency and danger. The exorbitant rates of interest which were in all cases demanded for the use of money, materially checked active commercial operations.

False ideas of Usury.

Absurd as it seems in the present day, an idea generally prevailed, that the receipt of interest for loans came within the scriptural denunciation of usury, and, notwithstanding the enlightened views which were beginning to gain ground, there were not wanting learned doctors of the church who maintained the guilt of those who received pay for the risk they took in loaning their capital. The merchants of Italy, or, as they were called in the North of Europe, the Lombards, were the bankers as well as the carriers of the age, and finding themselves engaged in a business which was considered disgraceful and irreligious by the mass of the people, naturally became extravagant in their demands in the ratio of the infamy of their transactions. The consequence was, that extravagant profits were required to remunerate traders, and traffic was confined almost exclusively to barter and exchange. The merchant accompanied his goods to their destination, sold them himself, and purchased a new stock, which was saleable in his own country; and in most cases this transaction was effected without the medium of gold or silver.

Evidence of a change in mercantile affairs.

But evidence of an approaching change was not wanting. The demands of advancing civilization had begun to develop a vast alteration in the face of Europe. The increasing demand for the fabrics of the East stimulated the enterprise of the inhabitants of the South of Europe, and efforts were made to cultivate the plants of India, while manufactories, already established in Italy, gave fair promise of success and profit. The looms of her silk-weavers had already begun to clothe her citizens in garments which heretofore, from their costliness, could only be obtained by princes and nobles.

Comparative luxury of nations.

It is curious to contemplate the vast difference in luxury and comfort which existed between those countries which, from their natural geographical position, were placed in the course of trade, and those more secluded or out of the way of travellers. In England, for instance, an isolated country, many of the inhabitants of her largest towns lived in huts, without window or chimney. The fire was built on the ground, in the centre of the house, and its smoke was left to find its way out by the door, or escaped by a hole in the roof. Chairs and tables, the commonest articles of domestic utility, were almost unknown to the largest part of the population. How different the scene in Ghent, or Bruges, or Venice, or Genoa! There, costly palaces for the wealthy, furnished with most of the luxuries of later times, and comfortable habitations for the poorer classes, every where abounded. Art and literature flourished by the side of commerce, and universities and schools were established, which disseminated knowledge far and wide among mankind.

Conquest of the Eastern Empire.

The manufacturing spirit of Southern Europe was brought to life mainly by the fact that the old-established ways of transporting goods from India, which had gradually been growing more and more precarious, were then almost entirely abandoned, on account of their danger. The Turks, a nation of ferocious religious warriors, had overrun the Greek provinces of Asia bordering upon the Mediterranean, and annihilated the Christian power in the East by the conquest of Constantinople. They were as a people little adapted to commercial pursuits, even had they possessed the willingness to engage in them which characterized their predecessors, and their lawless character and marauding habits rendered the passage of the deserts, even by their own countrymen, a task of great uncertainty and danger.

CHAPTER I.

Efforts to [illegible] a new [illegible]

It was not to be supposed that the shrewd spirit of mercantile enterprise and speculation would remain dormant in this state of affairs. Traders in every part of Europe were alive to the advantages to be derived from the discovery of a new route of transportation. Several efforts were made, and in some few cases attended with immense profit and success, to communicate with India by the long and arduous journey round the Black Sea, and through the almost unexplored regions of Circassia and Georgia. The far-off shores of the Caspian were reached by some travelling traders, and the geographical knowledge they circulated on their return gave a new impulse to the growing spirit of adventure. Apocryphal as the narratives of Marco Polo and Mandeville appeared, there was a sufficient mixture of truth with exaggeration to stimulate the minds of men, ever greedy of gain, and the endless wealth of the Grand Khan and his people were the subjects of many eager and longing anticipations.

Invention of the compass and astrolabe.

The inventions of the Compass and the Astrolabe, while they increased the facilities of navigators most opportunely, added greatly to the confidence of merchants. They began to perceive that they must, in future, rely mainly upon water carriage in transporting their goods, and ships and seamen multiplied rapidly in consequence. Ability to define their position with accuracy led mariners to undertake longer voyages, and at length nautical enterprise was powerfully roused by the influence of a sagacious mind, whose energies for many years had been devoted to the elucidation of a grand problem. This was no less than the possibility of reaching the Indies by the circumnavigation of Africa.

Prince Henry of Portugal. Robertson's character of him.

Prince Henry of Portugal is justly entitled to the grateful remembrance and respect of the world. The character which is given by Dr. Robertson of this truly great man is indeed enviable. "That prince," he says, "added to the martial spirit which was the characteristic of every man of noble birth at that time, all the accomplishments of a more enlightened and polished age. He cultivated the arts and sciences, which were then unknown and despised by persons of his rank. He applied with peculiar fondness to the study of geography, and by the instruction of able masters, as well as by the accounts of travellers, he early acquired such knowledge of the habitable globe, as discovered the great probability of finding new and opulent countries by sailing along the coast of Africa. Such an object was formed to awaken the enthusiasm and ardour of a youthful mind, and he engaged, with the utmost zeal, to patronize a design that might prove as beneficial as it appeared to be splendid and honourable. In order that he might be able to pursue this great scheme without interruption, he retired from court immediately after his return from Africa, and fixed his "residence at Sagres, near Cape St. Vincent, where the prospect of the Atlantic Ocean invited his thoughts continually towards his favourite project,

CHAPTER I.

and encouraged him to execute it. In this retreat he was attended by some of the most learned men in his country, who aided him in his researches. He applied for information to the Moors of Barbary, who were accustomed to travel by land into the interior provinces of Africa, in quest of ivory, gold-dust, and other rich commodities. He consulted the Jews settled in Portugal. By promises, rewards, and marks of respect, he allured into his service several persons, foreigners as well as Portuguese, who were eminent for their skill in navigation. In taking those preparatory steps, the great abilities of the Prince were seconded by his private virtues. His integrity, his affability, his respect for religion, his zeal for the honour of his country, engaged persons of all ranks to applaud his design, and to favour the execution of it. His schemes were allowed by his countrymen to proceed neither from ambition nor the desire of wealth, but to flow from the warm benevolence of a heart eager to promote the happiness of mankind, and which justly entitled him to assume a motto for his device that described the quality by which he wished to be distinguished,—The talent of doing good."[1]

Vasco de Gama doubles Cape of Good Hope, 1497.

It is impossible to avoid a feeling of regret that this great Prince was not permitted to live long enough to behold all his ardent aspirations realized.

[1] Vide Robertson's History of America, vol. i. p. 43, 44. This volume has been frequently referred to while this chapter was in progress, and has been of much service, which is gratefully acknowledged.

CHAPTER I.

Vasco de Gama, 1497.

When, at last, in the year 1497, Vasco de Gama, proceeding from the port of Lisbon, with four ships, coasted the shores of Africa to their farthest extent, and doubled the Cape of Good Hope, he must have regarded with veneration the memory of the able and patriotic Prince who first prompted to the design he had now brought to such a glorious conclusion. It is worthy of remark, that the Portuguese Admiral found in use, among the mariners of the Red Sea and the Persian Gulf, a nautical instrument answering, very nearly, the description of the astrolabe, which that noble prince had so recently assisted in perfecting in Portugal.[1]

[1] Vasco de Gama was born in Portugal, in the town of Synis. The historians who have recorded his discoveries have omitted to give many particulars of his life previous to his departure for the Indies. It was the current opinion at the time De Gama sailed, that there existed on the eastern shores of Africa a nation of Christians under the dominion of a powerful prince, whom they called Prester John, and the Portuguese, who had so recently seen the magnificent discoveries of Columbus enuring to the benefit of Spain, were stimulated to a determination of finding this country, which they imagined would bring equal advantage to their own nation.

De Gama set sail with a small fleet on the 8th of July, 1497, and arrived on the 17th of December at the point where the discoveries of Diaz had ceased. There the Portuguese entered the seas of India for the first time, and stretched away to the North.

In the early part of March he arrived before the city of Mozambique, then inhabited by Moors and Mahometan Arabs, under the dominion of a prince of their own faith.

These people carried on an extensive commerce with the Red Sea, and the hope of commercial connection with a new people led them to give a friendly reception to De Gama. But their friendship was of short duration, and as soon as they discovered them to be Christians, they formed a plan to massacre them. The admiral, however, escaped from their snares, and proceeded on his voyage, touching at various places, until he arrived at Calicut, on the 20th of May, 1498.

This was the richest and most commercial city of India at the time, and was under the rule of a

CHAPTER I.

Early discoveries.

The earliest efforts for maritime discovery were of the most trifling nature, and impeded by the most fanciful fears and apprehensions. Accustomed to think nothing of a passage across the ocean, the mariners of the present day can have no idea how extensive and important, appeared to the Portuguese an undertaking to explore the coast of Africa beyond Cape Non. The very name of the Cape itself, was indicative of the impossibility of sailing

monarch called Zamorin. Luckily for De Gama, he found there a Moor who, with the aid of one who accompanied the fleet, acted as interpreter, and was the means of his opening a communication with the king. The Portuguese naturally distrusted the faith of the Mahometans; but their commander was not to be deterred by any ordinary danger, and selecting twelve brave men from the fleet, he landed.

He was obliged to go about five miles into the interior to a country palace where Zamorin resided, and was followed through the city of Calicut by an immense crowd of persons, all anxious to gaze at the newly-arrived strangers. He was at first received favourably, but after a while, jealousies and suspicions rose in the minds of the natives, and rendered it necessary to re-embark and set sail somewhat suddenly upon his return.

After refitting his ships at some neighbouring islands, he steered a homeward course, stopping on his way back at Melinda, where he took on board his fleet an ambassador to the King of Portugal from the ruler of that country. This nation was the only friendly one which the Portuguese found in India.

The fleet doubled the Cape of Good Hope once more in March, 1499, and arrived in Lisbon in September of the same year, after an absence of more than two years.

Emmanuel received De Gama with the greatest honours and magnificence, and created him Admiral of the Indies. The admiral subsequently made another voyage with a powerful armed fleet to the Indies, and compelled by force of arms his old enemy, Zamorin, to admit of Portuguese establishments in his dominions. He was afterwards created Viceroy of the Indies, but died soon after his arrival from his third voyage to take control of his new dominions.

A history of his discoveries was written by Barros, and published in 1628. Camoens, it is well known, made him the subject of his Lusiad.—*Biog. Univ.*, t. xvi., p. 398—404.

CHAPTER I.

beyond it, and even after it was passed, more than twenty years elapsed ere the timid navigators ventured beyond the rocky promontory of Bajador, less than two hundred miles distant, an exploit, which, when it was at last accomplished, was proclaimed over Europe as one of the most daring and intrepid actions, ever recorded in the pages of history.

False ideas and unfounded apprehensions.

The belief which generally prevailed, that the torrid zone was a region of impassable heat, where no vegetation existed, and where the very waters of the ocean boiled as in a caldron, under the influence of a vertical sun, had effectually checked any attempts at discovery; and as the Portuguese penetrated within the tropics, the sights they saw, all tended to confirm the old opinion.

Beyond the Senegal River they found a new race of beings, with complexions black as ebony, with hair crisped as though burnt, with features flat and inexpressive, and evidently possessing intelligence vastly inferior to their own. This was all attributed to the fatal influence of the climate, and they dreaded any further exploration, lest by some sudden catastrophe, they also might be reduced to the state in which they found the unhappy denizens of Africa.

The active and capacious mind of Prince Henry alone opposed itself to the representations which they made to him. The discoveries which they had already made, served to undermine his confidence in the views of the ancient geographers, and supported in his determination by his brother

CHAPTER I.

Pedro, who then ruled in Portugal, as guardian of his minor nephew, Alphonso, he persevered in his plans with eagerness.

Sanction of the Church.

One circumstance contributed materially to animate the hearts of the Portuguese navigators, which must not be overlooked. Well knowing the effect which an apparent sanction of his movements by the Church would have upon the bigoted minds of his countrymen, Prince Henry applied directly to the Head of the Church, and, by representing the labours and religious zeal with which he had exerted himself for many years to discover unknown regions then sunk in the darkness of Paganism, with a view to their conversion to the true faith, he obtained from the Pope a Bull, conferring upon the crown of Portugal the exclusive right of dominion over all the countries which they might discover on the coast of Africa, as far as the Indies. Absurd as this grant appears at the present day, no power then existed, that disputed the right of the papal see to make it, or that ventured to interfere with it. The religious zeal of the discoverers was highly inflamed by the encomiums bestowed upon them, and they were encouraged to prosecute their undertakings by a new and powerful motive.

Death of Prince Henry, 1643.

In 1463 the cause of discovery received a severe blow in the death of Prince Henry. From that time until the accession of John II. to the throne of Portugal, little worthy of note was added to the maritime knowledge of the world. The new monarch, however, entered at once into the schemes of his grand uncle, and revived them with great vigour. Powerful fleets were despatched from time to time; forts were erected along the African coast, and at length when the line was crossed, the delusions which had long held the minds of men in bondage, were dissipated. Two great errors of the ancients were exposed: the first, that respecting the unconquerable heat of the tropics; the second, that the continent of Africa increased in breadth as it extended to the south.

Bartholemew Diaz, 1486.

The return of Bartholemew Diaz, a mariner of great sagacity and boldness, who, in 1486, had coasted the shores over a thousand miles, and finally reached the southernmost point of Africa, filled the sanguine mind of the king with the warmest hopes of success. In the plenitude of his joy, and confident that he had at last attained the great object of his enterprises, he re-named the promontory which Diaz had appropriately designated, Cabo Tormentoso, or the Stormy Cape, and gave it the more euphonious and attractive title, The Cape of Good Hope.

Active preparations were immediately commenced to bring to a conclusion their long and arduous labours. But, notwithstanding the skill which the Portuguese sailors had gained, the reports which the companions of Diaz widely circulated filled the minds of all with fear, and some years elapsed before they were sufficiently calmed to take advantage of the knowledge already ac-

CHAPTER I.

quired. While the possibility of doubling in safety a cape, washed by seas so tempestuous, was eagerly debated, Europe was electrified by the astounding discovery of a new world in the Western Ocean, a direction which the boldest in nautical affairs had hitherto scarcely dared to contemplate.

Growth of the Spirit of Discovery.

The impetus which was given to the spirit of discovery by these voyages of the Portuguese, may be compared with the vast conceptions, and magnificent projects, which have followed the applica- of the power of steam in the present day. The public mind was excited beyond measure, and the wildest tales of imaginary regions beyond the trackless waste of waters, hitherto unexplored, found ready and enthusiastic believers, who were willing to peril life and reputation in efforts to test their truth. As is almost always the case, those who were most earnest in their faith, possessed the smallest means to carry out their views.

But their day of success was fast approaching. The science of cosmography became the favourite subject of speculation among philosophers and learned men, affording, as it did, a brilliant field for the imagination, and, at the same time, an opportunity of deep research. The works of ancient writers were ardently sought for, and diligently collated; the vague hypotheses of some of the old geographers were revived; theories which had lain undisturbed beneath the dust of ages were brought to light again; and, when compared with the accounts of Eastern travellers, lent a semblance of truth to the dim visions of distant islands in the Atlantic, which haunted the minds of navigators; the coast of Africa gave immense scope to nautical enterprise, and the court of Portugal, hitherto hardly known in Europe, became at once the resort of hardy adventurers from all nations, while the kingdom rose immediately from the inferior position it had previously occupied, to one of the greatest importance. Lisbon was in a continual fever of excitement, which affected all classes of society, and the constant succession of new expeditions which were fitted out were eagerly joined by men of rank and celebrity, as well as the more common class of mariners.

Speculation on the subject of a passage to the Indies.

The idea of a passage by the west to India was not, even at that time, one of recent date. Various indefinite accounts were current of seamen driven by tempestuous gales far out of their course, who, on their return, had reported that they had fallen in with land, which was supposed to be a part of the islands on the eastern coast of India. The rediscovery of the Grand Canaries, in the fourteenth century, the Fortunate Islands of the ancients, from which Ptolemy calculated longitude, had familiarized navigators with the wide waters of the Atlantic, and occasionally, for a century past, they had ventured even farther out on the ocean, in the doubtful hope of meeting with the fabled Atalantis of Plato, or the equally visionary islands of the

CHAPTER I.

Seven Cities and St. Brandan.[1] Each of these phantasies found firm believers, and the age required only a master-mind to arrange the crude

[1] The fabulous history of both of these islands is full of romantic interest, which the reader may gratify by the perusal of Mr. Irving's account of them in the appendix to his history of Columbus. A short sketch is all that our space admits, and is abridged from that work.

The story which was current at the time of Columbus, respecting the Island of the Seven Cities, was to this effect. When the Moors overrun and conquered the countries of Spain and Portugal, seven bishops of the Christian church fled by sea, and abandoning themselves to the waves, were cast upon an island in the midst of the ocean, where they destroyed their ships to prevent the desertion of their followers, and founded seven cities. This story was very generally credited at the time of Prince Henry, who was said to have received accounts of the island from some Portuguese sailors, and in the maps of the era it was located in the Atlantic under the name of Antilla.

The origin of the belief in the Island of St. Brandan is still more singular. It was supposed by many to be identical with the Island of the Seven Cities, and originated in a very remarkable optical delusion of the inhabitants of the Canaries. They imagined that in clear weather they could see from the summits of their highest hills, an island, apparently about ninety leagues in length, and varying in distance from the point of view from fifteen to one hundred leagues, according to the accounts of different persons. The name was derived from that of a Scotch abbot, St. Borondon, who went with a numerous train of monks and enthusiasts, as the tale was told, in search of a terrestrial paradise in the ocean, and who at last were thrown upon this island.

It is astonishing how many expeditions were fitted out and sailed in search of this imaginary country, but it always eluded the pursuit of the navigators. Even as late as the year 1721 a fleet was sent in search of it, and in 1755 it still figured in some geographical charts. In a letter written by a Franciscan monk from the Island of Gomara in 1759, it is distinctly described as having been seen by himself and upwards of forty witnesses, whom he called to verify his own eyesight. He describes it as consisting of two high mountains, with a valley between, and when viewed through a telescope, the ravine appeared filled with trees and verdure. A belief in the existence of this island is still prevalent among the more superstitious of the lower classes in the Canaries.

Unwilling to disbelieve what appears to them to be the evidence of their senses, they prefer to attribute the impossibility of reaching it to supernatural causes, and

imaginings which were rife, and direct them to a useful end. Such a mind existed.

The reflections of Christopher Columbus.

For many years previous to his first voyage, Columbus pondered over the idea of a western passage to India; he collected by degrees all the information which was to be derived from the works of the ancients, and from the accounts of certain recent travellers who had penetrated the countries of Eastern Asia, far beyond the regions described by Ptolemy. The narrations of Marco Polo and Mandeville, who visited Asia in the thirteenth and fourteenth centuries, and gave marvellous accounts of the wealth and grandeur of the potentates who inhabited those unknown countries, were diligently studied and connected with more trifling evidence. The inhabitants of the newly discovered Canaries, or of the Azores, had found on their shores pieces of wood strangely carved, or of trees unknown in Europe, and once, it was said, there had come to their islands two messengers from the far-off land, whose swollen and disfigured lips, could they have spoken, might have told of a new race of beings and a new world. They were speechless corpses, yet their lineaments were strange, and it was evident that

maintain that it is inaccessible to mortals. If such sights are still seen, they are undoubtedly the effects of atmospherical deceptions, similar to that of the Fata Morgana, seen at times in the Straits of Messina, where the town of Reggio is reflected in the air above the sea. The inhabitants on the borders of the great American lakes sometimes witness a phenomenon very similar, when the Canadian shore is distinctly visible, though at a distance beyond the possibility of actual observation.

the blood which had once circulated in their veins, came not from the same source as that of the wondering islanders.

Columbus gave heed to these and many other similar circumstances, and his views were strengthened almost to certainty by the receipt of a letter from a learned cosmographer of Florence, by name Paolo Toscanelli, with whom he had opened a correspondence, and who had sent him a map, projected according to Ptolemy in part, and in part from the accounts of Marco Polo.[1] Therein ap-

[1] Toscanelli (Paul del Pozzo) or Paul the Physician, was born at Florence in 1397. He devoted himself with great ardour to the study of astronomy, and became so celebrated for his learning that at the age of thirty years, in 1428 he was appointed one of the curators of the valuable library which Niccoli had placed under the care of the most illustrious citizens of Florence.

The reading of the travels of Marco Polo excited the imagination of Toscanelli, who compared his accounts with the information he derived from some Eastern merchants, and pondered incessantly upon the means of opening a communication with the magnificent countries which he described.

After a while he conceived the idea of a passage by the west, and in reply to the letter of Columbus, who, hearing of his learning, wrote to consult him, he sent a long explanatory letter, accompanied by a hydrographical chart.

On this chart a line was projected from Lisbon, on the western extremity of Europe, to the great city of Quinsai, on the opposite shores of Asia. This line was divided into twenty-six spaces of two hundred and fifty miles each, making the total distance between the two cities sixty-five hundred miles, being, as Toscanelli supposed, one-third of the circumference of the earth. His ideas took strong hold of the mind of Columbus, and influenced him in all his voyages.

In consequence of his constant study of the heavenly bodies, many of the superstitious of his day were disposed to look upon him as an astrologer, but he did nothing to encourage the notion, and was free from any of the absurd views which many astronomers still kept alive. He replied to those who questioned him on the subject, that he found in his own case a proof of the fallacy of astrological calculations, for he had attained to a great age in spite of the constellations which figured in his horoscope, and which all

peared the eastern regions of Asia, invitingly pictured at a few days sail from the western shores of Europe, while, as stopping-places for the weary navigator, at convenient distances lay the wealthy islands of Cipango and Antilla.

Discoveries of the Scandinavians.

It is not to be supposed that the researches which Columbus was engaged in, left him ignorant of the wild accounts of the discoveries of the Northmen, some centuries before. Mysterious legendary tales, of a land beyond the Thule of the ancients, must have reached his ears. He sailed himself, in 1477, in the direction indicated by the Scandinavian mariners. If the antiquarian researches of the nineteenth century are to be credited, these adventurous voyagers were not contented with the discovery of Greenland and Vinland, but coasted the shores of North America to a low latitude, and left upon the rocks of New-England sculptured evidence of their daring navigation. But whatever reliance may be placed upon the accounts of their voyages now, in the days of Columbus they were effectually lost to the world, and were of no more advantage to him in the prosecution of his plans, than the wildest tales of the inhabitants of the Canaries.[1]

predicted an early death. Notwithstanding his longevity, he did not have the satisfaction of knowing the discoveries of Columbus. He died at Florence, 15th of May, 1482.—*Biog. Univ.*, tom. xlvi., p. 303—305.

[1] The following account of the celebrated Dighton Rock, one of the most remarkable remains alluded to, is extracted from a letter addressed by Thomas H. Webb, Esq., Secretary of Rhode Island Historical Society, to the Royal Society of Northern Antiquarians, which is published in their great

CHAPTER I.

Cotemporary Navigators, natives of Italy.

The mention of Columbus naturally brings to mind other navigators of his own country and epoch. It would reasonably be supposed that

work on the subject of Scandinavian remains in America.

Providence, R. I., Sept. 22, 1830.

* * * * * That the existence of the continent of America was known to European nations at a period anterior to the voyages of Columbus, has long been the received opinion of many of our most learned antiquaries. In the western parts of our country may still be seen numerous and extensive mounds similar to the tumuli met with in Scandinavia, Tartary, and Russia; also the remains of fortifications that must have required for their construction a degree of industry, labour, and skill, as well as an advancement in the arts, that never characterized any of the Indian tribes. Various articles of pottery are found in them, with the method of manufacturing which, they were entirely unacquainted. But, above all, many rocks inscribed with unknown characters, apparently of very ancient origin, have been discovered, scattered through different parts of the country—rocks, the constituent parts of which are such as to render it almost impossible to engrave on them such writings, without the aid of iron, or other hard metallic instruments. The Indians were ignorant of the existence of these rocks, and the manner of working with iron they learned of the Europeans after the settlement of the country by the English. * * * * * *

A rock similar to those alluded to above, lies in our vicinity. It is situated about six and an half miles south of Taunton, on the east side of Taunton River, a few feet from the shore, and on the west side of Assonet Neck, in the town of Berkeley, County of Bristol, and Commonwealth of Massachusetts: although probably from the fact of being generally visited from the opposite side of the river, which is in Dighton, it has always been known by the name of the Dighton Writing Rock. It faces northwest toward the bed of the river, and is covered by the water two or three feet at the highest, and is left ten or twelve feet from it at the lowest tides. It is also completely immersed twice in twenty-four hours. The rock does not occur in situ, but shows indubitable evidence of having occupied the spot where it now rests, since the period of that great and extensive disruption, which was followed by the transportation of immense boulders to, and a deposit of them in, places at a vast distance from their original beds. It is a mass of well-characterized, fine-grained greywacke. Its true colour, as exhibited by a fresh fracture, is a bluish grey.

There is no rock in the immediate neighbourhood which would at all answer as a substitute for the purpose for which the one bearing the inscription was selected, as they are aggregates of those nations whose extended commerce gave them the greatest opportunities to acquire familiarity with nautical affairs would have derived the widest benefit from the experience of their citizens, but such was not the case. It is worthy of remark, that while all the prominent powers of Europe availed themselves of the services of Italian navigators in prosecuting the discovery of new regions, and in acquiring new possessions; not a foot of territory was obtained by any of the governments of that country. The skill in nautical science, which the citizens of her republics had acquired, in the course of a long and prosperous career of mercantile enterprise, was rendered entirely useless to them by the petty feuds and factions which occupied the attention of their rulers.

No Italian possessions in the New World.

the large conglomerate variety. Its face, measured at the base, is eleven feet and an half, and in height it is a little rising five feet. The upper surface forms with the horizon an inclined plane of about sixty degrees. The whole of the face is covered, to within a few inches of the ground, with unknown hieroglyphics. There appears little or no method in the arrangement of them. The lines are from half an inch to an inch in width, and in depth generally one third of an inch, though generally very superficial. They were, inferring from the rounded elevations and intervening depressions, pecked in upon the rock, and not chiselled or smoothly cut out.

The marks of human power and manual labour are indelibly stamped upon it. No one who examines attentively the workmanship will believe it to have been done by the Indians. Moreover, it is a well-attested fact, that nowhere throughout our widespread domain is a single instance of their recording, or having recorded, their deeds or history on stone.—*Antiquitates Americanæ*, p. 356—358.

The work from which the above is taken contains evidence, collected with great pains and ability, and proving conclusively the discoveries of the Northmen, and will well repay the antiquarian reader. It is published in the Danish language, with a Latin translation subjoined.

CHAPTER I.

State of the Italian Republics.

Venice, Genoa, Florence, and Pisa, though fully awake to the importance of the undertakings which were in progress, and sensible that their success would inevitably be the beginning of ruin to their own commerce, were yet so much engrossed in the unfortunate conflicts of the times, they heeded not the warnings which occasionally reached them. While Columbus was giving a new world to Castile, while Sebastian Cabot projected immense and promising plans of vast commercial advantage to England, for which that country owes him a debt of imperishable gratitude; while Vespucius, in the service of Portugal and Spain, added immeasurable regions to the dominion of both powers, and while Verazzani, another noble Florentine, braved the dangers of the Atlantic, and coasted the shores of the New World, in the employment of France, they all remained passive spectators of the progress of discovery, and, as it were, unconcerned at their own impending fate.

What a lesson for the statesmen and philosophers of modern times does the position of the Italian States, in the fifteenth century, present! Divided among themselves, they possessed no external power, and expended all their resources in contemptible efforts to add a few roods of ground to the territories of their own particular cities and principalities, at the expense of some weaker neighbour, while continents were divided among the more sagacious nations of Europe. Even Rome, once the mistress of the world, displayed

CHAPTER I.

her pitiable imbecility, in grants of domains more extensive than the broadest empires of the Cæsars, and reposed sluggishly upon her seven hills, while greater prizes than ever before had tempted her, were within her grasp.

How different would have been the case had a federative union subsisted in Italy in the fifteenth century! Each separate province, linked with the others in bonds of common interest and unity, and directing their joint efforts for the common good, Genoese, Florentine, and Venetian, all alike Italians! Once more might Italy have been the centre of the universe, and Rome have received the tribute of the world.

A short sketch of the lives of Verazzani and Cabot may not be without interest to the reader, and is given in this place, although both are worthy of a more elaborate notice.

Giovanni Verazzani, 1524.

Giovanni Verazzani, a Florentine navigator, was born towards the close of the fifteenth century. He was of noble descent, and was employed by Francis I. to make discoveries in the northern part of America. Authors differ concerning the date of his departure; but it appears that he went to sea before the month of July, in the year 1524, since, on the 8th of that month, he wrote a letter to the French monarch, informing him, that, in consequence of a violent gale, he had been obliged to put back into a port of Brittany.

Sails in the Dauphin.

On the 17th of January, in the same year, he set sail with the frigate Dauphin, which he com-

CHAPTER I.

manded, from a desert island near Madeira, where he had previously come to anchor. After having experienced a violent hurricane, he coasted the shores of some parts of North America.

Fate of Giovanni Verazzani.

His letters give a curious description of the savages he met with, and of the plants, birds, and animals of the unknown region. His discoveries were considered highly important at the time, as he visited more than seven hundred leagues of coast, running from 30° north latitude as far as Newfoundland. It is said, by some authorities, that he met with a horrible fate on these inhospitable shores; having been taken, with many of his companions, and roasted alive by the Indians. Others, however, with less appearance of truth, say that he was taken prisoner by the Spaniards, who sent him to Madrid, where he was hung.

In the library of the Palazzo Strozzi, at Florence, is preserved a cosmographical description of the coasts and countries which Verazzani visited, while seeking for a passage to the East Indies by the north, which was the great object of his voyages, as it was of almost all the enterprises of the day. An account of his voyage, which was originally sent by him to the King of France, may be found in the collection of Ramusio.[1]

Sebastian Cabot.

Sebastian Cabot was born in Bristol, England, in 1467, whither his father, John Cabot, had gone from Venice, to propose to the king a scheme for

[1] Vide Biographie Universelle, tom. xlviii. p. 158.

the discovery of a passage to Cathay and the East Indies. The whole family, consisting of the father and his three sons, were treated with great attention by Henry VII.

Decree of Henry VII.

An authentic decree is extant, dated March 5th, 1495, in which that king grants to him and his children the liberty of navigating in all seas under the English flag, and authorizes him to form establishments and build forts, ceding to him and his heirs a monopoly of commerce in all the countries he might discover.

Cabot's Voyage.

The only fragments of any voyages made by this family of navigators which have been preserved, mention the name of Sebastian alone. It seem that, setting sail from England, he chose the northwest route, and fell in with land which tended to the north. He endeavoured to discover a gulf stretching to the west, but after sailing as high as 56° north latitude, and finding that the course of the land was easterly, he despaired of meeting with a passage, and turned in a southerly direction and proceeded as far as the southernmost Cape of Florida.

Ramusio gives no account of the voyages of Sebastian Cabot, but contents himself with quoting, in the preface to his third volume, a passage from a letter which he had received from him. It appears to be from the pen of a man of much experience and uncommon acquirements in the arts of navigation and cosmography. Subsequently he transcribes part of his letter, from which it appears that Cabot advanced as far as 67° north latitude, and sailed behind many of the islands which he found upon the coast. Peter Martyr relates, in his History of the East Indies, that Cabot met with icebergs, which impeded his progress towards the north. The same author adds, that in this part of the sea there was no night, and that at midnight it was possible to see with as much distinctness, as in the twilight of other countries.

If these accounts can be relied upon, it would seem that Cabot had gone as far as Hudson's Bay, but it is more probable that he only penetrated the Gulf and River of St. Lawrence.

Cabot goes to Spain.

After having made these discoveries for the King of England, Cabot went to Spain and made several voyages in Spanish vessels, in one of which he ascended the River La Plata. At the death of Vespucius, in 1512, he succeeded him in the office of chief pilot. This office he only held a short time; but, disgusted with the ignoble commencement of the reign of Charles V., he returned to England, where he found honourable employment under Henry VIII., and performed another westerly voyage in 1517, which, however, resulted unsuccessfully. In 1518 he again went to Spain, but finally returned to England to end his days. There he exercised a general superintendence of the English maritime expeditions, receiving a handsome salary.

It was at his instigation that the important expedition was undertaken which resulted in the opening of a trade with Russia; and in the charter of the company of merchants, which was granted by the government, his name was mentioned as "the chiefest setter forth" of the project. Cabot lived to a very advanced age, and died in London; but neither the date of his death nor the place of his interment is authentically known.

Variation of the Needle.

On his last voyage he satisfied himself that the variation of the needle was regulated by fixed natural laws, and disclosed his discovery of the principles of that remarkable phenomenon to Edward VI. on his return. This discovery alone should render his name immortal.[1]

Intellectual aspects of different eras.

In reading the pages of history, it is impossible not to be struck with the prevalence, or, so to speak, the pre-eminence, of particular ideas and phrases in particular epochs. In all the works originating in the thirteenth and fourteenth centuries, which have come down to modern times, the Crusades and Crusaders are almost inevitably constant themes. This is but an example, but the same remark applies equally well to other periods of the world. For a while the Reformation weighed down the pens of authors, and all their writings were, as it seemed involuntarily, tinged with the colouring of that great event. In this nineteenth century, who does not recognize the marked effect of that most astonishing of all the astonishing occurrences in the annals of nations, the French

[1] Biog. Univ. Art. Cabot.

CHAPTER I.

Revolution? Thus it was in the sixteenth century. One great idea filled the minds of men, and was made as familiar as household words in all the writings of the era. It appeared in all shapes, and scarcely a volume was written that was not sympathetically infected with it, to a greater or less degree. It was the great event of the discovery of a new world.

Revival of Letters.

How fortunate it was for succeeding ages that this discovery took place at a period when the revival of letters and civilization had brought forth authors competent to record the remarkable events which attended it with accuracy and judgment The fall of the Eastern Empire not only shifted the current of the commerce and enterprise of the world from the course in which it had flowed for ages, but it was the means of bringing to the light of day valuable stores of learning and wisdom. The literature of the ancient world had to a great extent been concealed, though preserved, by recluse Byzantine scholars, whom the Moslem conquest forced from their retirement, and drove out as wanderers over the face of Europe.

On the capture of Constantinople they fled to Italy, bearing with them their precious parchment scrolls of ancient lore, like the old prophets when they fled from the falling temples of Judah. Received by the princes and republics of the peninsula with enthusiasm, these exiled scholars repaid their hospitality by the instruction of youth and the dissemination of the valuable works which they had brought with them from the East.

Invention of the art of printing.

The recent invention of the printing-press was brought into full play, and copies of rare manuscripts were multiplied a thousand-fold. The value of many of these may be estimated, when it is considered that they were the only known copies, existing in the world, of the works of some of the ancient classics and philosophers. Men of letters perceived immediately how much might have been lost to themselves, and lamenting their own wants, turned their eyes to posterity, and chronicled the times in which they lived, for the benefit of their children.

This spirit spread rapidly, and infected not only those who had been, from their professional pursuits, accustomed to wield the pen, but the actors themselves in the important scenes of the new drama which was in progress, applied themselves to the task of perpetuating their doings for the benefit of succeeding ages. The writers whose works bear most immediate reference to the discovery, and are of the greatest value in furnishing correct statements, are of the latter class.

The son of Columbus, the venerable Bishop Las Casas, Bernal, the Curate of Los Palacios, Oviedo, and Americus Vespucius, are entitled to the gratitude of the world on this account. These cotemporaries were followed by another class of authors, whose writings, dating from the sixteenth century, are scarcely of less importance. They

CHAPTER I.

were enabled to collect and examine the accounts of their predecessors, to compare and revise them, to fill up the gaps which were unavoidably left, and supply from authentic documents any inadvertent omissions. Among these Gomara and Herrera are the most prominent. The lives of all of these writers are full of interest, but only a trifling sketch of them can be given in this work.

Fernando Columbus.

Fernando Columbus was the natural son of the great admiral, and was born about 1487. Though still a boy, he accompanied his father on his fourth expedition, and received great praise from him, for the fortitude with which he bore its hardships and privations. His most important work is his history of his father's life, which is really invaluable to the American antiquarian. He was the author of other works, however, which might have been of equal importance, had they been preserved to modern times. Devoted to literature, he made a collection of nearly twenty thousand books and manuscripts of great value, which, at his death, he bequeathed to the cathedral church of Seville, where he died on 12th July, 1559. Notwithstanding his relationship, he writes of his father with great fairness and clearness; and from the facilities which he enjoyed of examining his charts and papers, is entitled to the highest credit.

Bartholomeo de Las Casas.

Bartholomeo de Las Casas was born at Seville, in the year 1474, and went to America soon after its discovery. He was subsequently made a bishop in the newly-found diocese, and devoted a long life to the service of the Indians, who were cruelly oppressed and enslaved by their Spanish conquerors. He was the author of several works on the Indies, of which his "General History," from the period of their discovery to the year 1520, is the most important. Las Casas has been accused of counselling the Spaniards to import slaves from Africa, rather than use the Indians in this way, and thus to have been the originator of the slave traffic; but the assertion has in later times been contradicted and disproved. Las Casas returned to Spain in 1564, and died at Madrid in 1566.

Gonzalo Fernandez de Oviedo.

Gonzalo Fernandez de Oviedo was born in Madrid, in the year 1478. He was descended from a noble family, and went, in 1513, to the New World, to superintend the gold mines. His works are very voluminous, for he was a most industrious writer and compiler. Among other things, he wrote a Chronicle of the Indies, in fifty books. An eyewitness of most of what he describes, his works contain a great many valuable and curious particulars concerning the New World, and the manners and habits of the natives. He held, at his death, the appointment of Historiographer of the Indies, conferred upon him by Charles V.

Andrez Bernal.

Andrez Bernal, who is generally called The Curate of Los Palacios, was a warm supporter of Columbus, and wrote a history of the reign of Ferdinand and Isabella, into which he introduced a narrative of his voyages. No work of his was ever published, but it still exists in manuscript, and is

CHAPTER I.

often quoted by historians. He was a believer in the tales of Mandeville, and frequently quotes him with much approbation. His visionary ideas of a terrestrial paradise, which affected materially the imagination of Columbus also, were derived from this author.

Antonio Herrera.

Antonio Herrera de Tordesillas was born in the year 1565, and died in 1625. He was appointed by Philip II. to the post of Historiographer of the Indies, and wrote many books, the most celebrated of which is his General History of the American Colonies. From his position in Spain, he ought to have been much more accurate in his accounts, than he actually was. All the royal archives were thrown open to him; yet, though he availed himself freely of them, he frequently was guilty of suppressing facts and altering circumstances, which tended to injure the character of his countrymen. Still he was an industrious writer, and his work contains a great deal of information not to be found in other quarters, although much of it is, in a measure, liable to be received with suspicion, on account of his prejudices and partiality. A large part of his work is little more than a transcript from the manuscripts of Las Casas, who deserves much more credit as a faithful historian. In a subsequent part of this work, this author's attempt to injure the reputation of Vespucius will be the subject of remark.[1]

[1] The above sketches of cotemporary authors have been abridged from the accounts given of them by the author of the life of Columbus, though in our estimate of Herrera, it is our misfortune to differ materially from him

Francisco Lopez de Gomara.

Francisco Lopez de Gomara was born at Seville, in 1510, and for many years filled the chair of the Professorship of Rhetoric at Alcala. He was well versed in ancient and modern history, and particularly in that of his own country. His style is more polished and pure than that of any historian of the time. His most important work—A General History of the Indies—was published in 1558, and contains many valuable facts.

Peter Martyr.

Peter Martyr is another cotemporary writer, who must not be forgotten. He was born in Milan, in 1455; was educated at Rome, where he early acquired a distinguished reputation for learning, and was invited by the Spanish ambassador at the Papal See to proceed to Spain. He wrote an account of the discovery of the New World in Ten Decades, originally in Latin; but the most interesting of his works are his letters, which he addressed daily to distinguished persons, giving statements of the events which were taking place around him. A collection of these epistles was published in 1530. He died at Valladolid, in 1526.

It appeared desirable, before commencing the narration of the life of one of the prominent navigators of the age, to give the foregoing general view of matters which bear immediate reference to the discovery of the New World. This, though very imperfectly accomplished, will serve to prepare the reader for the occurrences which follow in the life of the distinguished man, whose name and fame are so intimately linked with that great event.

CHAPTER II.

Birth of Vespucius, 1451.—His Parents.—Anastasio Vespucci and Elizabetta Mini.—Origin of the Vespucci Family.—Peretola.—Extract from Ugolino Verini.—Estates of the House.—Old Family Mansion.—Inscription over its Door.—Simone Vespucci.—His great Wealth.—Offices of State of Florence held by the Vespucci.—Guido Antonio di Giovanni Vespucci.—Immediate Relatives of Americus.—Antiquity of Family.—Destiny of Americus.—Commerce and Italian Bankers.

Birth of Americus Vespucius, 1451.

AMERIGO VESPUCCI, or, as he will be designated in this work by his Latin name, Americus Vespucius, was the third son of Anastasio Vespucci and Elizabetta Mini, and was born in Florence, on the ninth day of March, A. D. 1451. At the time of his birth, his family was in moderate circumstances in respect of wealth; but they traced their descent through a long line of noble progenitors, and took a high rank among the aristocratic families of the Republic. His earliest biographer, Bandini, devotes a number of pages of his work to an account of the illustrious members of the Vespucci family who preceded Americus, and as every thing connected with him becomes a matter of interest, some parts of this genealogical narrative are extracted, divested as much as possible of unnecessary detail.[1]

[1] Bandini, Vita e Lettere, chap. i. p. 1—24.

Origin of the family of the Vespucci.

The family originated in the town of Peretola, distant only a few miles from Florence, where they possessed considerable estates, and were celebrated for their hospitality, and the patronage they bestowed upon men of letters. Ugolino Verini commemorates them in a Latin poem, and says,

> Venit et ex isto soboles Vespuccia vico
> Egregiis ornata viris, nec inhospita musis.[1]

About the commencement of the thirteenth century the Vespucci family removed to Florence. It was then the custom for the noble families of the Republic, to establish their residences near the gates of the city, which led to their country estates.

There was more of the leaven of democracy in the Florentine constitution than in that of any other of the Italian republics, and as the nobles never gave up their power till they were finally crushed by the people, the state was, in consequence, more liable to sudden convulsions and outbreaks. It was almost a matter of necessity for the prominent families to provide for themselves some easy way of escape from these turmoils, and they consequently adopted the course, of living as close as possible to that outlet of the city which was nearest to their strongholds in the country, where they could at least find temporary security.

The Vespucci family mansion.

The house of the Vespucci stood in the quarter

[1] Bandini, Vita e Lettere, chap. i. p. 3.

of S. Lucia di Ogni Santi, adjacent to the Porta della Cana, which, at the present day, is known as the Porta del Prato. In the street called Borgongnisanti, of modern Florence, may now be seen, by any traveller whose curiosity leads him to the spot, a large edifice, occupied as a hospital for the sick poor, under the direction of the monks of San Giovanni di Dio, which, for centuries before the discovery of America, was the dwelling-place of the ancestors of Americus Vespucius, and his own birthplace. Over the doorway of this mansion, a worthy abbot, by name Antonio Salvini, caused a marble tablet to be placed, in the beginning of the 18th century, which is still in existence, and on which the following inscription appears:

AMERICO VESPVCCIO PATRICIO FLORENTINO
OB REPERTAM AMERICAM
SVI ET PATIÆ NOMINIS ILLVSTRATORI
AMPLIFICATORI. ORBIS. TERARVM.
IN HAC OLIM VESPVCCIA DOMO
A TANTO VIRO HABITATA
PATRES SANCTI IOANNES DE DEO CVLTORES
GRATÆ MEMORIÆ CAVSSA.
MDCCXIX.[1]

The family were possessed of many houses in this same quarter of the city, if the number of doors

To Americus Vespucius, a noble Florentine,
Who, by the discovery of America,
Rendered his own and his country's name illustrious,
The Amplifier of the World,
Upon this ancient mansion of the Vespucci,
Inhabited by so great a man,
The Holy Fathers of St. John of God,
Have erected this Tablet, sacred to his memory,
A.D. 1719.

over which their coat-of-arms appeared is any evidence. Their wealth was acquired chiefly by an ancestor, Simone di Pero Vespucci, who left a memorial of his liberality to the church, as well as of his riches. He embarked largely in mercantile operations, and devoted no inconsiderable portion of his gains to the erection of hospitals for suffering

"This morning the young Cavaliere Amerigo Vespucci called to go with me to the house in which his illustrious ancestor was born. It is a stately and massive building, and in any other land than this, might have been the palace of a prince, but there is nothing to distinguish it in its architecture from an hundred other houses of the old nobility of the Florence of the Medici. Over the entrance a huge marble scroll is placed, on which the following inscription is cut, offering only a just tribute to so great a name.

* * * * * * *

"I always feel almost as great a desire to visit the precise house where an illustrious man was born, or the place where he ended his days, as I do even to read his history. So many associations of deep interest are connected with all that one sees in such spots. When we stood in the frescoed hall of the mansion, or wandered through the different apartments, it seemed, as Monti beautifully says, like "walking through the frescoed gallery of time," and I could almost see the family of the navigator collected under their own roof. We talked in the chamber where Vespucius was born, of his early days, and of the little that was accurately known of them; and in the saloon, of the wealthy and enterprising nobles who used to congregate there. When we turned to go away, with my mind occupied with other thoughts, I forgot, until too late, the usual ceremony of giving a small douceur to the porter, for his trouble in showing us the house—and only remembered it when he slammed the great door violently behind us, before we had left the steps. For an instant the blood suffused the cheek of the young cavalier, and a half-suppressed look of indignation told his feelings, though he said not a word. The time had been, when the porter who guarded that ponderous door bowed low as any one passed in whose veins flowed the blood of the Vespucci, but now, the only living descendant of that proud race, was like any other stranger in the halls of his fathers. There was food enough for reflection in the change which time produces, and we walked on in silence together." — *MSS. Note Book, Florence, 15th March,* 1845.

CHAPTER II.

poor. Jointly with his wife he built a magnificent chapel in the church of Ogni Santi, in the centre of which, his tomb is placed.[1]

Florentine offices held by the Vespucci.

The citizens of Florence availed themselves very frequently of the services of the members of the Vespucci race, and continually, for a long series of years, elevated them to offices of great distinction. Three of the name were, at different times, Gonfaloniere di Justiria, which was the highest office in the state. No less than twenty-five of the family became Priori, and numerous others are inscribed upon the records of the Republic, as the occupants of posts of distinction. In the year 1336, the office of Secretary of the Republic, in those days one of considerable importance, was filled by Amerigo di Stagio Vespucci, which is the first instance on record, where the pre-name which descended to the navigator is found.

The immediate relations of Americus, living ir his own day, were numerous, and although the

[1] This sepulchre still exists, and on the tomb is the following inscription in Gothic characters :

Sepulcrum Simonis Petri De Vespuccis
Mercatoris ac Filiorum et descendentium,
Et uxoris, quæ Fieri ac Pingi fecit
Totam istam capellam pro anima sua,
Anno MCCCLXXXIII.

The tomb of Simone Piero Vespucci,
A merchant—and of his children and descendants,
And of his wife, who caused this Chapel to be erected
And decorated, for the salvation of her soul.
A. D. 1383.

Bandini, Vita, &c., ch. i. p. 12

wealth of the family had in a great measure disappeared, still maintained the respectability of their house. His father was the Secretary of the Signori, the Senate of the Republic. His uncle Juliano was ambassador to Genoa, and subsequently Governor of Pistoia. Nor was Americus the only navigator of the family. His cousin Piero commanded the Florentine fleet of galleys, destined for an attack upon the Corsairs of Barbary, and was afterwards sent Ambassador to the King of Naples, by whom he was highly honoured, and returned to his own country, covered with dignities conferred by that monarch.

CHAPTER II.

Guido Antonio Vespucci.

In his time, also, appeared Guido Antonio di Giovanni, who was distinguished in letters, and for his profound knowledge of law. He established a court of purely mercantile jurisdiction in Florence, and served his country on many important embassies.[1]

[1] Andrea D'azzi, a celebrated literary character of the 15th century, wrote the following quaint epitaph upon this Antonio Vespucci:—

Interpres gravis utriusque juris,
Qui se mellifluæ fluore linguæ
Non vespæ ast apium genus probavit,
Guido Antonius hoc jacet sepulchro,
Is, quem vivere oportuit perenne,
Vel nunquam superum videre lumen.

A sound interpreter of the law,
Who by the flow of his mellifluous language
Proved himself more of the genus of the bee than of the wasp,
Guido Antonio, lies in this sepulchre.—
He, who should have lived forever,
Or else never have seen the light.

Bandini, ch. i. p. 16.

CHAPTER II.

These family details, to which much might be added, did space permit, are in themselves of trifling importance, except in so far as they show what must have been the natural early associations of Americus in his youth. Fernando Columbus, in his life of the Admiral, whose origin he leaves in obscurity, well remarks, that he thinks it better to content himself with dating his descent from the glory of his father, than to waste time in researches to prove that his father was noble by birth. Antiquity of blood is, in truth, a paltry score on which to exalt oneself; yet, differing from Fernando, many places contended, after his death, for the honour of being the birthplace of Columbus, and many efforts were made to attach his name to a lordly line; but where, as in the case of the family of Vespucius, those best ornaments of a genealogy, personal merit and distinguished virtue and talent, appear, it becomes the biographer not to pass them over in silence.

Prevailing Custom of Florentine families.

A custom had long prevailed among the noble families of Florence to select one of the younger members of each, and devote him to mercantile pursuits. It was not then considered as derogatory to the loftiest and purest blood among them, to engage in honourable traffic. A nation of merchants, and ruled by a family who were indebted for their rank and celebrity mainly to their successful business operations, they appreciated the position which an intelligent merchant occupies, and were not restrained from embarking in commerce by any ridiculous pride of birth. Florentine bankers and capitalists had more than once, before the time of Americus, made their influence felt with powerful effect in the affairs of nations; and prosperity in business brought not only wealth, but high consideration in the state, in its train. Americus was accordingly chosen by his father, almost from his birth, to advance the fortunes of his family by commerce, and high hopes were entertained of his success. It was not within the power of human wisdom to foresee, that his after life would contribute more to prejudice the mercantile interests of his native city, than to his own benefit, or that of his relatives.

CHAPTER III.

The Youth of Great Men.—Lack of Detail in this Respect.—Early Education of Americus.—Georgio Antonio Vespucci.—His Uncle.—Brilliant Expectations of his Family.—Studies in Astronomy and Cosmography.—Friendship for Piero Soderini.—Tomaso Soderini.—The Plague in Florence, 1478.—Dissolution of the School of the Friar Vespucci.—Early Letters of Americus.—Lorenzo de Medici.—His Brilliant Administration.—Paolo Toscanelli, the Learned Florentine Physician.—Religious Education of Americus.—Letter of Americus to his Father.

THE saying has been attributed to Bacon, tha the youth of a great man often furnishes data of more importance than any other portion of his life, in guiding posterity to a just estimate of his character. The traveller who looks off from the hills where a river rises, can easily determine the direction it must take as it pursues its course. Sometimes its passage is obstructed by a mountain, around whose base the stream must flow, and sometimes a winding valley leads it away from its nearest track to the sea. In like manner, circumstances over which a man can have little or no control determine the course of his life. His parentage, his country and its institutions; the times in which he is born, and the character of those by whom he is in early life surrounded, decide in a great measure his future history. The first acquisition, therefore, of the biog-

CHAPTER III.

rapher should be, an enlightened and philosophical understanding of those events which have influenced the life or coloured the history of his hero.

It is true that the youth of many of the most distinguished of mankind is veiled in obscurity, but all the historian needs, to form a correct idea of their character, is generally preserved in the few facts that escape oblivion. It would be easy to supply this deficiency in the case of Americus, for there are not wanting ingenious accounts of the history of his early days, in antiquated Italian books and manuscripts, and equally incredible stories are still told by his countrymen.

But, not to follow the uncertain gleamings of traditionary light, and believing that the materials in hand may be made serviceable to the scholar and inquirer of the present and future times, an attempt will be made to give a clear and impartial account of all which has been gathered that is authentic and interesting in the Life and Voyages of Americus.

Georgio Antonio Vespucci.

All the advantages derived by Americus from his patrician descent, were trifling in comparison with the education which his connexion with an eminent teacher of that day procured for him. His paternal uncle, Georgio Antonio Vespucci, had been from his youth distinguished as a scholar. Devoted in early life to the church, he became a monk of the order of San Marco, and won much reputation both for learning and piety. About a year before the birth of Americus, he opened a school in his convent for the sons

CHAPTER III.

of the principal nobles of Florence; and there, as soon as his years permitted, in company with many youthful Florentines, Americus daily repaired, to ponder over the mysteries of grammar and mathematics.

End kept in view in his education.

In his education, it may reasonably be supposed that the worthy friar was not unmindful of the claims of consanguinity, and that he paid particular attention to the progress of one, who, in the imagination of his parents, was destined to restore, by his success in commercial affairs, the decaying fortunes of his family. While this end was kept studiously in view, and his young mind continually exercised by application to the more abstruse sciences of astronomy and cosmography, no small portion of his attention was directed to the acquisition of classical lore, and he left the hands of his uncle, an accomplished scholar, in an age when it was difficult to find many such out of the cloister or the university.

That such was the case, the subsequent life of Americus sufficiently proves; while, at the same time, it affords another demonstration of the fallacy of human expectations. Little dreamed the worthy friar, Georgio Antonio, that the rudiments he daily instilled into the mind of his pupil would be of small avail in the acquisition of worldly goods, and still less thought he, that, when disgusted with the vicissitudes of commerce, those same instructions would open to his nephew a new path to honour, if not to fortune.[1]

[1] Bandini, Vita, &c., p. 19.

DEPARTURE FROM CADIZ.

In the year of our Lord, 1497, on the tenth day of May, as before stated, we left the port of Cadiz with four Ships

Friendship with Piero Soderini.

At this period Americus contracted a friendship with Piero Soderini, a noble youth, of his own age, who was also a pupil of the friar, which continued, with unchanging constancy, through his lifetime, and was the source of much gratification and pride to the future navigtor. Soderini afterwards became the Gonfaloniére of Florence; and to him, in all the confidence of early friendship, are addressed those letters which will appear in another part of this work, and which give the most interesting account of the subsequent voyages of Americus.

Piero was the son of the celebrated Tomaso Soderini, who, at the death of Pietro de Medici in 1469, was at the head of the most powerful family in Florence. He was treated with the greatest reverence, as the leader of the commonwealth, both by foreign princes and citizens; but modestly and with patriotism declining the honours they would have bestowed upon him, protected the fortunes of the young princes Lorenzo and Juliano, the first of whom afterwards became so celebrated, and who always, in his youth, adhered closely to the counsels of his protector.[1]

The plague in 1478.

The studies of Americus were suddenly interrupted by the appearance of the plague in Florence, in the year 1478. This terrible visitor always brought in its train general consternation and confusion. The utter want of precaution and preventive sanatory regulations, which can scarcely be said to have existed at all in that age, rendered it

[1] Bandini, Vita, &c., p. 25.

CHAPTER III.

peculiarly violent, and almost uncontrollable. All business and pleasure were alike suspended; the ties of relationship and affection were in most cases forgotten, and the universal feeling was selfish regard for personal safety. Even the quiet institutions of learning felt its malignant influence, and those who were most secluded from social intercourse dreaded and fled from its attacks.[1]

The school of the Friar Vespucci was at once broken up, and his pupils scattered in various directions. Americus was taken by his parents into the country, to await the disappearance of the pestilence, and there for the first time, as far as any evidence exists, employed his pen. Some letters which are still preserved, written while in this temporary seclusion, give strong proof of a mind earnest for instruction; and though showing a gravity of thought hardly consistent with his years, are full of enthusiastic impulse and love of adventure. Although tempered throughout by filial respect and affection, they foreshadow the subsequent career of the man, and are replete with the sincerity and modesty which characterized his later productions.

Temptations of Florence in 1480.

The contagion had barely subsided, when Americus resumed his studies with renewed ardour. This is the more remarkable, when the temptations which surrounded the noble youth of that day are

[1] Bandini, Vita, &c., p. 28. See also Machiavelli's account of the plague in 1528, which speaks of this, and gives a thrilling description of its horrors.—*Opere de Niccolo Machiavelli*, tom. viii. p. 5[illegible].

considered. Lorenzo, the Magnificent, in the flush of youth and power, rendered the city of Florence and his own court the centre of attraction to all the gay nobility of Italy and Europe. Festivals of unequalled splendour drew an immense concourse of strangers to his capital, and the city was wild with dissipation and extravagance.

In the midst of all, and exposed to most of these allurements, Americus diligently occupied himself with the pursuits of learning. He gave particular devotion to the study of geometry and cosmography, and frequently surprised the sagest professors of those sciences by the acuteness of his remarks and conjectures.

Toscanelli, the Florentine Physician.

Among the cosmographers of the times, he encountered frequently the celebrated Toscanelli, who is mentioned in the introductory chapter, and derived from him many of the views respecting the position of the Indies, which that philosopher afterwards communicated to Columbus by letter.[1]

The subsequent celebrity of Americus was mainly owing to the direction of his labours at this time, and it appears that his chief ambition was to excel as a geographer; so that when he quitted the monastery of the good brother of St. Mark, he was, in all probability, better fitted to astonish the world with novel theories, than to acquire the fortune for which his family had destined him.

Only one portion of his uncle's instructions remains to be noticed. He cultivated in the mind of

[1] Bandini, Vita, p. 29.

CHAPTER III.

his nephew a warm and profound sense of dependance upon the protection of God, which supported him in many trials and sufferings of his after life, and nerved his soul to the accomplishment of heroic achievements, which have been reserved by Providence for those men who have reposed with the highest confidence upon its arm. The reader of his letters cannot fail to be struck with the ready reliance upon the favour of Providence, which many of his actions evinced, and his often recurring acknowledgment of thanks for protection received.

Letter from Americus to his father.

The translation of a short letter from Americus to his father, written while he was residing at the country estate of the family, during the prevalence of the plague in Florence, will close this chapter. It was originally written in Latin.

To the Excellent and Honourable Signor Anastasio Vespucci.

HONOURED FATHER—

Do not wonder that I have not written to you within the last few days. I thought that my uncle would have satisfied you concerning me. In his absence I scarcely dare to address you in the Latin tongue, blushing even at my deficiencies in my own language; I have, besides, been industriously occupied of late in studying the rules of Latin composition, and will show you my book on my return. Whatever else I have accomplished, and how I have conducted myself, you will have been able to learn from my uncle, whose return I ardently desire, that, under his and your own joint directions, I may follow with greater ease both my studies and your kind precepts. Georgio Antonio, three or four days ago, gave a number of letters to you, to a good priest, Signor Nerotto, to which he desires your answer. There is nothing else that is new to relate, unless that we all desire much to return to the city. The day of our return is not yet fixed, but soon will be, unless the pestilence should increase, and occasion greater alarm, which God avert.

He, Georgio Antonio, commends to your consideration a poor and wretched neighbour of his, whose only reliance and means are in our house, concerning which, he addressed you in full. He asks you, therefore, that you would attend to his affairs, so that they may suffer as little as possible in his absence.

Farewell, then, honoured father; salute all the family in my behalf, and commend me to my mother and all my elder relatives.

Your son, with due obedience,

AMERIGO VESPUCCI.[1]

Trivio Mugelli, Oct. 19, 1478.

[1] Bandini, Vita, p. 29.

CHAPTER IV.

Period from 1480 to 1490.—Cosmography.—High Value of Maps.—Gabriel de Velasca.—Mauro.—Causes of the Departure of Americus from Florence.—Girolamo Vespucci.—His Loss of Property.—Piero de' Medici commissions Americus.—Spain.—Wars against the Moors.—Giovanni Vespucci, the Nephew of Americus.—Account given of him by Peter Martyr.—Letter of Americus and Donato Nicollini.—Juan Berardi, 1492.—The necessary Reflections of Americus.—An Epoch of Enterprise and Improvement.

CHAPTER IV.

HISTORY throws little light upon that period of the life of Americus comprised between the completion of his studies and his departure for Spain, which took place some time in the year 1490. It is probable that he resided in Florence during the whole of this time, and it may be, that he was engaged in commercial pursuits in his native city, although no evidence of it has come down to modern times. Whether such was the case or not, it is well known that he continued to pursue his researches in cosmography.[1]

High price of Maps and and Charts.

He was very curious in collecting all the best maps, charts, and globes, of the time, the works of distinguished projectors. The value of these maps was most extraordinary, even considering that their scarcity enhanced their price; and the projectors were so highly esteemed, that the making of one good

[1] Bandini, chap. iii. p. 33.

map, rendered the name of the cosmographer illustrious. The Venetians struck a medal in honour of Mauro, an eminent friar, who drew a map which was considered the most accurate of the time, and it is recorded that Americus paid the high price of one hundred and thirty ducats, which is equal to five hundred and fifty-five Spanish dollars of the present day, for a map of sea and land, made at Mallorea, in 1439, by Gabriel de Velasca.[1]

Misfortunes of Girolamo Vespucci.

The immediate cause of his departure from Italy appears to have arisen in some measure from the misfortunes of another person, although there is little doubt he had contemplated a long absence, for many previous years. His elder brother Girolamo, following the bent of an enterprising spirit, had left Florence about the year 1480, to seek his fortune in foreign climes, and had established himself in business in one of the Grecian cities of Asia Minor. For some time he was extremely prosperous in his negotiations, and by degrees, with the view of increasing his means of operation, had taken the control of a large portion of the family property. Every thing went on fortunately with him, until one disastrous day, in the year 1489. While attending the matin service, at a convent in the neighbourhood of his residence, his house was broken open by thieves; and, as he writes to Americus, he was robbed of all he possessed, including the property of his father, and the accumulation of nine years of incessant toil and watchfulness.

[1] Irving's Works, Paris edition, vol. ii. p. 613.

CHAPTER IV.

This severe blow greatly cramped the resources of the whole family; and on the receipt of his brother's letter, dated July 24th, 1489, which was forwarded to him by a Florentine pilgrim, who had been to Jerusalem to visit the holy sepulchre, and was on his return to his native city, Americus at once determined to attempt to retrieve, in some measure, his brother's losses; and for that purpose to proceed to Spain, where fair prospects in mercantile life were opened to him.[1]

Americus is commissioned by Lorenzo de' Medici.

At this time, Lorenzo de' Medici, cousin of Lorenzo the Magnificent, who had some matters of importance to attend to in Barcelona, commissioned Americus as his agent; and he accordingly set sail from Leghorn, for the Spanish city. The dominions of Ferdinand and Isabella just then afforded a fine field for profit in merchandise. The splendid court of those illustrious sovereigns, and the wars they had for a long time prosecuted against the Moors, had drawn from all quarters of Europe large numbers of the chivalrous young nobility of the age, who were anxious to gain reputation and military experience on the field of battle, and regarded the contest with the infidels on the hills of Grenada, in the light of another Christian crusade.

Italian merchants and bankers were not backward in taking advantage of the wants occasioned by this great influx of foreigners, and such extensive military movements. A great many of them were to be found in all parts of the Peninsula, and

[1] Bandini, ch. iii. p. 32.

in the records of Simaacas, various royal decrees respecting them are extant. Among them is a warrant, dated in 1486, granting a safe conduct to Juan Berardi and other Florentine merchants, from Barcelona to Seville. The connexion of Americus with this individual, as will subsequently appear, was of much consequence, and must have taken place soon after his arrival in Spain, if not before. It is not at all improbable that it originated in Florence, but no accurate information can be obtained on the subject.[1]

Giovanni Vespucci, the nephew of Americus.

On his departure from his native city, he was entrusted with the charge of a number of youthful Florentines, who were placed by their friends under his care, and who went with him to acquire the advantages of travel. He took with him also his nephew Giovanni, a promising youth, to whom he was warmly attached, and who subsequently accompanied him in all his voyages, and became a skilful navigator. The following extract from a letter which is preserved by Bandini, was copied by that biographer from a manuscript in the handwriting of Americus, which was preserved in his time, in the collection of the Abbot Scarlatti.[2]

1 Navarréte, Collecion de Viages, tom. iii. p. 315.

2 Bandini, chap. iii. p. 35. Irving, vol. ii. p. 883.

Peter Martyr speaks of this Giovanni Vespucci in the highest terms, and says, "Young Vespucius is one to whom Americus Vespucius, his uncle, left the exact knowledge of the mariner's faculties, as it were, by inheritance after his death, for he was a very expert master in the knowledge of his card, his compass, and the elevation of the Pole star by the quadrant. Vespucius is my very familiar friend, and a witty young man, in whose company I take great pleasure, and therefore use him oftentimes for my guest."

CHAPTER IV.

It indicates clearly what were his occupations as late as the early part of 1492; and is worthy of a translation, if only as a specimen of the style of mercantile correspondence of the age.

Extract from a Letter of Americus.

"And as it is necessary for one of us, either Americus or Donato, to proceed in a short time to Florence, we shall be able to give you better information all points by word of mouth than can possibly be done by letter.

As yet, it has been impossible to do any thing respecting the freight of salt, for want of a vessel. For some time past, we are sorry to say, no ship has arrived here which was not chartered; be consoled, if no one arrives here, that we shall be active for your interests.

You will have learned from the elder Donato the good fortune which has happened to his Highness the King; assuredly the most high God has given him his aid; but I cannot relate it to you in full—God preserve him many years, and us with him!

There is nothing new to communicate. Christ preserve you!

We date, January 30th, 1492.

DONATO NICOLLINI.
AMERICUS VESPUCIUS.[1]"

The Nicollini who signs the above letter jointly with Americus, was undoubtedly connected with him in business, at that period; but nothing further concerning him can be determined, and it is equally

[1] Bandini, chap. iii. p. 35, 36.

CHAPTER IV.

doubtful when he first became acquainted with Berardi. It must, however, have been soon after this time; for very shortly after the date of this letter, Americus went to Seville, where Berardi was established.

Contract of the Spanish Government with Berardi.

After the return of Columbus from his first voyage, Ferdinand and Isabella contracted with Berardi to furnish and equip four armaments, to be forwarded at different times to the New World, and Americus is found to be busily occupied, in connexion with him, receiving payments and entering into obligations in his behalf and name. Some have supposed that he was only the agent of Berardi in these transactions; but it is more probable that he became a partner in the house, as, after the death of Berardi, Americus still continued to manage all the affairs of the armaments, and was paid large sums of money by the government, for equipments previously effected.[1]

It has been thought, by some historians, that Americus accompanied Columbus upon his second voyage; but there is no evidence, which is of

[1] Entre varias partidas de maravedis que en cuenta del flete de estas naves se abonaron á Berardi, por el tesorero Pinelo, de órden de D. Juan Fonseca, hay dos que recibió Amerigo Vespuche á nombre del mismo Berardi, y habiendo este fallecido, en Diciembre de 1495—"Vespuche se encargo de tener la cuenta con los Maestres del flete y suelde que hobiesen de haber, segun el asiento, que el dicho Juanoto hizo con ellos, (y del mantenimiento, &c. Para lo cual recibió—Amerigo de Pinelo 10.000 maravedis en 12 de Enero de 1496." Siguio Vespucio disponiendo todas las cosas hasta despachar la armada en San Lucar.—*Navarrête*, tom. iii. p. 315—317.

CHAPTER IV.

much weight, to sustain the opinion, and his own accounts tend to contradict it.[1]

An important epoch in History. 1490.

The period at which Americus may be said to have first commenced active life was, without doubt, the most important epoch in modern history. If it were possible to transport oneself back, in propria persona, to the year 1490, it would be easy to analyze the probable condition of his mind at the date of his departure from Florence, and imagination can only partially supply the vacuum, which is felt in the lack of any writings of his own. Remarkable events had followed each other with startling rapidity, during the century which was then drawing to its close. The sudden advancement of literature, the revival of art, and the improvement in the science of navigation, must each have exerted a direct influence over his mind. He was no longer a youth, but in the fullest vigour of manhood, competent to think, and think deeply, on all

[1] The four voyages of Vespucius are described by Munster, in his Cosmography, printed in Latin in 1550. He says, "Americus Vespucius, after having been sent by Ferdinand, King of Castile, about the year 1492, in company with Columbus, to seek out unknown lands, after a few years elapsed, being learned in navigation, made voyages by himself,—two for the said King Ferdinand, and two for Emanuel, King of Portugal, and wrote concerning them in the following manner." But it is rendered certain that Munster was in error in his statement.—*Bandini*, ch. iv. p. 58. Canovai says, "Accordingly, in 1493 Vespucius was deputed by Ferdinand to accompany Columbus in his second voyage, in the quality of an apprentice." But he gives no authority but Munster for his statement.—*Canovai*, *Vita*, &c. tom. ii. p. 50. Irving says, "The first notice of a positive form which we have of Vespucci as resident in Spain is early in 1496." This is as manifest an error, as that of Munster.—*Irving*, vol. ii. p. 881.

the great subjects of thought which agitated the age. It was an age, too, of great intellectual activity, resembling more nearly the present, than any which had preceded it. Knowledge was taking vast strides. No solitary subject of contemplation, like the Crusades, occupied the minds of all, to the exclusion of every thing else. Every science, every theory of politics or religion, every department of art, attracted and received its share of attention.

It may reasonably be supposed that Americus experienced his proportion of the restlessness and anticipation which filled the public mind. He, with the rest of the world, was looking out anxiously, though with indefinite hopes, for the coming of great events. Perhaps, even as he entered the ship which was to bear him from his native country, he felt in his heart a presage of his future fame; and while visions of yet undiscovered lands floated before his eyes, inwardly resolved to take a prominent part himself, in the drama of progress and improvement then being enacted in the theatre of the world.

CHAPTER V.

Meeting of Americus with Columbus, 1492, '93.—Description of the Personal Appearance of Columbus.—Personal Appearance of Americus.—Sketch of their different Views.—The Problem of Longitude.—Discussion at Salamanca.—Conversation between Columbus and Americus.—Singular Vow of the Former.—He Repels the Imputation of Mercenary Motives.—Doubts of Americus as to the Territories of the Khan, drawn from the Appearance of the Natives, &c.—His Ideas of a large Island between Europe and Asia.—Confidence of Columbus.—Considers himself Divinely Commissioned.—His Plan of Attack upon the Infidels.—Cites Paolo Toscanelli.—Vespucius States his View of the Question of Longitude.—Terrestrial Paradise.—Enthusiasm of Columbus on this Subject.—Exaggeration of Marco Polo.—Criticism of Americus.

CHAPTER V.

It is hardly necessary to recall to the reader's mind the great event of the year 1492. After a long series of disappointments and reverses, Columbus had induced the Spanish sovereigns to lend their ears to his representations; and that memorable year, an epoch nearly as familiar to the memory of all, as that of the coming of the Saviour, crowned his hopes with triumph.

Personal appearance of Columbus.

It must have been soon after his return from his first voyage of discovery, when the acquaintance of Americus with the admiral commenced. Columbus is described by his contemporaries as being of a commanding personal appearance. Tall and muscular, and well proportioned in form, he happily blended in his address a certain suavity and affability of manner, with the greatest dignity. His complexion was fair, and his hair, which had once been light, had changed to grey. Piercing grey eyes, which, when he was engaged in discussion or conversation, would kindle and flash with peculiar brightness, gave life to features otherwise rather melancholy in their general effect. His temper was naturally hasty, but he seldom allowed it to appear in his conversation by any want of courtesy in his language.[1]

Personal appearance of Americus.

Americus is described as being of about the middle height, of rather a brawny and thickset frame. The shape of his head was peculiarly striking. His forehead was low and retreating, but of great breadth and massiveness, and his temples were unusually expanded. One look at the formation of his skull, which showed that there existed a vast preponderance of the intellectual, over the animal developments of the brain, would have satisfied a phrenologist that he beheld a remarkable man. His eyes were large and black, his nose aquiline, and his cheek bones rather prominent. His mouth was singularly expressive of firmness mingled with amiability. His complexion was dark, and inclining to sallow. His hair was originally black, but at this time was slightly mixed with grey. His beard was thick and bushy, and was preserved entire. The portrait of him, from which was taken the engraving that appears at the commencement of this

[1] Irving's Works, Paris Ed., vol. ii. p. 613.

CHAPTER V.

volume, was painted many years after the date of his first interview with Columbus, when he had become nearly bald. In his address, although possessed of less dignity of demeanour than Columbus, there was a gentleness and retiring modesty, which was highly attractive. His temper was mild and equable, and he never suffered it to gain the mastery over him in his speech.

Such, as nearly as can be ascertained at this period, was the personal appearance of the two great men, when they first came together. Americus, as has been said before, was greatly excited by the reports of the discoveries of Columbus, and had eagerly investigated them. There is evidence in his writings, that he arrived at very different conclusions as to their ultimate tendency, from those of the admiral; and it is scarcely probable that two such men should have met as they did, without an interchange of their peculiar sentiments, on a subject which was engrossing the attention of both. It has seemed best to set before the reader a brief sketch of some of the different views which influenced them, in the form of a friendly dialogue between the two, rather than in the shape of a dissertation.

Different views of Americus and Columbus.

Care has been taken that no idea should be attributed to either which their several writings do not indicate as existing in their own minds. At the same time, it must not be supposed that the views expressed by Americus were the settled convictions of his mind; they were rather the speculations of an active spirit, acting upon the natural doubts suggested by inquiry into a subject, where all was vague and undecided. Columbus appears, as he really existed, in all the confidence of enthusiasm; Americus rather as a sceptic, anxious to extract the truth from the mass of mingled truth and error, which lay before him. That neither of the two was free from error, is not to be wondered at; but that the speculations of Americus were much the most divested of absurdities, subsequent discoveries have amply proved.[1]

The doubts of Americus.

The greatest doubt which existed in the mind of Americus, was in relation to the distance between Europe and the eastern shores of Asia. He always discredited the measurement of longitude, which was invented by Toscanelli, and communicated to Columbus, and the recent discoveries of the latter tended to strengthen those doubts, rather than to abate them.

The conversation which follows, should be looked upon as the commencement of a discussion, and not as a discussion itself. Abstruse and minute calculations were doubtless entered into by the two navigators, to confirm their peculiar views. Co-

[1] Mr. Irving says, "When Vespucci wrote his letters, there was not a doubt entertained but that Columbus had discovered the main land in his first voyage. Cuba being always considered the extremity of Asia, until circumnavigated in 1508. Vespucci may have supposed Brazil, Paria, and the rest of that coast part of a distinct continent, &c." — *Irving's Works*, Paris Ed. p. 885, 886. This admission is striking, inasmuch as the Letters of Americus were all written previous to 1508, and contain ample confirmation of the opinion that he thought he had arrived at a new continent.— *Vide infra, Letter to Soderini.*

CHAPTER V.

lumbus was a man ever ready to receive suggestions and acquire information from whatever source, and it is not to be supposed that he considered the opinions of Americus, though materially at variance with his own, as he did the absurd objections which were raised to his first voyage by some of the over-wise doctors at Salamanca. Though pertinacious in his adherence to his own enthusiastic theories, he was ever ready to give ear to any doubt which carried with it the semblance of reason, or was susceptible of being supported by plausible argument.[1]

1 The two navigators agreed upon many important theories entirely. The great difference of their discussion, from that which Columbus held with the conclave at Salamanca, will be better understood after a perusal of the account of the absurd objections which were then raised to his theories, which is found in Mr. Irving's Life of the Admiral. He says,

"At the very threshold of the discussion, instead of geographical objections, Columbus was assailed by quotations from the Bible and the Testament, the Book of Genesis, the Psalms of David, the Prophets, the Epistles, and the Gospels. To these were added the expositions of various saints and reverend commentators, St. Chrysostome and St. Augustine, St. Jerome and St. Gregory, St. Basil and St. Ambrose, and Lactantius Firmianus, a redoubted champion of the faith. Doctrinal points were mixed up with philosophical discussions, and a mathematical demonstration was allowed no truth, if it appeared to clash with a text of Scripture, or a commentary of one of the fathers. Thus the possibility of antipodes in the southern hemisphere, an opinion so generally maintained by the wisest of the ancients, as to be pronounced by Pliny the great contest between the learned and the ignorant, became a stumbling-block with some of the sages of Salamanca. Several of them stoutly contradicted this basis of the theory of Columbus, supporting themselves by quotations from Lactantius and St. Augustine, who were considered in those days as almost evangelical authority. But though these writers were men of consummate erudition, and two of the greatest luminaries of what has been called the golden age of Ecclesiastical learning, yet their writings were calculated to perpetuate darkness in respect to the sciences

CONVERSATION BETWEEN AMERICUS AND COLUMBUS.

COLUMBUS

It grieves me much, worthy Signor Vespucci, to learn from our friend the Signor Berardi, that you

Dialogue between Americus and Columbus.

"The passage cited by Lactantius to confute Columbus is in a strain of gross ridicule, unworthy of so grave a theologian. 'Is there any one so foolish,' he asks, 'as to believe that there are antipodes with their feet opposite to ours; people who walk with their feet upwards and their heads hanging down? That there is a part of the world in which all things are topsy-turvy; where the trees grow with their branches downward, and where it rains, hails and snows upward? The idea of the roundness of the earth,' he adds, 'was the cause of inventing this fable of the antipodes with their heels in the air: for these philosophers having once erred, go on in their absurdities, defending one another.' More grave objections were urged on the authority of St. Augustine. He pronounces the doctrine of the antipodes incompatible with the historical foundations of our faith; since to assert that there were inhabited lands on the opposite side of the globe, would be to maintain that there were nations not descended from Adam, it being impossible for them to have passed the intervening ocean. This would be, therefore, to discredit the Bible, which expressly declares, that all men are descended from one common parent.

"Such were the unlooked-for prejudices which Columbus had to encounter at the very outset of his conference, and which certainly relish more of the convent than of the university. To his simplest proposition, the spherical form of the earth, were opposed figurative texts of Scripture. They observed that in the Psalms, the heavens are said to be extended like a hide, that is, according to commentators, the curtain, or covering of a tent, which, among ancient pastoral nations, was formed of the hides of animals; and that St. Paul, in his epistle to the Hebrews, compares the heavens to a tabernacle or tent, extended over the earth, which they thence inferred must be flat. Columbus, who was a devoutly religious man, found that he was in danger of being convicted, not merely of error, but of heterodoxy. Others, more versed in science, admitted the globular form of the earth, and the possibility of an opposite and inhabitable hemisphere, but they brought up the chimera of the ancients, and maintained that it would be impossible to arrive there in consequence of the insupportable heat of the torrid zone. Even granting this could be passed, they observed, that the circumference of the earth must be so great as to require at least three years for the voyage, and those who should undertake it must

CHAPTER V.

do not estimate, as I do, the result of our recent navigation in the West. With your well-known skill in cosmography, I fear me, you combine more of doubt than would be becoming to a Christian navigator.

AMERICUS.

Your Excellency mistakes my views greatly, or has been misinformed of them. Far from undervaluing the effect of the discoveries which your genius has accomplished, I am the rather disposed to place a greater estimate upon them, than does the Admiral Colon himself. If I judged them in the light in which they are viewed by the most of those who hope to profit by them, then indeed the imputation would be just, considering that I have freely expressed what has occurred to my own thoughts: but I look not to such things, and well I know that your own mind is above them.

COLUMBUS.

In that respect you do me but justice. If I look for gain in aught that I have undertaken, it is only that I may devote it to a holy purpose. Have I

perish of hunger and thirst, from the impossibility of carrying provisions for so long a period. He was told, on the authority of Epicurus, that admitting the earth to be spherical, it was only inhabitable in the Northern Hemisphere, and in that section only was canopied by the heavens; that the opposite half was a chaos, a gulf, or a mere waste of water. Not the least absurd objection advanced was, that should a ship even succeed in reaching, in this way, the extremity of India, she could never get back again, for the rotundity of the globe would present a kind of mountain, up which it would be impossible for her to sail with the most favourable wind."—*Irving*, vol. ii. p. 627.

not, even within the last few days, recorded my solemn oath that I would, in the event of my prosperous arrival at the wealthy capital of the Grand Khan, (whom, by the favour of God, I hope to convert to the true faith), employ the riches I shall acquire in the equipment of a force of four thousand horse and fifty thousand foot, for the recovery of the holy sepulchre from the hands of the infidels? I am unwilling to think that your speech tends to the end of imputing to me mercenary motives, but wherein do we differ? Is not the way opened, and will not the intercourse I mean to establish with the Pagan monarch contribute greatly to the purposes I keep in view? The holy father at Rome himself lends me encouragement in my undertaking, and regards with approbation my efforts to lead into the true church so mighty a potentate.[1]

AMERICUS.

With all the deference that is due to your Excellency's superior wisdom and experience, I would state, that therein lies the very point of our difference.

[1] "While the mind of Columbus was thus teeming with glorious anticipations, his pious scheme for the deliverance of the Holy Sepulchre was not forgotten. It has been shown that he suggested it to the Spanish sovereigns at the time of first making his propositions, holding it forth as the great object to be effected by the profits of his discoveries. Flushed with the idea of the vast wealth that was now to accrue to himself, he made a vow to furnish within seven years an army consisting of four thousand horse and fifty thousand foot, for the rescue of the Holy Sepulchre, and a similar force within the five following years. It is essential to a full comprehension of the character of Columbus, that this wild and visionary project should be borne in recollection."—*Irving*, vol. ii. p. 680.

CHAPTER V.

I deem it by no means certain that your ships have touched the territories of the Grand Khan at all, but rather a land which has hitherto been alike unknown to him and to us. Thousands of leagues may yet intervene between that land and his dominions, whether of sea or earth remains to be discovered; and I judge in this wise, as well from the accounts of cosmographers, who have written upon the subject, as from the description of the barbarous natives, which you yourself have fallen in with, in your recent discoveries. The accounts of those who have penetrated to the distant regions of the East, lead us to understand that the subjects of the Grand Khan live in the midst of the most profuse wealth and luxury, and bedeck themselves with superfine garments, and much gold and jewelry. These people, however, are naked and wild, and may be looked upon as little superior to the beasts, and I think cannot be in any way connected with a monarch of such magnificence. My own thoughts lead me to the conviction, that there exists near unto the lands you have visited, an immense country, which may possibly belong to, and be part of, the Khan's dominions, though I doubt if such be the case. Marco Polo himself speaks of an island lying far out in the ocean which washes the eastern shores of Asia, the great Cipango, abounding in riches and precious stones, which has never been subdued by the sovereign of Cathay, although he has made many attempts to conquer it. This island I deem it necessary to discover, in the first place; then, even after it is circumnavigated or passed over, and the last may be the easiest way, a voyage of long duration will still have to be accomplished before the empire of Cathay is reached. When I speak of a passage over this unknown island, I do so in view of its great extent, as I estimate it to be of such size, that it might more properly be designated Terra Firma, being, according to my calculations, as large, if not larger, than the whole of Europe. And herein do I estimate most highly the worth of the discoveries which your excellency has made, and their importance to this realm, as it will now be comparatively easy to pass the lands you have fallen in with, by sailing either in a more northerly or a more southerly direction, in either case striking the country I have in my mind.[1]

Columbus.

Nay, nay, good Signor Vespucci, I have the confidence in my heart that you are mistaken. I feel persuaded, by the many and wonderful manifestations of Divine Providence in my especial favour, that I am the chosen instrument of God in bringing

[1] Vide infra—Letter to Soderini, chap. vii.—where Americus says, "We sailed so rapidly that at the end of twenty-seven days we came in sight of land, which we judged to be a continent, being about a thousand leagues west of the Grand Canaries," &c.

"Unless the reader bears in mind these sumptuous descriptions of Marco Polo, of countries teeming with wealth, and cities whose very domes and palaces flamed with gold, he will have but a faint idea of the splendid anticipations of Columbus when he discovered, as he supposed, the extremity of Asia."—*Irving*, vol. ii. p. 906.—Also, vide supra, the first note to this Chapter.

CHAPTER V.

to pass a great event—no less than the conversion of millions who are now existing in the darkness of Paganism.[1] I would, indeed, provide for the good of the poor natives we have already met with, as well by building cities on their islands, and cultivating their lands, as by the erection of churches, and the establishment of holy priests and Christian worship. But I would by no means forget the greater end in view: namely, that of bringing to bear upon the infidels the wealth and power of the vast kingdom of Cathay; that thus, being encompassed on all hands by armies from Europe on the one side, and by the innumerable hosts of Asia on the other, they may be utterly destroyed, and the tomb of our Lord be again placed in the possession of true believers. I will not think that so enlightened a sovereign as the Grand Khan is represented to us, would refuse to submit at once to the authority of Holy Mother Church; but if he does, it will become our duty to convert him by the sword of faith. In these things I marvel much at your incredulity, Signor Vespucci, seeing that you have had often opportunities of conversing with the

[1] On one occasion during the first voyage of Columbus, there was a heavy swell of the sea during a perfect calm, a phenomenon which is now perfectly understood by mariners, and which occurs very frequently. "Columbus, who considered himself under the immediate eye and guardianship of Heaven in the solemn enterprise, intimates in his journal that this swelling of the sea seemed providentially ordered to allay the rising clamours of his crew—comparing it to that which so providentially aided Moses when conducting the children of Israel out of the captivity of Egypt."—*Irving*, vol. ii. p. 643. *Navarrête*, tom. i. Journal of Columbus.

learned physician Paolo, your own countryman, (peace be to his ashes,) who, in his lifetime, coincided so nearly with me in opinion.

AMERICUS.

I have, indeed, as your Excellency observes, oftentimes disputed and argued with the venerable Toscanelli, and to him is due much of the little knowledge I have been able to acquire in cosmography and astronomy. But from him I also learned, that the descriptions which are given by Marco Polo were considered by many wise men as not altogether beyond the reach of doubt, and irrefutable. And even to his own apprehension there were many apparent exaggerations and mis-statements. If, then, he is in error in some particulars, how shall we draw the line, and say wherein he speaks the truth of his own knowledge? And how could he know the distance which exists between Cathay and the western shores of Europe, save by hearsay and the reports of mariners on that unknown shore, who themselves must have been falsifiers, as it is well known that not one of them has ever appeared here, who might have estimated the distance? I cannot think that we are so near to Cathay as your Excellency supposes, and had much rather follow the opinion, that you have possibly approached the shore, that has been hitherto represented as inaccessible to mortals.[1]

[1] Both Americus and Columbus were inclined to believe in the doctrine of the existence of a terrestrial paradise. With Americus,

CHAPTER V.

COLUMBUS.

You speak of the Paradise, which so many sound and able divines assert to be still in existence on the earth.

AMERICUS.

I do; though not as firmly believing in the relation as they do. If there is such a place existing as is described by the eloquent St. Basil, methinks it must be near unto the balmy islands which you have discovered, so similar in climate and verdancy.

COLUMBUS.

Such, indeed, has often been my own opinion, and I deem it not to be inconsistent with the other, which holds to the proximity of Cathay. Oh that I might, through the grace of God and intercession of the saints, ever arrive at that blessed spot, where

however, it was rather a subject of pleasant contemplation than actual belief. He speaks respecting it always with a qualification: "If there be a terrestrial paradise on earth, doubtless it cannot be far from these places."—*Vide infra*, Letter to Piero de Medici.

Columbus, on the contrary, was full of enthusiasm upon the subject, and looked upon it as having an undoubted existence. These opinions are not to be wondered at, as they were entertained by many philosophers of that and previous ages. The most fanciful accounts were given of this imaginary spot and its presumed locality.—Some placed it in the grand oasis of Arabia, others in the Holy Land, and others again in India. Wherever located, it was the garden of Eden, and the waters of the great fountain therein, are said by St. Ambrose to have emptied themselves into an immense lake, with such awful noise that all the people living in the neighbourhood were born deaf. Columbus thought that the immense mass of fresh water, which filled the Gulf of Paria, came from this fountain.—*Irving*, vol. ii. p. 922—924.

all is beauty and happiness; where the harmonious notes of the birds ever fall gratefully on the ear; where the air is filled with the aroma of sweet flowers, and a perpetual spring, combining with its own beauties those of every other season of the year, continually prevails; where the limpid waters flow smoothly and gently, or gush forth in pure fountains, ever ready for the thirsty mouth, the liquid exhilarating, but never cloying; where all is perennial youth, and neither decay nor death are known. But I perceive, Signor Vespucci, that you are incredulous, also, as to this blissful region, and even smile at my belief. Remember, then, that herein I only follow the opinions of wise and learned fathers of the church; but in regard to Cathay, that I am supported by ample proof, from the discoveries of travellers and the relations of cosmographers.

AMERICUS.

I am ever willing to yield to proof; but methinks that the foundation of the error under which I conceive your Excellency to labour is this: that you do not make a sufficient allowance for exaggeration in the accounts of the great traveller, Marco Polo. It appears to me that he has deceived himself as to the extent to which he penetrated, and that thereby he has carried out the eastern coast of Cathay too far into the ocean. That being done, the learned physician, my countryman, in following him, finds it necessary to shorten the extent of ocean, which intervenes between Cathay and Europe, in order to render accurate his estimate of the circumference of the globe.

COLUMBUS.

I note your objections, but cannot deem them correct, and yet hope to deliver the letters of our sovereigns, with which I was charged in my recent voyage, to the Grand Khan in person. But let us examine accurately into this question of longitude, for therein I am interested deeply, and have small doubt that I can turn you to my opinions.

AMERICUS.

Most gladly will I do so, noble Admiral, for I am strongly moved to tempt the ocean myself, in the hope of adding something to the knowledge of mariners.

It requires but a slight effort of the imagination, to fancy the two great navigators seated at a table covered with charts, and busily occupied in explaining to each other their peculiar views. Intense thought is pictured on the countenances of both. Both are striving to fill up the vast void of the Atlantic, as it was drawn on those imperfect maps, with new islands and continents, and as the world grows, as it were, beneath their hands, they seem themselves half amazed at the boldness of their own conceptions, and turn, one to the other, for encouragement and approval.

CHAPTER VI.

Death of Berardi.—Payments to Americus.—Wreck of Fleet fitted out by him.—His Letter to Soderini.—Modesty displayed by him.—Position held by Americus in his First Voyage.—Cosmography of Ilacomilo.—Bibliotheca Riccardiana.—René, Titular King of Sicily and Jerusalem.—Date of the Voyage.—Herrera's Statements.—The Name of America.—Spanish Archives.—Voyages of Alonzo de Ojeda.—His Evidence in the Lawsuit of Don Diego Columbus.—Silence of the Cotemporary Historians.—Negative Evidence.—Extract from Gomara on the Subject.—No Disparagement of Columbus.—Authenticity of the Letters.—Feelings of Columbus.—His Letter respecting Americus to his Son.—General Licenses of the Crown for other Voyages.

Death of Berardi. 1495.

In consequence of the death of Juan Berardi, which occurred in the month of December, 1495, the entire management of their business affairs devolved upon Americus, and he devoted himself steadily to the settlement of all the outstanding accounts of the house, while he continued to conduct the preparations for the forwarding of new fleets to the Indies. The researches and industry of Navarrête have brought to light many documents bearing upon this period of his history. The payment of various sums of money in liquidation of the old demands of the house, and orders of the public officers for various other sums, clearly indicate the occupation of his time. On the 12th of January, 1496, Bernardo Pinelo, the treasurer of the king-

CHAPTER VI.

dom, paid to Americus the sum of 10,000 maravedis, on account of the pay and subsistence of the mariners of one of the expeditions which Berardi had forwarded. An armament which was in course of preparation at the time of his partner's death, under the contract which he held with the government, was despatched by Americus on the 3d of February, 1496. This expedition, on the 18th of the same month, was overtaken by a violent gale and totally wrecked; the crews, with the exception of three men who were lost, barely escaping with their lives.[1]

Letter to Piero Soderini, filling the gap in his history.

When the public records cease to mention the name of Americus, his own letter to Piero Soderini, his old schoolmate and friend, which is given in the next chapter, and which describes the events of the first voyage of the navigator to the New World, opportunely fills up the gap which was left in his history. There, in his own words, exists an interesting and minute account of the perils of the navigation and of the strange countries which he visited in his absence, with the manners and customs of their inhabitants. It is only to be regretted that the modesty of the writer did not permit him to dwell more at large upon his own personal adventures, and the immediate part which he took in the prosecution of the discoveries.

There is no way of determining the rank or position which Americus occupied in his first expedi-

[1] See Translation of Documents from the Collection of Navarréte. —See also *Irving*, vol. ii. p. 881.

tion. It is evident, however, from his own letters, as well as from the records of the times, that he did not hold the command. He says himself that he was chosen to "assist" in the discoveries by the King of Spain, and that expression confirms the view which is taken below, that he accompanied the fleet as an aid to the commanders in their navigation, and as a private agent of the king; that he occupied a position analogous to that of the members of scientific corps, who are usually despatched at the present day in exploring voyages. It is possible, however, that he might have held a recognized rank, and that the movements of the ships might have been in some measure under his control, for he is spoken of by some historians who have written concerning him, as "one of the principal pilots and sea captains."[1]

Proper address of the letter of Americus

It would not be proper to lay the letter of Americus to Piero Soderini before the reader, without noticing, as briefly as possible, consistently with a fair statement of the case, the question which has been discussed by historical critics, touching the accuracy of its date and its authenticity. It seems hardly worth while to enter into any argument respecting the direction of the epistle, although this also has been the subject of much dispute among authors. As far as can now be ascertained, the most ancient impression of the letter is found in a volume of cosmography, written by Martin Ilaco-

[1] Dissertazione Giustificativa, tom. iii. p. 101. Giuntini, tom. ii. Questione III. sec. 25. Canovai, p. 832, 833.

CHAPTER VI.

milo, which was published in Latin at Strasburg, in the year 1509. Neither of the biographers, Bandini or Canovai, appear to have been cognizant of this edition, and in it the letter is addressed to Réné, Duke of Lorraine and Bar, and King of Jerusalem and Sicily. All the letters in the work of Bandini are taken from records in the celebrated collection of the Bibliotheca Riccardiana, from the text of Ramusio, and from a pamphlet which Canovai calls the edition of Valori.[1]

[1] Canovai, tom. i. p. 11. The edition of Valori was a pamphlet of sixteen maps, with the four voyages of Americus attached to it, which Canovai found in the possession of the Marchese Gino Capponi, whom he describes as "a great and very studious lover of good books." He says, moreover, that "this edition exhibits corrections in various places; and time, and if I am not mistaken, fire, has done considerable damage to the margin of many pages." He calls it "the edition of Valori," because Bacci Valorii, χτημα, was found written on the title-page. Ramusio, in the first volume of his collection of voyages, preserves the two voyages of Americus in the service of Portugal and the second letter to Lorenzo de' Medici.

Réné II., Duke of Lorraine and Bar, was born in the year 1451, and succeeded his grandfather Nicholas on the throne of the duchy in 1473. This prince was much celebrated in the age in which he lived. He was more than once expelled from his dominions by the Duke of Burgundy, with whom he carried on continual wars, which ended at last in the death of his rival, in a fierce battle fought under the walls of his capital, Nancy. In the year 1486, the Neapolitan nobility, who were in insurrection against their king, Ferdinand, offered him the throne of that kingdom. He made an attempt to take possession of it aided by French troops, but was obliged to return without success to his own domains, in consequence of troubles which the King of France caused there. Nevertheless, he assumed the title of King of Sicily and Jerusalem, and quartered their arms with his own. It was but an empty title, however, for he never succeeded in establishing his claims. He died on the 10th of December, 1508.

This Prince was noted as well for his love of literature as for the prowess of his arms, and rendered his capital and court a favourite resort for learned men of all countries. It is more than probable that he caused the pub-

Bandini considers it useless to speculate upon this subject of the direction, and accounts for the fact that it is different in different copies, by supposing that after the original had been sent to Soderini, Americus forwarded copies to various friends and persons of quality, one of which was afterwards published by the King of Sicily and Jerusalem, as directed to himself. Navarrête adopts the Latin edition above mentioned, and gives the same address, but it is said that since the publication of his collection of voyages, the original Latin manuscript itself has been discovered among the scrolls of the Riccardi palace, which is directed to Soderini. As far as any judgment can be formed from the internal evidence of the document itself, the address was that which is given in this work, for it speaks of the old student-friendship of the writer with his correspondent, in a manner which he would not have been likely to have made use of toward a person of a royal birth.[1]

Authenticity of the letter undoubted. Slander of Herrera.

Whatever may be the opinion of critics as to the address, the authenticity of the letter itself is undoubted. No one undertakes to question that it was written by Americus himself; and, until the publication of the History of Herrera, in 1601, it was received by all literary and scientific men as an accurate and veracious account. That writer

lication of the accounts of Americus, as addressed to himself, with a view of adding to his literary celebrity.—*Chronologie Historique des Rois et Ducs de Lorraine,* from *St. Allai's L'Art de verifier les dates des faits Historiques,* tom. xiii. p. 410—412.

[1] Letter to Soderini, chap. vii.

asserted, without a particle of proof, and on his own unsupported authority, that Vespucius had artfully and wilfully falsified in his narrative, and that he did so with the view of stealing from Columbus the honour of being the discoverer of the continent of America, changing, for this purpose, the date of his first voyage, from 1499 to 1497. Spanish authors of that day, and ever since, have gladly seized upon this charge, and given it currency in their writings; while foreign historians, from indifference to the subject, or want of means of correct information, circulated the slander. In this way it became the generally received opinion of the world, and most people consider Americus Vespucius as little better than an impostor, while the few who acquit him of intentional fraud, attribute the mistake, as they are pleased to consider it, to an error of the press, or some similar accident.

Historical evidence of the accuracy of Americus.

This latter class of critics, as well as the maligners of the navigator, assume, that one of the principal effects of this change of date was, to confer upon the new continent the name of America. That this, at least, was not the case, will be satisfactorily shown to the reader in another place. If a plausible, though hardly a fair argument, had been wanting to substantiate the accuracy of Americus, surely the fact that his name was attached to the New World so soon after his voyages, might be adduced, and brought to bear with much more force in his favour than it could ever be used against him. But it is much more satisfactory and convincing to examine the proof which history affords, than to speculate upon probabilities. The Spanish archives of the day make no mention of Americus after the year 1496, until 1505, an interval of about eight years; while, both before that interval and subsequently, his name appears very often in the documents which have been brought to light. If he did not sail in 1497, why did not Herrera inform the world how and in what way he was occupied from that time till 1499? That historian and Navarrête, who follows in his footsteps, admit his connexion with Berardi, the agent of the fleets of Columbus, and the latter finds evidence of his continued connexion with the business, but only until 1496. Now Columbus sailed in 1498, and it is probable that Americus would have aided in the fitting out of his third voyage, as he did of the second, had he been in Spain at the time. Herrera himself, though accusing Americus of unblushing impudence and fraud, copies the principal portion of his narrative of the first voyage of Alonzo de Ojeda, from the letter to Soderini. He mingles in his account many of the occurrences of the second voyage of Americus, with matters relating exclusively to Ojeda; and then, being unable to deny that the Florentine navigator actually made two voyages, in the service of Spain, makes Americus accompany Ojeda in the second voyage of the latter, which took place in 1502. But in 1502 it appears, from indisputable evidence, the authority of Gomara and many others, besides that of the

CHAPTER VI.

navigator himself, that Americus was in the service of Portugal.

Evidence of Ojeda in the lawsuit of Diego Columbus.

The evidence Ojeda gave in the lawsuit which the son of Columbus, Don Diego, commenced after the death of his father, and prosecuted against the crown of Spain, is much relied upon to prove inaccuracy in the date of this letter. He testifies, that when he sailed in 1499, "he took with him Juan de la Cosa, Americus Vespucius, and other pilots." Admitting that Americus did sail with Ojeda at this time, it by no means follows that he did not make a previous voyage in 1497, and it is unfair to infer that he did not. The silence of the cotemporary historians of the day, with respect to this voyage, is the main reliance of Dr. Robertson, when he follows the lead of Herrera. Gomara, Benzoni, Peter Martyr, and Oviedo do not, it is true, mention the fact of this discovery in 1497; but if an argument drawn from this source proves any thing, it undoubtedly proves too much. Neither Gomara nor Oviedo allude at all to the voyages of Ojeda, any more than they do to the voyages of Americus, yet it is universally admitted that both of these mariners, either singly or in company, did make two voyages to the New World at about this time. Martyr also neglects Ojeda more than he does Americus, and only speaks of the third voyage of the navigator, which was performed in the service of the King of Portugal, while he omits the companion of Columbus altogether. Benzoni did not pretend to write a history of the discovery, but

CHAPTER VI.

merely gives an account of what he himself saw and did when he went to the New World in 1541, nearly half a century after the disputed event.[1] A solution of this difficulty may be found in the statement of Gomara himself, who says: "Learning that the territories which Christopher Columbus had discovered were very extensive, many persons proceeded to continue the exploration of them. Some went at their own expense, others at that of the king; all thinking to enrich themselves, to acquire honour, and to gain the royal approbation. But as most of these persons did nothing but discover, memorials of all of them have not come to my knowledge, especially of those who sailed towards the north, nor even of all those who went in the direction of Paria, from the year 1495 to the year 1500."[2]

Absence of testimony in the lawsuit is but negative evidence.

Another, and perhaps the strongest argument adduced by the followers of Herrera to support their views, is taken from the absence of any testimony in the same lawsuit concerning the alleged discoveries of Americus. The object of this pro-

1 Robertson, History of America, vol. i. note 22.

2 Gomara, Historia de las Indias, chap. xxxvi., from Barcia's Early Histories of the West Indies, vol. ii.

"Entendiendo quan grandissimas tierras eran las que Christoval Colon descubria, fueron muchos a continuar el descubrimiento de todas; unos á sua costa, otros á la del Rey, y todos pensando enriquecer, ganar fama, y medrar con los Reyes. Pero como los mas de ellos no hicieron sino descubrir, y gastarse, no quedó memoria de todos, que yo sepa: especialmente de los que navegaron ácia el norte, —ni aun de todos los que fueron por la otra parte de Paria, desde el año de mil quatro-cientos y noventa y cinco hasta el de mil y quinientos."

ceeding, on the part of Don Diego Columbus, was to obtain from the crown the government of certain territories on the mainland of America, and a share of the revenue arising from them, according to the stipulations of the government with his father; and the crown, in contesting this claim, are supposed to have brought forward all possible proof, that Columbus did not discover the coast of Paria.

In this trial nearly one hundred witnesses were examined on oath, yet no mention is made of the voyage of Americus in 1497, but on the contrary, Ojeda testifies directly that Columbus discovered Paria. On being asked how he knew this, he replied that he had seen the map which Columbus sent home to the government, of the lands he had discovered in 1498, and immediately started himself on a voyage of exploration, on which he used the map, and found it to be correct. It is urged that Ojeda must have known the fact, if Vespucius had made a previous discovery, because he accompanied him in 1499: and the crown must have known it also, and would have insisted upon it in this suit, if it had ever taken place.[1]

All this is but negative evidence at the best, and should weigh but lightly against the positive statements of one whose integrity, good sense, and character are unquestionable. It is easy to conceive of numerous reasons which might have prevented the government from bringing forward evidence of this voyage; and the very fact that Ojeda navigated

[1] Navarréte, Colleccion, &c., tom. iii. p. 539.

in 1499, with a chart which Columbus had sent home in 1498, while Americus himself was on board of his fleet, may have been the reason which led him to look upon Columbus as its first discoverer, and to forget the date of the expedition of Americus in 1497, which, according to the statement of Gomara, was one out of many that were undertaken about that time. It must not be forgotten, that this evidence was given in the latter part of the year 1512, and the commencement of 1513, after the death of Americus had taken place, and at a distance of nearly fifteen years from the date of the events concerning which Ojeda testifies.[1]

A decision of the question is after all important.

After all that can be said, it is unimportant to come to any decision on this point. Even if Americus did discover the mainland before Columbus by a few months, the fact takes nothing from the name and fame of that great man. He at any rate arrived at the continent without assistance from any source but his own strength of mind, and to him, whatever may have been the good fortune of any of his cotemporaries, belongs the glory of the grand discovery of a New World. The first glimpse that he obtained of the luxuriant islands of the Western Ocean rendered him immortal, and all subsequent discoveries followed his own almost as a matter of course.

The character and renown of Columbus belong to the world, and it is impossible to sympathize with any of those historians who strive to depre-

[1] Navarréte, tom. iii. p. 538.

CHAPTER VI.

ciate either, for the sake of exalting a favourite or fellow-countryman of their own. Americus needs no such advocacy, and the subject has been considered in the foregoing pages solely to relieve his character from the gross aspersions which have been cast upon it, by those who foolishly consider this secondary question as one affecting materially the reputation of Columbus. "In fact," as is well observed by the distinguished author of the life of the great Admiral, "the European who first reached the mainland of the New World was most probably Sebastian Cabot, a native of Venice, sailing in the employ of England. In 1497 he coasted the shores from Labrador to Florida, yet neither the English nor the Venetians have set up any pretensions on his account."[1]

General arguments in favor of the accuracy of Americus.

It is much more charitable to attribute an error in the date of the first voyage, if the reader can suppose any such to exist, after a candid consideration of the arguments on both sides of the question, to the negligence of the early publishers, rather than to a wilful deception on the part of the writer. It would have been strange indeed, had he attempted any misrepresentation of the kind. The letters are universally acknowledged to have been written with the pen of Americus himself; they purport to be the account of an eyewitness of the events which he describes; they were addressed to persons of great celebrity in the world, whom it certainly would have been a hard, if not a perilous task, to deceive;

[1] Irving, vol. ii. p. 886.

they give full accounts of events which, from their extraordinary nature, must have flown upon the wings of the wind to the remotest quarters of civilized Europe; if falsified in any particular, there were hundreds who stood ready to contradict and expose to public indignation their author; yet that author occupies, for years after the contested accounts are published and translated into various tongues, a high and responsible post at the court in whose service the voyage in question was made. No voice is raised to condemn the shameless impostor; for such Americus must have been, if his calumniators spoke the truth; but so far from it, the very man whose honours and merits he was endeavouring to appropriate remains his warm friend, and commends him to his own son, in a letter which has been fortunately preserved to us, as one well entitled to his esteem and affection.

Letter of Columbus highly commending Americus.

Can any one suppose that Columbus would have written a letter like the one which follows, concerning a man who was wickedly engaged in injuring the reputation so dear to him?

To my very dear Son, Don Diego Columbus.
At the Court.

My dear Son,

Diego Mendez departed from this place on Monday, the third of this month. After his departure, I held converse with Americus Vespucius, the bearer of this letter, who goes to court on some business connected with navigation. He has always been

CHAPTER VI.

desirous of serving me, and is an honourable man, though fortune has been unpropitious to him, as to many others, and his labours have not been as profitable as he deserves. He goes on my account, and with a great desire to do something which may redound to my advantage, if it is in his power.

I know not, here, what instructions to give him that will benefit me, because I am ignorant what will be required there. He goes determined to do for me all that is possible. See what can be done to advantage there, and labour for it, that he may know and speak of every thing, and devote himself to the work; and let every thing be done with secresy, that no suspicions may arise. I have said to him all that I can say touching the business, and have informed him of all the payments which have been made to me, and what is due.

This letter is intended also for the Adelantado, that he may avail himself of any advantage and advice on the subject. His highness believes that his ships were in the best and richest portion of the Indies, and if he desires to know any thing more on the subject, I will satisfy him by word of mouth, for it is impossible for me to tell by letter. May our Lord have you in his holy keeping. Done at Seville, February 5th, 1505.

Thy father, who loves thee better than himself,

CHRISTOPHER COLUMBUS.[1]

[1] Navarréte, tom. i. p. 351. Irving, vol. ii. p. 882. The signature of Columbus is curious. It is written thus, ap-

CHAPTER VI.

In rescuing this letter from the dust of the Spanish archives, Navarrēte has done good service in the cause of truth, and furnished an important link in the chain of evidence which will establish, it is trusted satisfactorily, in the mind of the reader, the credibility of Americus. But if any thing be still wanting to confirm him in such an opinion, the fact that Fernando Columbus, the biographer of his father, who throughout his work gives constant proof of his sensitiveness with regard to anything touching the honour and renown of the Admiral, makes not the slightest mention of any attempt on the part of Americus to appropriate to himself any portion of his father's fame. Is it probable, that he would have passed it over in silence, had such an attempt been made?

General Licence granted by the Court for other voyages.

As far as was possible, a candid statement of the point in dispute, with the reasoning on both sides of the question, has been given, and with but one

to this letter as well as locuments.

S.
S. A. S
X M Y
XPO FERENS

In the early part of his life Columbus subscribed himself, Columbus de Terra Rubra, according to the history of Fernando his son, but when he had acquired celebrity, he adopted the form above. A great many opinions have been formed as to the meaning of these characters, which are an incongruous mixture of Greek and Latin, savouring very strongly of the pedantry of his times. Xristus, Sancta Maria, Josephus, is one reading; Salva me Xristus, Maria, Josephus, another. Neither appears very satisfactory, and the reader has the same right to exercise his ability in deciphering it, and may arrive as nearly at the truth as any conjectures of the critics will lead him. It is undoubtedly a pious exclamation, which it was very customary in those days to prefix to writings as well as signatures.—*Fernando Columbus*, chap. xi.

additional suggestion, the subject will be dropped. It is a well-known fact that for a number of years previous to his departure upon his third voyage, Columbus was annoyed and persecuted by the attacks of his enemies at court, and by the doubts and vacillation of King Ferdinand; and as Herrera emphatically declares, he made frequent remonstrance against the various expeditions which were undertaken, under the general license which had been given by the crown for private adventurers, to prosecute discoveries in the Indies, and only succeeded, after long solicitation, in obtaining a small squadron for his enterprise in 1498. There is nothing to contradict the supposition that the expedition of Americus was one of those which the Admiral supposed to interfere with his own rights: a private undertaking altogether, but at the same time one in which Vespucius went, at the command of the king, to "assist in the discoveries." With this view of the case, it is easy to account for the non-appearance of any public documents in the archives relating to the voyage.

CHAPTER VII.

Sketch of the Life of Piero Soderini.—His Character.—Elected Gonfaloniére of Florence.—His Fall and Banishment.—His Death at Rome.—Letter of Americus to him, describing his First Voyage.—His Reasons for Writing.—Sails from Cadiz, May 10th, 1497.—Arrives at the Grand Canaries.—Arrives at the New World.—Appearance of the Inhabitants.—Sails along the Coast.—Their Weapons and their Wars.—Mode of Life.—Religion and Laws.—Their Riches.—Their System of Physic.—Burial Rites.—Their Food.—Ignami.—Finds trifling Indications of Gold.—Venezuela.—Treachery of the Inhabitants.—Fight with them.—Five Prisoners.—Their Artful Escape.—Singular Animals.—Fish made into Flour.—Americus received by another Tribe with great Honour.—Laughable Occurrence.—Establishes Baptismal Fonts.—Lariab.—Cannibalism.—Repairing the Ships.—Sail for the Islands.—Battle with the Natives.—Slave Prisoners.—Return Voyage.—Arrival at Cadiz, 15th of October, 1498.

CHAPTER VII.

Sketch of the Life of Piero Soderini.

PIERO SODERINI, to whom the following letter was addressed by Americus, was born in Florence, in the year 1450. He was the son of Tomaso Soderini, of whom mention has been made in a previous chapter, and was educated by the good Friar Georgio Antonio, in company with the navigator. As he grew up, the friendship which subsisted between the two young men was strengthened by a great similarity of character in many respects. Both were devotedly attached to their country, and both lived to do it honour.

When, a few years after the death of Lorenzo the

CHAPTER VII.

Magnificent, the Florentines returned to their ancient democratic form of government, and expelled Piero, his son, with all the members of that powerful family from the city, they sought among their distinguished citizens for one whom they might trust to restore and preserve their rights and liberties. The state was in great confusion and anarchy, and it behooved them to select for their chief magistrate a man of undoubted patriotism, who would administer the laws with prudence and firmness. After much deliberation, their choice fell upon Piero Soderini. His known probity, his wealth, his love for the arts and sciences, and the prominent part he took in the measures which resulted in the revolution, all influenced his election, and, on the 16th of August, 1502, he was unanimously called to preside over the destinies of the republic, with the title of Perpetual Gonfaloniēre.

His Character.

The character of Soderini was too mild and amiable to allow him to abuse the privileges of his high station. On the contrary, he hardly insisted sufficiently upon his rights, to ensure the stability of his power. He loved to lend his patronage to men of letters and artists, and his palace was thronged with all the sculptors and painters of the day who had attained any celebrity in their professions. Poets and philosophers flocked to his court as they did to that of the great Lorenzo, but, unlike him, Soderini left more memorials of his devotion to literature and art, than of his statesmanship. During his administration, however, the republic waged war with

Pisa, with great activity, and finally, in the year 1509, succeeded in subduing that city.

His deposition and banishment.

The assistance of the French had been of great assistance to Soderini, in the expulsion of the Medici and his own elevation, and he always remained warmly attached to that nation. He gave his consent to the measure which Louis XII. projected, of assembling a council at Pisa for the purpose of deposing Pope Julius II., and that pontiff never forgave him for the affront. When the French evacuated Italy in 1512, he stimulated the Viceroy of Naples in Tuscany to attempt the re-establishment of the Medici family. The movement was successful. The city was taken by surprise on the 30th of August, 1512, and was given up to pillage and massacre. The partisans of the Medici broke into the public palace tumultuously, and surprised Soderini in his apartments. They confined him in chains, and the next day the Signory passed an act deposing him from his office, after he had served the state for upwards of ten years, without giving occasion for the slightest murmur of dissatisfaction among the peaceable citizens.

The day following his deposition, he was conducted to the frontiers of the republic, escorted by a strong guard, and banished for ever. He went immediately to Ragusa, where he remained till the election of Leo X. to the papal chair. Though a Medici himself, this pontiff was too generous to cherish an old enmity, and invited Soderini to Rome, remembering rather the services of the fa-

CHAPTER VII.

ther of Piero towards his family, than the more recent doings of the son. At the pontifical court he was received with much distinction, although he never wavered in his attachment to the rights of his countrymen and the cause of liberty. He ended his days at Rome, and died regretted and respected by all the intelligent and patriotic men of the day.[1]

Letter of Americus to Piero Soderini, Perpetual Gonfaloniere of the Republic of Florence, giving an account of his First Voyage.[2]

MOST EXCELLENT SIR:—

(After my humble reverence and due commendation)—It may be that your Excellency, with your well-known wisdom, will be astonished at my temerity, in that I have been so absurdly moved to address you my present very prolix letter, knowing that your Excellency is continually occupied in the arduous duties and pressing business of State. I may be termed not only presumptuous, but idle, in writing things neither convenient nor pleasing to your state, and which were formerly written in barbarous style, destitute of the polish of literature, and directed to Don Ferdinand, king of Castile; but the confidence I have in your virtues, as well as in the truth of what I write, concerning things

[1] Biog. Universelle, tom. xlii. p. 567, 568.

[2] The direction of the letter in the edition of Gruniger, which is followed by Navarréte, reads as follows: To the Most Illustrious, the King of Jerusalem and Sicily, the Duke of Lorraine and Bar. —*Navarréte*, tom. iii. p. 191.

described neither by ancient nor modern authors, has emboldened me in my undertaking.

CHAPTER VII.

Reasons of Americus for writing.

The principal reason why I am induced to write, is the request of the bearer, Benvenuto Benvenuti, the devoted servant of your Excellency, and my very particular friend. He happened to be here in this city of Lisbon, and requested that I would impart to your Excellency a description of the things seen by me in various climes, in the course of four voyages which I have made for the discovery of new lands, two by the authority and command of Don Ferdinand VI., the King of Castile, in the great Western Ocean, and the other two by order of Don Emanuel, King of Portugal, towards the south. So I resolved to write to your Excellency, and set about the performance of my task, because I am certain that your Excellency counts me among the number of your most devoted servants; remembering that in the time of our youth, we were friends, going daily to study the rudiments of grammar, under the excellent instruction of the venerable and religious Brother of St. Mark, Friar Georgio Antonio Vespucci, my uncle, whose counsels, would to God I had followed! for then, as Petrarch says, I should have been a different man from what I am.

However that may be, I do not complain, inasmuch as I have always delighted in those things which are virtuous, and in literary pursuits; and now that these my trifling affairs may not be disagreeable to your virtuous mind, I will say to you, as Pliny said to Mecœnas, "You were once accustomed to be

CHAPTER VII.

pleased with my prattling."[1] However constantly employed you may be in public affairs, you can snatch some hours of relaxation, for the purpose of reading those things which, however trifling, will amuse by their novelty; for with the cares and engrossment of business, these letters of mine will mingle, as it is customary to mingle fennel with savoury viands, to dispose them for better digestion. And if perchance I am more prolix than I ought to be, I ask your Excellency's pardon.

Your Excellency will please to observe, that I came into the kingdom of Spain for the purpose of engaging in mercantile affairs, and that I continued to be thus employed about four years, during which time I saw and experienced the fickle movements of fortune, and how she ordered the changes of these transitory and perishing worldly goods; at one time sustaining a man at the top of the wheel, and at another returning him to the lowest part thereof, and depriving him of her favours, which may truly be said to be lent.[2] Thus having experienced the continual labour of one who would acquire her favours, subjecting myself to vastly many inconveniences and dangers, I concluded to abandon mercantile affairs, and direct my attention

1 He meant to have said, "as Catullus said to Cornelius Nepos." This mistake goes but little way to prove a want of classical information, which Navarréte seems inclined to impute to the navigator.

2 These four years may be considered to be the four which preceded his departure on his first voyage in 1497, embracing the time of his connexion with Berardi, and his management of the business after his partner's death.

to something more laudable and stable. For this purpose I prepared myself to visit various parts of the world, and see the wonderful things which might be found therein. Time and place were very opportunely offered me.

King Ferdinand of Castile had ordered four ships to go in search of new lands, and I was selected by his highness to go in that fleet, in order to assist in the discoveries. We sailed from the port of Cadiz on the tenth day of May, A. D. 1497, and steering our course through the great Western Ocean, spent eighteen months in our expedition, discovering much land, and a great number of islands, the largest part of which were inhabited.[1] As these are not spoken of by ancient writers, I presume they were ignorant of them. If I am not mistaken, I well remember to have read in one of their books which I possessed, that this ocean was considered unpeopled; and our poet Dante also held this opinion, judging by the twenty-sixth canto of L'Inferno, where he sings the fate of Ulysses.[2] In

[1] Giuntini writes 17 as required by the departure on 10th May, 1497, and return on 15th October, 1498. But Giuntini also has the departure on the 20th of May, and arrival on 25th of October. It is easy to infer that the first translator of this voyage took from his manuscript the figure 2 for the figure 1.—*Canovai, Viaggi*, &c., tom i. p 49, note. Navarrète cavils unnecessarily at this very natural inaccuracy. The voyage actually took seventeen months and five days, but in his introductory remarks, Vespucius speaks approximately.—*Navarrète*, tom. iii.

[2] 'Oh! brothers,' I began, 'who to the west
Through perils without number now have reached
To this the short remaining watch, that yet
Our senses have to wake, refuse not proof
Of the unpeopled world, following the track
Of Phœbus.'
Carey's Dante, Canto xxvi. p. 181, 182.

CHAPTER VII.

this voyage I saw many astonishing things, as your Excellency will perceive by the following relation:

VOYAGE THE FIRST.[1]

Departure from Cadiz, May 10th, 1497.

In the year of our Lord 1497, on the tenth day of May, as before stated, we left the port of Cadiz with four ships in company.[2] The first land we made was that of the Fortunate Islands, which are now called the Grand Canaries, situated in the Western Ocean, as far as the habitable world was supposed to extend, being located in the third climate, where the North Pole is elevated twenty-seven and a half degrees above the horizon, and distant from the city of Lisbon (where this letter is written) two hundred and eighty leagues. Having arrived here, with south and southerly winds, we tarried eight days, taking in wood and water and other necessaries, when, having offered up our prayers, we weighed anchor and set sail, steering a course west by south.

We sailed so rapidly, that at the end of twenty-

[1] Giuntini, Canovai, and Navarréte, all introduce this with the following heading, which is omitted in the text. "Description of various lands and islands not spoken of by ancient authors found in the year 1497, and thereafter in four voyages, that is, two in the Western Ocean under the authority of Ferdinand, King of Castile, and the other two in the South Sea, in the name of Emanuel, King of Portugal. Americus Vespucius, one of the principal pilots and sea captains, sending the following account of them to the aforesaid Ferdinand, King of Castile."

[2] The addition of Gruniger gives the date of the departure as 20th of May. On comparison with other editions, this appears to be an error.

seven days we came in sight of land, which we judged to be a continent, being about a thousand leagues west of the Grand Canaries, and within the Torrid Zone, as we found the North Pole at an elevation of six degrees above the horizon, and our instruments showed it to be seventy-four degrees farther west than the Canary Islands.[1] Here we anchored our ships at a league and a half from the shore; and, having cast off our boats, and filled them with men and arms, proceeded at once to land.

First landing on the Continent.

Before we landed we were much cheered by the sight of many people rambling along the shore. We found that they were all in a state of nudity, and they appeared to be afraid of us, as I supposed from seeing us clothed, and of a different stature from themselves. They retreated to a mountain, and, notwithstanding all the signs of peace and friendship we could make, we could not bring them to a parley with us; so, as the night was coming on, and the ships were anchored in an insecure place, by reason of the coast being exposed, we agreed to leave there the next day, and go in search of some port or bay where we could place our ships in safety.

We sailed along the coast with a northwest

[1] The degrees of which he speaks were, as mariners then calculated, fifteen leagues each.—*Navarréte*, tom. iii. 199, note. The true longitude or distance from the Canaries to the land which he reached is fifty-four or fifty-five degrees. The instruments of the sailors of that day were so very inaccurate, and it was almost impossible to measure correctly with them.—*Canovai*, tom. i. 53.

CHAPTER VII.

wind, always keeping within sight of land, and continually seeing people on shore; and having sailed two days, we found a very safe place for the ships, and anchored at half a league from the land, and the same day we landed in the boats—forty men leaping on shore in good order. The people of the country, however, appeared very shy of us, and for some time we could not sufficiently assure them to induce them to come and speak with us; but at length we laboured so hard, in giving them some of our things, such as looking-glasses, bells, beads, and other trifles, that some of them acquired confidence enough to come and treat with us for our mutual peace and friendship. Night coming on, we took leave of them and returned to our ships.

Received in a friendly manner by the natives.

The next day, as the dawn appeared, we saw on the shore a great number of men, with their wives and children; we landed, and found that they had all come loaded with provisions and materials, which will be described in the proper place. Before we reached the land, many of them swam to meet us, the length of a bow shot into the sea (as they are most excellent swimmers), and they treated us with as much confidence as if we had had intercourse with them for a long time, which gratified us much.

All that we know of their life and manners is, that they go entirely naked, not having the slightest covering whatever; they are of middling stature, and very well proportioned; their flesh is of a reddish colour, like the skin of a lion, but I think that if they had been accustomed to wear clothing, they would have been as white as we are. They have no hair on the body, with the exception of very long hair upon the head—and the women especially derive much beauty from this: their countenances are not very handsome, as they have large faces, which might be compared with those of the Tartars: they do not allow any hair to grow on the eyelids or eyebrows, or any other part of the body, excepting the head, as they consider it a great deformity. Both men and women are very agile and easy in their persons, and swift in walking or running; so that the women think nothing of running a league or two, as we many times beheld, having, in this particular, greatly the advantage of us Christians.

Characteristics of the natives.

They swim incredibly well—the women better than the men—as we have seen them many times swimming without any support, fully two leagues at sea. Their arms are bows and arrows beautifully wrought, but unfurnished with iron or any other hard metal, in place of which they make use of the teeth of animals or fish, or sometimes substitute a slip of hard wood, made harder at the point by fire. They are sure marksmen, who hit whereever they wish, and in some parts the women also use the bow with dexterity. They have other arms, such as lances and staves with heads finely wrought. When they make war they take their wives with them, not that they may fight, but because they carry

CHAPTER VII.

their provision behind them; a woman frequently carrying a burden on her back for thirty or forty leagues, which the strongest man among them could not do, as we have many times witnessed.

Their motives in making war.

These people have no captains, neither do they march in order, but each one is his own master; the cause of their wars is not a love of conquest or enlarging their boundaries, neither are they incited to engage in them by inordinate covetousness, but from ancient enmity which has existed between them in times past; and having been asked why they made war, they could give us no other reason, than that they did it to avenge the death of their ancestors. Neither have these people kings nor lords, nor do they obey any one, but live in their own entire liberty, and the manner in which they are incited to go to war, is this: when their enemies have killed or taken prisoners any of their people, the oldest relative rises and goes about proclaiming his wrongs aloud, and calling upon them to go with him and avenge the death of his relation. Thereupon they are moved with sympathy, and make ready for the fight.

They have no tribunals of justice, neither do they punish malefactors; and what is still more astonishing, neither father nor mother chastises the children when they do wrong; yet, astounding as it may seem, there is no strife between them, or, to say the least, we never saw any. They appear simple in speech, but in reality are very shrewd and cunning in any matter which interests them.

They speak but little, and that little in a low tone of voice, using the same accentuation that we use, and forming the words with the palate, teeth, and lips, but they have a different mode of diction. There is a great diversity of languages among them, inasmuch that within every hundred leagues we found people who could not understand each other. Their mode of life is most barbarous; they do not eat at regular intervals and as much as they wish at stated times, but it is a matter of indifference to them, whether appetite comes at midnight or mid-day, and they eat upon the ground at all hours, without napkin or table-cloth, having their food in earthen basins, which they manufacture, or in half gourd shells.

CHAPTER VII.

They sleep in nets of cotton, very large, and suspended in the air, and although this may seem rather a bad way of sleeping, I can vouch for the fact, that it is extremely pleasant, and one sleeps better thus, than on a mattress. They are neat and clean in their persons, which is a natural consequence of their perpetual bathing.

* * * * * * * *

* * * * * * * *

[It is deemed inexpedient to translate certain passages which occur at this stage of the letter, referring to personal habits of the natives, which are unfit for publication at the present day.]

Their villages and houses.

We are not aware that these people have any laws. Neither are they like Moors or Jews, but are worse than Gentiles and Pagans, because we

CHAPTER VII.

have never seen them offer any sacrifice, and they have no houses of prayer. From their voluptuous manner of life, I consider them Epicureans. Their dwellings are in communities, and their houses are in the form of huts, but strongly built, with very large trees, and covered with palm leaves, secure from wind and storms; and in some places they are of such great length and breadth that in a single house we found six hundred people, and we found that the population of thirteen houses only amounted to four thousand.[1] They change their location every seven or eight years, and on being asked why they did so, they said that it was on account of the intense heat of the sun upon the soil, which by that time became infected and corrupted with filthiness, and caused pains in their bodies, which seemed to us very reasonable.

Their ide of wealt

The riches of these people consist in the feathers of birds of the most magnificent colours, of paternosters, which they fabricate of fish bones, of white or green stones, with which they decorate the cheeks, lips, and ears, and of many other things which are held in little or no esteem with us. They carry on no commerce, neither buying nor selling, and, in short, live contentedly with what nature gives them. The riches which we esteem so highly in Europe and other parts, such as gold, jewels, pearls, and other wealth, they have no regard for at all, and make no effort to obtain any

1 The edition of Gruniger says, eight houses and ten thousand inhabitants.

CHAPTER VII.

thing of this kind which exists in their country. They are liberal in giving, never denying one any thing, and, on the other hand, are just as free in asking. The greatest mark of friendship they can show, is to offer you their wives and daughters, and parents consider themselves highly honoured by an acceptance of this mark of favour.

* * * * * * * *
* * * * * * * *

Their funeral rites.

In case of death, they make use of various funeral obsequies. Some bury their dead with water and provisions placed at their heads, thinking they may have occasion to eat, but they make no parade in the way of funeral ceremonies. In some places, they have a most barbarous mode of interment, which is thus: when one is sick or infirm, and nearly at the point of death, his relatives carry him into a large forest, and there attaching one of their sleeping hammocks to two trees, they place the sick person in it, and continue to swing him about for a whole day, and when night comes, after placing at his head water and other provisions sufficient to sustain him for five or six days, they return to their village. If the sick person can help himself to eat and drink, and recovers sufficiently to be able to return to the village, his people receive him again with great ceremony; but few are they who escape this mode of treatment; most of them die without being visited, and that is their only burial.

Medical treatment.

They have various other customs which, to avoid prolixity, are not here mentioned. They use in

CHAPTER VII.

their diseases various kinds of medicines, so different from any in vogue with us, that we were astonished that any escaped. I often saw, for instance, that when a person was sick with a fever, which was increasing upon him, they bathed him from head to foot with cold water, and then making a great fire around him, they made him turn round within the circle for about an hour or two, until they fatigued him, and left him to sleep. Many were cured in this way. They also observe a strict diet, eating nothing for three or four days; they practise bloodletting, but not on the arm, unless in the armpit; but generally they take blood from the thighs and haunches, or the calf of the leg. In like manner they excite vomiting with certain herbs, which they put into their mouths, and they use many other remedies, which it would be tedious to relate.

Cannibalism.

Their blood and phlegm is much disordered on account of their food, which consists mainly of the roots of herbs, of fruit and fish. They have no wheat or other grain, but instead, make use of the root of a tree, from which they manufacture flour, which is very good, and which they call Huca; the flour from another root is called Kazabi, and from another, Ignami.[1] They eat little meat except hu-

[1] "The Castilians found there very large parrots, honey, bees' wax, and an abundance of those plants which the islanders called Cazabi, from which the French Cassave is derived."—*Hist. Gen. des voy.* tom. xlv. p. 167. "They brought much Cazabi, which is the name of the bread."—*Ferd. Col.* p. 117. Alvarez Cabral, speaking of the Igname of the Brazilians, says, "A root called

man flesh, and you will notice that in this particular they are more savage than beasts, because all their enemies who are killed or taken prisoners, whether male or female, are devoured with so much fierceness, that it seems disgusting to relate, much more to see it done, as I with my own eyes have many times witnessed this proof of their inhumanity. Indeed, they marvelled much to hear us say that we did not eat our enemies.

And your Excellency may rest assured that their other barbarous customs are so numerous that it is impossible herein to describe all of them. As in these four voyages I have witnessed so many things at variance with our own customs, I prepared myself tó write a collection, which I call "The Four Voyages," in which I have related the major part of the things which I saw, as clearly as my feeble capacity would permit. This work is not yet published, though many advise me to publish it. In it every thing will appear minutely, therefore I shall not enlarge any more in this letter, because in the course of it we shall see many things which are peculiar. Let this suffice for matters in general.

In this commencement of discoveries we did not see anything of much profit in the country, owing, as I think, to our ignorance of the language, except

Igname, and their bread which they eat."—*Ram.* t. i. p. 121. "Linnæus calls this plant, 'Dioscorea oppositi folia,' the root of which is eaten, or cut in pieces and baked under the coals, or, when it is of middling size, it is boiled whole, and it serves some times also to make bread of."—*Cook*, vol. i. p. 90. *Canovai*, tom. i. p. 67, 68.

CHAPTER VII.

some few indications of gold. In whatever relates to the situation and appearance of the country we could not have succeeded better. We concluded to leave this place and go onward, and having unanimously come to this resolution, we coasted along near the land, making many stops, and holding discourses with many people, until after some days we came into a harbour, where we fell into very great danger, from which it pleased the Holy Spirit to deliver us.

Arrival at Venezuela and battle with the natives.

It happened in this manner. We landed in a port where we found a village built over the water, like Venice.[1] There were about forty-four houses, shaped like bells, built upon very large piles, having entrances by means of drawbridges, so that by laying the bridges from house to house, the inhabitants could pass through the whole. When the people saw us, they appeared to be afraid of us, and to protect themselves, suddenly raised all their bridges, and shut themselves up in their houses. While we stood looking at them and wondering at this proceeding, we saw coming toward us by sea about two and twenty canoes, which are the boats they make use of, and are carved out of a single tree. They came directly toward our boats, appearing to be astonished at our figures and dresses, and keeping at a little distance from us. This being the case, we made signals of friendship, to induce them to come nearer to us, endeavouring

[1] The natives called this place Coquibacoa: it is the modern Venezuela.

to reassure them by every token of kindness; but seeing that they did not come, we went toward them. They would not wait for us, however, but fled to the land, making signs to us to wait, and giving us to understand that they would soon return.

They fled directly to a mountain, but did not tarry there long, and when they returned, brought with them sixteen of their young girls, and entering their canoes, came to our boats and put four of them into each boat, at which we were very much astonished, as your Excellency may well imagine. Then they mingled with their canoes among our boats, and we considered their coming to speak to us in this manner, to be a token of friendship. Taking this for granted, we saw a great crowd of people swimming toward us from the houses, without any suspicion. At this juncture, some old women showed themselves at the doors of the houses, wailing and tearing their hair, as if in great distress. From this we began to be suspicious, and had immediate recourse to our weapons, when suddenly the girls, who were in our boats, threw themselves into the sea, and the canoes moved away, the people in them assailing us with their bows and arrows. Those who came swimming toward us brought each a lance, concealed as much as possible under the water. Their treachery being thus discovered, we began not only to defend ourselves, but to act severely on the offensive. We overturned many of their canoes with our boats, and making considera-

CHAPTER VII.

ble slaughter among them, they soon abandoned the canoes altogether and swam to the shore. Fifteen or twenty were killed and many wounded on their side, while on ours five were slightly wounded, all the rest escaping by favour of Divine Providence, and these five being quickly cured. We took prisoners two of their girls and three men, and on entering their houses found only two old women and one sick man. We took from them many things of little value, but would not burn their dwellings, being restrained by conscientious scruples. Returning to our boats and thence to our ships, with five prisoners, we put irons on the feet of each, excepting the young females, yet when night came, the two girls and one of the men escaped in the most artful manner in the world.

Continue their voyage along the coast.

These events having occurred, the next day we concluded to depart from the port and proceed further. Keeping our course continually along the coast, we at length came to anchor at about eighty leagues distance from the place we had left, and found another race of people, whose language and customs were very different from those we had seen last. We determined to land, and while proceeding in our boats, we saw standing on the shore a great multitude, numbering about four thousand people. They did not wait to receive us, but fled precipitately to the woods, abandoning their things. We leaped ashore, and taking the way which led to the wood, found their tents within

VILLAGE BUILT OVER THE WATER.

We landed in a port where we found a village built over the water like Venice. The houses were shaped like bells, built upon very large piles, having entrances by means of drawbridges. (See P. 126.)

CHAPTER VII

the space of a bow-shot, where they had made a great fire, and two of them were cooking their food, roasting many animals and fish of various kinds.

Remarkable Animal.

We noticed that they were roasting a certain animal that looked like a serpent; it had no wings, and was so filthy in appearance, that we were astonished at its deformity. As we went through their houses or tents, we saw many of these serpents alive. Their feet were tied, and they had a cord round their snouts, so that they could not open their mouths, as dogs are sometimes muzzled, so that they may not bite. These animals had such a savage appearance, that none of us dared to turn one over, thinking they might be poisonous. They are about the size of a kid, about the length and a half of a man's arm, having long coarse feet armed with large nails. Their skin is hard, and they are of various colours. They have the snout and face of a serpent, and from the nose there runs a crest, passing over the middle of the back to the root of the tail. We finally concluded that they were serpents, and poisonous; and, nevertheless, they were eaten.[1]

[1] The navigator has perhaps drawn somewhat upon his imagination in his description of this animal, although Canovai adopts it seriously, and says in a note that "this is the serpent Tuana which is spoken of in Ramus, tom. iii. p. 130."—*Canovai, Viaggi*, &c. tom. i. p. 75. Navarrête mentions this as one of the absurdities of Vespucius.—*Navar. Colleccion*, tom. iii. p. 225. But though it is rather hard to believe in a domestic serpent as large as a kid, yet the whole difficulty vanishes, if for the word serpent, which seems to have been misapplied by the navigator, we substitute reptile or animal.

CHAPTER VII.

We found that this people made bread of small fish which they caught in the sea, by first boiling them, then kneading together and making a paste of them, which they baked upon the hot coals; we tried it, and found it good.[1] They have so many other kinds of eating, chiefly of fruits and roots, that it would be very tedious to describe them minutely. Seeing, then, that the people did not return, we resolved not to meddle with or take away any of their things, in order to reassure them; and, having left in their tents many of our own things, in places where they might be seen, returned to our ships for the night. Early the next morning we saw a great number of people on the shore, and landed. Though they seemed fearful of us, they were sufficiently confident to treat with us, and gave us all that we asked of them. Finally they became very friendly; told us that this was not their place of dwelling, but that they had come there to carry on their fishery. They invited us to go to their villages, because they wished to receive us as friends—their amicable feelings toward us being much strengthened by the circumstance of our having the two prisoners with us, who were their enemies. They importuned us so much, that, hav-

1 "The ancient fish-eaters also dried their fish, and made flour out of them. A large quantity of dried fish was presented to him (Nearchus); these people eating fish as their common food."—*Ramus*, t. i. p. 271, B. In our times the same custom prevails in those countries. Barbosa writes, "In this country they attend much to fishing, and catch very large fish, which they salt, and also feed their horses with them."—*Ram.* t. p. 295. *Canovai*, tom. i. p. 75, 76, note.

ing taken counsel, twenty-three of us Christians concluded to go with them, well prepared, and with firm resolution to die manfully, if such was to be our fate.

CHAPTER VII.

Americus journeys inland and reaches a village.

After we had remained here three days, we accordingly started with them for a journey inland. Three leagues from the shore we arrived at a tolerably well-peopled village, of a few houses—there not being over nine—where we were received with so many and such barbarous ceremonies, that no pen is equal to the task of describing them. There was dancing and singing, and weeping mingled with rejoicing, and great feasting. Here we staid for the night. * * * * *
* * * * * * * *
* * After having passed the night and half of the next day, an immense number of people visiting us from motives of curiosity—the oldest among them begging us to go with them to other villages,as they desired to do us great honour—we determined to proceed still further inland. And it is impossible to tell how much honour they did us there. We visited so many villages, that we spent nine days in the journey; having been so long absent, that our companions in the ships began to be uneasy on our account.

Return to the ships.

Being now about eighteen leagues inland, we deliberated about returning. On our return, we were accompanied by a wonderful number, of both sexes, quite to the seashore; and when any of us grew

CHAPTER VII.

weary with walking, they carried us in their hammocks much at our ease; in passing rivers, which were numerous and quite large, they conveyed us over with so much skill and safety, that we were not in the slightest danger. Many of them were laden with the presents they had made us, which they transported in hammocks. These consisted in very rich plumage, many bows and arrows, and an infinite number of parrots of various colours. Others brought loads of provisions and animals. For a greater wonder, I will inform your Excellency, that when we had to cross over a river, they carried us on their backs.

A ludicrous incident.

Having arrived at the sea, and entered the boats which had come on shore for us, we were astonished at the crowd which endeavoured to get into the boats to go to see our ships; they were so overloaded that they were oftentimes on the point of sinking. We carried as many as we could on board, and so many more came by swimming, that we were quite troubled at the multitude on board, although they were all naked and unarmed. They were in great astonishment at our equipments and implements, and at the size of our ships. Here quite a laughable occurrence took place at their expense. We concluded to try the effect of discharging some of our artillery, and when they heard the thundering report, the greater part of them jumped into the sea from fright, acting like frogs sitting on a bank, who plunge into the marsh on the approach of any thing that alarms them. Those who remained in the ships were so timorous that we repented of having done this. However, we reassured them by telling them that these were the arms with which we killed our enemies. Having amused themselves in the ships all day, we told them that they must go, as we wished to depart in the night. So they took leave of us with many demonstrations of friendship and affection, and went ashore.

I saw more of the manners and customs of these people, while in their country, than I wish to dwell upon here. Your Excellency will notice, that in each of my voyages, I have noted the most extraordinary things which have occurred, and compiled the whole into one volume, in the style of a geography, and entitled it "The Four Voyages." In this work will be found a minute description of the things which I saw, but as there is no copy of it yet published, owing to my being obliged to examine and correct it, it becomes necessary for me to impart them to you herein.

This country is full of inhabitants, and contains a great many rivers. Very few of the animals are similar to ours, excepting the lions, panthers, stags, hogs, goats, and deer, and even these are a little different in form. They have neither horses, mules, nor asses, neither cows, dogs, nor any kind of domestic animals. Their other animals, however, are so very numerous, that it is impossible to count them, and all of them so wild, that they cannot be employed for serviceable uses. But what shall I say of their birds, which are so numerous and of so

CHAPTER VII.

many species and varieties of plumage, that it is astounding to behold them!

The country and its climate.

The country is pleasant and fruitful, full of woods and forests, which are always green, as they never lose their foliage. The fruits are numberless, and totally different from ours. The land lies within the Torrid Zone, under the parallel which describes the Tropic of Cancer, where the pole is elevated twenty-three degrees above the horizon, on the borders of the second climate. A great many people came to see us, and were astonished at our features and the whiteness of our skins. They asked us where we came from, and we gave them to understand that we came from heaven, with the view of visiting the world, and they believed us. In this country we established a baptismal font, and great numbers were baptized, calling us, in their language, Carabi, which means men of great wisdom.

The natives called this province Lariab.[1] We left the port, and sailed along the coast, continuing in sight of land, until we had run, calculating our advances and retrogressions, eight hundred and seventy leagues towards the northwest, making many stops by the way, and having intercourse with many people. In some places we found traces of gold, but in small quantities, it being sufficient for us to have

[1] This name is read Lariab in the edition of Valori, and also in that of Gruniger. Giuntini substitutes Paria, which is, doubtless, the same region. The change of one name for the other was simply a corruption.

CHAPTER VII.

discovered the country and to know that there was gold in it.

Preparations for the return voyage.

We had now been thirteen months on the voyage, and the ships and rigging were much worn, and the men weary. So by common consent we agreed to careen our ships on the beach, in order to calk and pitch them anew, as they leaked badly, and then to return to Spain. When we took this resolution, we were near one of the best harbours in the world, which we entered, and found a vast number of people, who received us most kindly.[1] We made a breastwork on shore with our boats and our casks, and placed our artillery so that it would play over them; then having unloaded and lightened our ships, we hauled them to land, and repaired them wherever they needed it. The natives were of very great assistance to us, continually providing food, so that in this port we consumed very little of our own. This served us a very good turn, for our provisions were poor, and the stock so much reduced at this time, that we feared it would hardly last us on our return to Spain. Having stayed here thirty-seven days, visiting their villages many times, where they paid us the highest honour, we wished to depart on our voyage.

Before we set sail, the natives complained to us, that at certain times in the year, there came from the sea into their territory, a very cruel tribe, who, either by treachery or force, killed many of them,

[1] This was probably the modern port of Mochina, on the coast of Cumana.

CHAPTER VII.

and eat them, while they captured others, and carried them prisoners into their own country, and that they were hardly able to defend themselves. They signified to us that this tribe were islanders, and lived at about one hundred leagues distance at sea. They narrated this to us with so much simplicity and feeling, that we credited them, and promised to avenge their great injuries; at which they were highly rejoiced, and many offered to go with us. We did not wish to take them for many reasons, and only carried seven, on the condition, that they should come back in their own canoes, for we would not enter into obligations to return them to their own country. With this they were contented, and we parted from these people, leaving them very well disposed toward us.

Discover new islands.

Our ships having been repaired, we set sail on our return, taking a northeasterly course, and at the end of seven days, fell in with some islands. There were a great many of them, some peopled, others uninhabited. We landed at one of them, where we saw many people, who called the island Iti. Having filled our boats with good men, and put three rounds of shot in each boat, we proceeded toward the land, where we saw about four hundred men and many women, all naked, like those we had seen before. They were of good stature, and appeared to be very warlike men, being armed with bows and arrows, and lances. The greater part of them carried staves of a square form, attached to their persons in such a manner that they were not prevented

CHAPTER VII.

from drawing the bow. As we approached within bow-shot of the shore, they all leaped into the water, and shot their arrows at us, to prevent our landing.

Severe battle and defeat of the natives.

They were painted with various colours, and plumed with feathers, and the interpreters who were with us told us that when they were thus painted and plumed they showed a wish to fight. They persisted so much in their endeavours to deter us from landing, that we were at last compelled to fire on them with our artillery. Hearing the thunder of our cannon, and seeing some of their people fall dead, they all retreated to the shore. We, having consulted together, forty of us resolved to leap ashore, and if they waited for us, to fight with them. Proceeding thus, they attacked us, and we fought about two hours with little advantage, except that our bowmen and gunners killed some of their people, and they wounded some of ours. This was because we could not get a chance to use the lance or the sword. We finally, by desperate exertion, were enabled to draw the sword, and as soon as they had a taste of our arms, they fled to the mountains and woods, leaving us masters of the field, with many of their people killed and wounded. This day we did not pursue them, because we were much fatigued, but returned to our ships, the seven men who came with us being very highly rejoiced.

The next day we saw a great number of people coming through the country, still offering us signs of battle, sounding horns and various other instru-

CHAPTER VII.

ments which they use in war, and all painted and plumed, which gave them a strange and ferocious appearance. Whereupon, all in the ships held a grand council, and it was determined that since these people were resolved to be at enmity with us, we would go to meet them, and do every thing to engage their friendship; but in case they would not receive it, we resolved to treat them as enemies, and to make slaves of all we could capture. Having armed ourselves in the best manner possible, we immediately rowed ashore, where they did not resist our landing, from fear, as I think, of our bombardment. We disembarked in four squares, being fifty-seven men, each captain with his own men, and engaged them in battle.

After a long battle, having killed many, we put them to flight, and pursued them to a village, taking about two hundred and fifty prisoners.[1] We burned the village, and returned victorious to the ships with our prisoners, leaving many killed and wounded on their side, while on ours not more than one died, and only twenty-two were wounded. The rest all escaped unhurt, for which, God be thanked We soon arranged for our departure, and the seven men, of whom five were wounded, took a canoe from the island, and with seven prisoners, four women and three men that we gave them, returned to their own country, very merry and greatly aston-

1 The edition of Gruniger reads, "twenty-five slaves;" but it does not appear probable that the number was so small, and the text is in accordance with Canovai.

ished at our power. We also set sail for Spain, with two hundred and twenty-two prisoners, slaves, and arrived in the port of Cadiz on the fifteenth day of October, 1498, where we were well received, and found a market for our slaves. This is what happened to me, in this my first voyage, that may be considered worth relating.[1]

[1] The edition of Gruniger makes the date of the return of Americus the 15th of October, 1499, and, immediately after, gives as the date of his departure on his second voyage, May, 1499. So manifest an error of print, one would think, ought not to have afforded any ground from which to argue the incredibility of the writer, yet Navarréte makes use of it for this purpose.

CHAPTER VIII.

The Arrival of Columbus on the Coast of Paria, and at Hispaniola, August 30th, 1498.—Distracted State of the Colony he had left.—Despatches News of his Discovery of the Continent on 18th of October, 1498, from Isabella.—Americus arrives at Cadiz, 15th of October, 1498.—News made Public.—Consequent Excitement.—Alonzo de Ojeda.—His Plan of an Expedition.—Bishop Fonseca.—His Hatred of Columbus.—Commission of Ojeda.—His Companionship with Americus.—Interval between First and Second Voyage.—Marriage of Americus with Maria Cerozo.—He goes to Court.—Is importuned by Ojeda.—Consents to go with him.—Juan de la Cosa.—Preparations for sailing at Seville.—Lorenzo di Pier-Francesco de' Medici.—Sketch of his Life.

It appears in the history of Columbus, that the Admiral, after visiting the coast of Paria, in 1498, arrived, on the 30th of August in that year, at the settlement which he had founded on the island of Hispaniola. He found the affairs of the colony in the greatest state of confusion and anarchy. Notwithstanding the sagacious and vigorous government of his brother Bartholomew, whom he had left behind him as his lieutenant or adelantado, a serious insurrection, headed by an ambitious man named Roldan, had broken out, and threatened the utter destruction of the new colony. Roldan was the last man who should have rebelled against the authority of Columbus, for he had been raised by the Admiral from poverty and a low position, to one of usefulness and distinction; but he was "one of those base spirits, which grew venomous in the sunshine of prosperity."[1]

Condition of Hispaniola, and despatches of Columbus.

Columbus saw at once the necessity of vigorous measures to quell the growing spirit of discontent and rebellion. He was well aware that many of the colonists were extremely anxious to return to Spain. They were composed mostly of refugees from justice, and convicts who had been pardoned, on the condition of accompanying him on his second and third voyages, and looked upon their residence in Hispaniola as a punishment. He deemed it advisable, therefore, to get rid of as many of these unruly subjects as possible, and accordingly, on the 12th of September, 1498, he made proclamation, offering a free passage home to such of the colonists as wished to avail themselves of the chance, in five vessels, which he determined to despatch at once for Spain. He hoped by this means to weaken the force of the disaffected, and was desirous, also, of sending to his sovereigns an account of his further discoveries.[2]

These ships set sail, on the 18th of the next month, from the port of Isabella, in the island of Hispaniola, just three days after the date of the arrival of Americus from his first voyage, in Cadiz. They reached Spain in the month of December, after a passage of about two months, bringing with them an account of the recent voyage of Colum-

[1] Irving, vol. ii. p. 771. Fernando Columbus, chap. lxxiv.

[2] Fernando Columbus, chap. lxxiv.

CHAPTER VIII.

bus, with some specimens of the gold and pearls which he had picked up on the coast of Paria. This account was accompanied by a chart of the track of the expedition, and discoursed in glowing terms of the beauties and wealth of the country which he had visited.[1]

It is probable that this was the first news which was published in Spain of the newly-found continent. Following out the idea adopted and illustrated in the sixth chapter of this work, that the expedition which Americus first accompanied was a private enterprise, joined by him as an agent in behalf of the king, it is reasonable to conclude that secresy was at first maintained concerning it, for purposes of private advantage. It is very likely, however, that it was communicated to the government by Americus, and this supposition is corroborated by what followed.

Alonzo de Ojeda.

Alonzo de Ojeda, a young man of great courage and enterprise, who, when only twenty-one years of age, had accompanied Columbus on his second voyage, and distinguished himself much by his gallantry and audacious spirit, was at that time lingering about the court, in search of some service or employment, in which to gain new laurels by his prowess. He was brought up as a page by the

[1] Irving, vol. ii. p. 781.

In this account Columbus still adhered to his first views and, did not imagine for a moment that when he touched the coast of Paria, he had found a continent. Ferdinand Columbus says that "he called it the Holy Island, believing that land of Paria to be no continent."—*Ferd. Columbus,* chap. lxxi.

CHAPTER VIII.

Duke of Medina Celi, one of the earliest supporters of Columbus at the court of Ferdinand and Isabella, and had been trained to hardy exercises and daring exploits in the Moorish wars. Possessing influential connexions and friends, he found little difficulty in organizing an expedition to continue these discoveries, which were the first that had roused the cupidity of the Spaniards, by their enticing descriptions of pearls, and gold, and spices.[1]

Enthusiasm respecting the New World.

Hitherto the accounts of the New World had fallen far short of the sanguine anticipations of men, and, as appears above, the disappointment in the expectations of all was so great, that it had been found necessary to force sailors to accompany the second and third expeditions. Convicts and desperate characters of all descriptions had been pressed into the service; but the great sensation produced by the later intelligence entirely altered the face of affairs. A multitude of adventurers, noble as well as of low degree, came eagerly forward to enrol themselves as volunteers in every new armament, and the only difficulty was, to make a judicious selection from the crowd of applicants.

Commission granted by the Bishop Fonseca.

The Bishop Fonseca, who held the chief control of all matters appertaining to the affairs of the Indies, had been since the year 1493 a bitter enemy to Columbus, and was always ready to seize upon any opportunity to annoy and impede him in his

[1] Irving, vol. ii. p. 945.

undertakings.[1] He gladly encouraged Ojeda to proceed in his attempt, and issued a commission, giving him full authority. Well knowing that the representations of Columbus, before his departure on his third voyage, had procured a revocation of the edict of general license to private adventures, he did not seek the approval of the sovereigns, and the commission appears signed by him alone, in virtue of his general superintendence of such affairs.[2] It was worded with great caution and address, for the Bishop knew that King Ferdinand would be gratified at the prospect of extending his dominions at the expense of private persons, although he did not wish to appear guilty of any public breach of faith with Columbus. Accordingly, the only provisos which the license of Ojeda contained, were to the effect, that he should not visit any lands belonging to the King of Portugal, or any of those which had been discovered for Spain previous to the year 1495; thus leaving him entire liberty to explore the coast of Paria and the adjacent countries, and

[1] The origin of the difficulty between Columbus and the Bishop Fonseca was this. While at Seville, making preparations for his second voyage, Columbus found that the expenses would be greater than he had anticipated, and much delay and demurring was occasioned in the settlement of his accounts. Fonseca was very captious in the matter, and in particular refused the application of Columbus for the appointment of certain members of his household retinue. Columbus appealed to the sovereigns, who rebuked the Bishop in a letter, in which they ordered that he should be allowed ten squires or unmounted footmen, and twenty additional servants, in various domestic capacities. Fonseca cherished the memory of this affront, as he chose to consider it, to the latest period of his life.—*Irving*, vol. ii. p. 687.

[2] Navarréte, tom. ii.

NATIVES JUMPING OVERBOARD.

When they heard the thundering report of the big guns, the greater part of them jumped into the sea from fright, acting like frogs sitting on a bank, who plunge into the marsh on the approach of anything that alarms them. (See P. 132.)

giving him an opportunity to reap the first fruits of the golden harvest, which the accounts of Americus and Columbus represented as awaiting him.

The voyages of Ojeda and Americus identical.

The near resemblance of its incidents, the similarity of dates of departure and arrival, and the direct testimony of Alonzo de Ojeda himself, in the course of the lawsuit of Don Diego Columbus, referred to in a previous chapter, render it almost certain that this voyage of Ojeda and the second voyage of Americus are identical. It is true that the Italian biographers of the navigator arrive at a different conclusion, but they had not the benefit of the valuable mass of testimony which has recently been brought to light by the researches of Navarrête among the dusty archives of Spain, and are in some degree carried away by their desire to exalt Americus to a separate command and authority, rather than leave him in the less showy and consequential, but more useful position of a skilful navigator and scientific astronomer. Before proceeding, however, to give the descriptions which Americus has left of his second voyage, the few events which have come down to the present time, relating to his personal history during the interval between his arrival and second departure, demand attention.

Marriage of Americus with Maria Cerezo

It was during this interval of about seven months, that Americus, notwithstanding the multifarious employments and negotiations in which he was engaged, found time to complete a matrimonial engagement, which he had entered into before his first voyage. Donna Maria Cerezo, the lady whom he

19

CHAPTER VIII.

married, became known, and subsequently betrothed to him, while he was conducting the affairs of the house of Berardi, in Seville, but either from prudential motives, or some other cause which cannot now be ascertained, their nuptials did not take place till after his first voyage. This lady was a native of Seville, of an honourable though not wealthy family, and it is reasonable to conclude that her alliance with Americus was based upon motives of affection alone, as the navigator was neither at that time, nor ever afterwards, in affluent circumstances. Very little is known respecting this lady, excepting that her union with Americus was unproductive of children, and that she survived him, receiving from the government, after his death, a handsome pension in consideration of her husband's services.[1]

Americus goes to the court.

Soon after his marriage, Americus visited the court, where he was received with marked attention by the king, Ferdinand. Bishop Fonseca paid him particular attention and honour. He was consulted respecting new expeditions, and his accounts, of what he had already seen, were listened to with the greatest interest. The cold and calculating spirit of the king was gratified by finding that others besides Columbus could add to his dominions and wealth, for he already repented the contract he had entered into with the Admiral. When that was agreed upon, he little dreamed of the vast concessions he was making to a subject, considering his

1 See the Illustrations and Documents. Translation of Documents from Navarréte.

schemes wild and visionary; but now that the brightest hopes of the advocates of Columbus seemed on the point of being realized, he was anxious to grasp as much as possible for himself, and bitterly repented his former bargain.

Alonzo de Ojeda, having comparatively little experience as a navigator, and viewing his projected voyage in the light of a marauding enterprise, rather than as an expedition of discovery, was naturally desirous of engaging the services of competent and scientific navigators to conduct his fleet. He made immediate application to Americus and to Juan de la Cosa, whose reputation for skill in nautical affairs was deservedly high, and urged strongly that they should accompany him.[1] Americus was at first disinclined to go, and represented the short time which he would have to enjoy the quiet and repose of home, after a long and arduous voyage, but his objections were of no avail. Seconded by the requests of the Bishop Fonseca, the entreaties of Ojeda prevailed, and Americus decided again to visit the New World.

A new fleet is equipped at the port of St. Mary.

Thus strengthened by the patronage of the Court, the next step for Ojeda was to find the means of equipping his expedition. The connection of Americus with many of the rich merchants of Seville was of material aid in this particular, and but little difficulty was experienced in finding among the

[1] For a sketch of the lives of Ojeda and Juan de la Cosa, the companions of Americus, in his second voyage, see *Illustrations and Documents*.

CHAPTER VIII.

wealthy capitalists of that enterprising city some who were willing to stake a portion of their fortunes on the successful issue of the schemes of the adventurer. A fleet of four vessels was speedily equipped at St. Mary, a port on the shore of the bay of Cadiz, opposite to that city, and by the latter part of the spring of 1499 was ready for sea. So tempting was the spirit of adventure, that many of the sailors who, at their own request, had been sent home by Columbus from Hispaniola, enrolled themselves in this new expedition.[1]

Sketch of the life of Lorenzo di Pier Francesco de' Medici.

A brief notice of the individual to whom Americus addressed his letters, giving an account of his second and third voyages, may not be without interest to the reader. Cosmo de' Medici, the grandfather of Lorenzo the Magnificent, had a brother by name Lorenzo, in connection with whom he carried on a very extensive trade, both in Florence and in other parts of the world. This Lorenzo left only one son, Pier Francesco, who inherited his wealth. It was retained, however, in the hands of Cosmo de Medici, for some years after his death, and a division of the family property did not take place until the year 1451. At that time a new agreement or partnership was entered into, by which it was stipulated that the business should be carried on for the joint benefit of Pier Francesco, and the two sons of Cosmo, Piero and Giovanni, and that their profits should be divided in equal thirds. Very large acquisitions were the result of this arrangement, but while Cos-

[1] Irving, vol. ii. p. 945.

mo and his sons expended immense amounts in public charities and in supporting the dignity of chief magistrates of the republic, Pier Francesco preferred the quiet of private life, and transmitted to his sons, Lorenzo, the subject of this notice, and Giovanni, a patrimony much more ample than that which Lorenzo the Magnificent inherited from his father, Piero.

The death of Pier Francesco took place in 1459. His sons continued in the same course which their father had pursued throughout life. They were both anxious rather to acquire wealth and increase their already overgrown property, than ambitious of political honours. In 1490, as appears previously in this work, Lorenzo gave certain commissions to Americus, which were one cause of his residence in Spain. At the time of the expulsion of Piero de Medici from Florence, in 1494, the two brothers, fearful of being themselves banished in the popular commotions which ensued, dropped the family name, which at that time was in so much odium from the inefficient management of Piero, and assumed the surname of Popolani. It appears that they were influenced to this course partly by a desire to acquire for themselves the power which had passed out of the possession of the elder branch of the family; but, if so, the subsequent elevation of Piero Soderini, and the return of the elder branch, after his fall, disappointed their hopes.

Both the correspondent of Americus and his brother passed through life in subordinate stations, and though the ducal house which afterwards furnished, for nearly three centuries, a line of monarchs for Tuscany, originated in their branch of the family, they themselves never acquired any political rank. They continued engaged in extensive mercantile operations throughout their lives, and were known all over Europe by their large commercial transactions. When Americus wrote to Lorenzo di Pier Francesco an account of his second voyage, they were living at Florence, under the government of Piero Soderini.[1]

[1] Roscoe, Life of Lorenzo de Medici, vol. i. 181; vol. ii. p. 404, 405

CHAPTER IX.

FIRST LETTER OF AMERICUS TO LORENZO DI PIER-FRANCESCO DE' MEDICI, GIVING AN ACCOUNT OF HIS SECOND VOYAGE.

Departure from Cadiz, May 18th, 1499.—Makes the Canary Islands.—Arrives at the New World in twenty-four Days.—Difficulty of Disembarcation.—Freshness of the Water at Sea.—Two large Rivers Discovered.—Ascent of one of them.—Description of the Scenery.—Remarkable Current.—Shadows of the Sun.—The Stars of the South Pole.—Remarkable Passage in Dante.—Calculation of Distance from Cadiz.—Calculation of Longitude, Aug. 23, 1499.—Occultation of Mars.—Sails Northwardly.—Discovers an Island.—Description of the Natives.—Their Hospitality.—Present of Pearls.—Voyage continued.—Meets with Unfriendly Natives.—Cannibalism.—Battle with them.—Valour of a Portuguese Sailor.—A very large Race of Natives.—Venezuela.—Proceeds to Hispaniola.—Refitting the Fleet.—Continue Homeward Voyage.—Take a Cargo of Slave-prisoners.—Arrive at the Azores and Cadiz.—Conclusion of the Voyage.

Most Excellent and dear Lord,

It is a long time since I have written to your Excellency, and for no other reason than that nothing has occurred to me worthy of being commemorated. This present letter will inform you, that about a month ago, I arrived from the Indies, by the way of the great ocean, brought, by the grace of God, safely to this city of Seville. I think your Excellency will be gratified to learn the result of my voyage, and the most surprising things which have been pre-

CHAPTER IX.

sented to my observation. If I am somewhat tedious, let my letter be read in your more idle hours, as fruit is eaten after the cloth is removed from the table. Your Excellency will please to note, that, commissioned by his highness the King of Spain, I set out with two small ships, on the 18th of May, 1499, on a voyage of discovery to the southwest, by way of the great ocean, and steered my course along the coast of Africa, until I reached the Fortunate Islands, which are now called the Canaries. After having provided ourselves with all things necessary, first offering our prayers to God, we set sail from an island which is called Gomera, and turning our prows southwardly, sailed twenty-four days with a fresh wind, without seeing any land.

Arrives at the continent in twenty-four days.

At the end of these twenty-four days we came within sight of land, and found that we had sailed about thirteen hundred leagues, and were at that distance from the city of Cadiz, in a southwesterly direction. When we saw the land we gave thanks to God, and then launched our boats, and, with sixteen men, went to the shore, which we found thickly covered with trees, astonishing both on account of their size and their verdure, for they never lose their foliage. The sweet odour which they exhaled (for they are all aromatic) highly delighted us, and we were rejoiced in regaling our nostrils.

We rowed along the shore in the boats, to see if we could find any suitable place for landing, but after toiling from morning till night, we found no way or passage which we could enter and disembark. We were prevented from doing so by the lowness of the land, and by its being so densely covered with trees. We concluded, therefore, to return to the ships, and make an attempt to land in some other spot.

CHAPTER IX.

Fresh currents of water at sea

We observed one remarkable circumstance in these seas. It was, that at fifteen leagues from the land, we found the water fresh like that of a river —and we filled all our empty casks with it. Having returned to our ships, we raised anchor and set sail—turning our prows southwardly, as it was my intention to see whether I could sail round a point of land, which Ptolomey calls the Cape of Cattegara (which is near the Great Bay).[1] In my opinion it was not far from it, according to the degrees of latitude and longitude, which will be stated hereafter. Sailing in a southerly direction along the coast, we saw two large rivers issuing from the land—one running from west to east, and being four leagues in width, which is sixteen miles,—the other ran from south to north, and was three leagues wide. I think that these two rivers, by reason of their magnitude, caused the freshness of the water in the adjoining sea. Seeing that the coast was invariably low, we determined to enter one of these rivers with the boats, and ascend it till we either found a suitable landing-place or an inhabited village.

Having prepared our boats, and put in provision for four days, with twenty men well armed, we entered the river, and rowed nearly two days,

[1] See the Dissertazione Gustificativa, Nos. 85, 86

CHAPTER IX.

making a distance of about eighteen leagues. We attempted to land in many places by the way, but found the low land still continuing, and so thickly covered with trees, that a bird could scarcely fly through them. While thus navigating the river, we saw very certain indications that the inland parts of the country were inhabited; nevertheless, as our vessels remained in a dangerous place, in case an adverse wind should arise, we concluded, at the end of two days, to return.

Sees beautiful birds and foliage.

Here we saw an immense number of birds, of various forms and colours; a great number of parrots, and so many varieties of them, that it caused us great astonishment. Some were crimson-coloured, others of variagated green and lemon, others entirely green, and others, again, that were black and flesh-coloured. Oh! the song of other species of birds, also, was so sweet and so melodious, as we heard it among the trees, that we often lingered, listening to their charming music. The trees, too, were so beautiful, and smelt so sweetly, that we almost imagined ourselves in a terrestrial paradise; yet not one of those trees, or the fruit of them, were similar to the trees or fruit in our part of the world. On our way back we saw many people, of various descriptions, fishing in the river.

Having arrived at our ships, we raised anchor and set sail, still continuing in a southerly direction, and standing off to sea about forty leagues. While sailing on this course, we encountered a current, which ran from southeast to northwest; so great was it, and ran so furiously, that we were put into great fear, and were exposed to great peril. The current was so strong, that the Strait of Gibraltar and that of the Faro of Messina appeared to us like mere stagnant water in comparison with it. We could scarcely make any headway against it, though we had the wind fresh and fair. Seeing that we made no progress, or but very little, and the danger to which we were exposed, we determined to turn our prows to the northwest.

His geographical position and the solar shadow.

As I know, if I remember right, that your Excellency understands something of cosmography, I intend to describe to you our progress, in our navigation by the latitude and longitude. We sailed so far to the south, that we entered the Torrid Zone, and penetrated the Circle of Cancer. You may rest assured, that for a few days, while sailing through the Torrid Zone, we saw four shadows of the sun, as the sun appeared in the zenith to us at mid-day. I would say that the sun, being in our meridian, gave us no shadow, and this I was enabled many times to demonstrate to all the company, and took their testimony of the fact. This I did on account of the ignorance of the common people, who do not know that the sun moves through its circle of the zodiac. At one time I saw our shadow to the south, at another to the north, at another to the west, and at another to the east, and sometimes, for an hour or two of the day, we had no shadow at all.

We sailed so far south in the Torrid Zone, that we found ourselves under the equinoctial line, and had both poles at the edge of the horizon. Having passed the line, and sailed six degrees to the south of it, we lost sight of the north star altogether, and even the stars of Ursa Minor, or, to speak better, the guardians which revolve about the firmament, were scarcely seen. Very desirous of being the author who should designate the other polar star of the firmament, I lost, many a time, my night's sleep, while contemplating the movement of the stars around the Southern Pole, in order to ascertain which had the least motion, and which might be nearest to the firmament, but I was not able to accomplish it with such bad nights as I had, and such instruments as I used, which were the quadrant and astrolabe. I could not distinguish a star which had less than ten degrees of motion around the firmament; so that I was not satisfied within myself, to name any particular one for the pole of the meridian, on account of the large revolution which they all made around the firmament.

While I was arriving at this conclusion as the result of my investigations, I recollected a verse of our poet Dante, which may be found in the first chapter of his "Purgatory," where he imagines he is leaving this hemisphere to repair to the other, and attempting to describe the Antartic pole, says:

CHAPTER IX.

"Io mi volsi a man destra e posi mente
All' altro polo, e vidi quattro stelle
Non viste mai, fuor che alla prima gente:
Goder pareva il Ciel di lor fiammelle:
O settentrional vedovo sito
Poiche privato sei di mirar quelle."[1]

The Southern Cross.

It appears to me that the poet wished to describe in these verses, by the four stars, the pole of the other firmament, and I have little doubt, even now,

1 To the right hand I turned, and fixed my mind
On the other pole attentive, where I saw
Four stars ne'er seen before save by the ken
Of our first parents. Heaven of their rays
Seemed joyous. Oh thou northern site, bereft
Indeed, and widowed, since of these deprived.

Carey's Dante, Vision of Purgatory, Can. i.

Venturi observes that "Dante here speaks as a poet, and almost in the spirit of prophecy; or what is more likely, describes the heavens about that pole according to his own invention. In our days," he adds, "the cross, composed of four stars, three of the second and one of the third magnitude, serves as a guide to those who sail from Europe to the south, but in the age of Dante these discoveries had not been made." "It appears probable," says Carey, in a note to this passage, "that either from long tradition, or from the relation of later voyagers, the real truth might not have been unknown to our poet. Seneca's predictions of the discovery of America may be accounted for in a similar manner. But whatever may be thought of this, it is certain that the four stars are here symbolical of the four cardinal virtues, Prudence, Justice, Fortitude, and Temperance. M. Artaud mentions a globe constructed by an Arabian in Egypt, with the date of the year 622 of the Hegira, corresponding to 1225 of our era, in which the Southern Cross is positively marked. See his *Histoire de Dante*, chap. xxxi. and xl. 8vo. Par. 1841.

The prediction of Seneca is contained in the well known lines from Medea,

Venient annis
Sæcula seris, quibus Oceanus
Vinculis rerum laxet, et ingens
Pateat tellus, Typhisque novos
Detegat orbes, nec sit terris
Ultima Thule.

See also the Illustrations and Documents—Eulogy of Americus.—Canovai says, in a note at this passage, that Pigafetta speaks as follows of the Antarctic Pole: "At the Antarctic Pole are seen many stars congregated together, which are like two mists, separated from each other, and a little obscure in the middle. Between these are two not very large or very bright, and which have little motion, and these two are the Antarctic Pole."—*Ramusio*, tom. i. p. 356. A Portuguese navigator, in the same

CHAPTER IX.

that what he says may be true. I observed four stars in the figure of an almond, which had but little motion, and if God gives me life and health, I hope to go again into that hemisphere, and not to return without observing the pole. In conclusion, I would remark, that we extended our navigation so far south, that our difference of latitude from the city of Cadiz was sixty degrees and a half, because, at that city, the pole is elevated thirty-five degrees and a half, and we had passed six degrees beyond the equinoctial line.[1] Let this suffice as to

collection, says, "As we arrived at the golden river, we began to see four stars of admirable size and lucidity, placed in the form of a cross, which are thirty degrees distant from the Antarctic Pole, and we called it the Cross, and raised an instrument to one of these four stars, which is the foot of the cross, and as it is found there in the south, we knew its centre to be the Antarctic Pole.' —*Ibid.* p. 117, D. Corsali speaks in terms more cogent yet, in confirming the observations and application of Americus. "In which place is the pole . . . . . two clouds of reasonable size evidently manifest it, moving around it continually in a circular motion, now rising and now descending with one star always in the middle, which, with them, revolves about eleven degrees distant from the pole. Above these appears a marvellous cross, in the midst of five stars which surround it . . . . . with other stars which go with it round the pole, revolving about thirty degrees distant, and it makes its revolution in twenty-four hours, and is so beautiful, that, it appears to me, no other heavenly sign can be compared with it . . . . . I think this may be the cross of which Dante speaks with prophetic spirit."—*Ib.* p. 177, E. And finally Giuntini, in the Comments on the Sfera del Sacro Bosco, writes, "Some Portuguese mariners, while seeking the noble emporium of India, now called Calcutta, sailing round the whole Atlantic Ocean, saw the other pole, meanwhile, elevated above fifty degrees, at the same time that our pole was depressed below the horizon."—*In. C. 1. Sphera de Sacro Bosco. Canovai*, tom. i. p. 103, note

[1] The following is the calculation of Americus more plainly expressed:

From the Pole to the Equator is . .	90°
From the Equator to his position at the time	6°
Total . .	96°
Deduct the Latitude of Cadiz . .	35½°
Difference of Latitude . . .	60½

See *Canovai*, tom. ii. p. 105

CHAPTER IX.

our latitude. You must observe that this our navigation was in the months of July, August, and September, when, as you know, the sun is longest above the horizon in our hemisphere, and describes the greatest arch in the day, and the least in the night. On the contrary, while we were at the equinoctial line, or near it, within four to six degrees, the difference between the day and night was not perceptible. They were of equal length, or very nearly so.

As to the longitude, I would say that I found so much difficulty in discovering it, that I had to labour very hard to ascertain the distance I had made by means of longitude. I found nothing better, at last, than to watch the opposition of the planets during the night, and especially that of the moon, with the other planets, because the moon is swifter in her course than any other of the heavenly bodies. I compared my observations with the almanac of Giovanni da Monteregio, which was composed for the meridian of the city of Ferrara, verifying them with the calculations in the tables of King Alphonso, and, afterwards, with the many observations I had myself made one night with another.

Transit of Mars, August 23d, 1499.

On the twenty-third of August, 1499 (when the moon was in conjunction with Mars, which, according to the almanac, was to take place at midnight, or half an hour after), I found that when the moon rose to the horizon an hour and a half after the sun had set, the planet had passed in that part of the east. I observed that the moon was about a degree and

CHAPTER IX.

some minutes farther east than Mars, and at midnight she was five degrees and a half farther east, a little more or less. So that, making the proportion: if twenty-four hours are equal to 360 degrees, what are five hours and a half equal to? I found the result to be eighty-two degrees and a half, which was equal to my longitude from the meridian of the city of Cadiz; then giving to every degree sixteen leagues and two thirds, I found myself distant west from the city of Cadiz thirteen hundred and sixty-six leagues and two thirds, which is five thousand four hundred and sixty-six miles and two thirds. The reason why I give sixteen leagues to each degree is, because, according to Tolomeo and Alfagrano, the earth turns twenty-four thousand miles, which is equal to six thousand leagues, which, being divided by 360 degrees, gives to each degree sixteen leagues and two thirds. This calculation I certified many times conjointly with the pilots, and found it true and good.[1]

It appears to me, most excellent Lorenzo, that by this voyage most of those philosophers are controverted, who say that the Torrid Zone cannot be inhabited on account of the great heat. I have found the case to be quite the contrary. I have found that the air is fresher and more temperate in that region than beyond it, and that the inhabitants

[1] Sacrobosco calculates the circumference of the earth at 31,500 miles, Baliani at 30,000, and modern astronomers at 21,600 at the equator, and 21,532 at the poles. It will be observed that Americus approximated more closely to the modern estimate than either.—*Canovai*, tom. i. p. 105, note.

BREASTWORK ON SHORE.

We made a breastwork on shore with our boats and our casks, and placed our artillery so that it would play over them; then having unloaded and lightened our ships, we hauled them to land, and repaired them wherever they needed it. (SEE P. 135.)

CHAPTER IX.

are also more numerous here than they are in the other zones, for reasons which will be given below. Thus it is certain, that practice is of more value than theory.

Description of the natives. A race of cannibals.

Thus far I have related the navigation I accomplished in the South and West. It now remains for me to inform you of the appearance of the country we discovered, the nature of the inhabitants, and their customs, the animals we saw, and of many other things worthy of remembrance, which fell under my observation. After we turned our course to the north, the first land we found to be inhabited was an island, at ten degrees distant from the equinoctial line. When we arrived at it, we saw on the seashore a great many people who stood looking at us with astonishment. We anchored within about a mile of the land, fitted out the boats, and twenty-two men, well armed, made for land. The people, when they saw us landing, and perceived that we were different from themselves (because they have no beard and wear no clothing of any description, being also of a different colour, they being brown and we white), began to be afraid of us, and all ran into the woods. With great exertion, by means of signs, we reassured them, and negotiated with them. We found that they were of a race called cannibals, the greater part, or all of whom, live on human flesh.

Your Excellency may rest assured of this fact. They do not eat one another, but navigating with certain barks which they call *canoes*, they bring

CHAPTER IX.

their prey from the neighbouring islands or countries inhabited by those who are enemies, or of a different tribe from their own. They never eat any women, unless they consider them outcasts. These things we verified in many places where we found similar people. We often saw the bones and heads of those who had been eaten, and they who had made the repast admitted the fact, and said that their enemies always stood in much greater fear on that account.

Still they are a people of gentle disposition and beautiful stature. They go entirely naked, and the arms which they carry are bows and arrows, and shields. They are a people of great activity and much courage. They are very excellent marksmen. In fine, we held much intercourse with them, and they took us to one of their villages about two leagues inland, and gave us our breakfast. They gave whatever was asked of them, though I think more through fear than affection, and after having been with them all one day, we returned to the ships, still remaining on friendly terms with them.

Sail along the shore and arrive at the Gulf of Paria.

We sailed along the coast of this island, and saw by the seashore another large village of the same tribe. We landed in the boats, and found they were waiting for us, all loaded with provisions, and they gave us enough to make a very good breakfast, according to their ideas of dishes. Seeing they were such kind people, and treated us so well, we dared not take any thing from them, and made sail till we arrived at a gulf which is called the

Gulf of Paria. We anchored opposite the mouth of a great river, which causes the water of this gulf to be fresh, and saw a large village close to the sea. We were surprised at the great number of people who were seen there. They were without arms, and seemed peaceably disposed. We went ashore with the boats, and they received us with great friendship, and took us to their houses, where they had made very good preparations for breakfast. Here they gave us three sorts of wine to drink, not of the juice of the grape, but made of fruits like beer, and they were excellent. Here also we ate many fresh acorns, a most royal fruit. They gave us many other fruits, all different from ours, and of very good flavour, the flavour and odour of all being aromatic.

They gave us some small pearls, and eleven large ones; and they told us by signs, that if we would wait some days, they would go and fish for them, and bring us many of them. We did not wish to be detained, so with many parrots of various colours, and in good friendship, we parted from them. From these people we learned that those of the before mentioned island were cannibals, and ate human flesh. We issued from this gulf and sailed along the coast, seeing continually great numbers of people, and when we were so disposed, we treated with them, and they gave us every thing we asked of them. They all go as naked as they were born, without being ashamed. If all were to be related concerning the little shame they have, it

CHAPTER IX.

would be bordering on impropriety, therefore it is better to suppress it.

Sail along the shores of the Continent four hundred leagues.

After having sailed about four hundred leagues continually along the coast, we concluded that this land was a continent, which might be bounded by the eastern parts of Asia, this being the commencement of the western part of the continent. Because it happened often that we saw divers animals, such as lions, stags, goats, wild hogs, rabbits, and other land animals, which are not found in islands, but only on the main land. Going inland one day with twenty men, we saw a serpent which was about twenty-four feet in length, and as large in girth as myself. We were very much afraid of it, and the sight of it caused us to return immediately to the sea. I oftentimes saw many very ferocious animals and large serpents.

Thus sailing along the coast, we discovered every day a great number of people, speaking various languages. When we had navigated four hundred leagues along the coast, we began to find people who did not wish for our friendship, but stood waiting for us with their arms, which were bows and arrows, and with some other arms which they use. When we went to the shore in our boats, they disputed our landing in such a manner that we were obliged to fight with them. At the end of the battle they found that they had the worst of it, for as they were naked, we always made great slaughter. Many times not more than sixteen of us fought with two thousand of them, and in the end defeated them, killing many, and robbing their houses.

Battle with the natives and gallantry of a Portuguese sailor.

One day we saw a great number of people, all posted in battle array to prevent our landing. We fitted out twenty-six men well armed, and covered the boats, on account of the arrows which were shot at us, and which always wounded some of us before we landed. After they had hindered us as long as they could, we leaped on shore, and fought a hard battle with them. The reason why they had so much courage and made such great exertion against us, was, that they did not know what kind of a weapon the sword was, or how it cuts. While thus engaged in combat, so great was the multitude of people who charged upon us, throwing at us such a cloud of arrows, that we could not withstand the assault, and nearly abandoning the hope of life, we turned our backs and ran to the boats. While thus disheartened and flying, one of our sailors, a Portuguese, a man of fifty-five years of age, who had remained to guard the boat, seeing the danger we were in, jumped on shore, and with a loud voice called out to us, "Children! turn your faces to your enemies, and God will give you the victory!" Throwing himself on his knees, he made a prayer, and then rushed furiously upon the Indians, and we all joined with him, wounded as we were. On that they turned their backs to us, and began to flee, and finally we routed them, and killed a hundred and fifty. We burned their houses also, at least one hundred and eighty in number. Then, as we

CHAPTER IX.

were badly wounded and weary, we returned tc the ships, and went into a harbour to recruit, where we staid twenty days, solely that the physician might cure us. All escaped except one, who was wounded in the left breast.

Continue the voyage and encounter a race of gigantic natives.

After being cured, we recommenced our navigation, and, through the same cause, we often were obliged to fight with a great many people, and always had the victory over them. Thus continuing our voyage, we came upon an island, fifteen leagues distant from the mainland. As at our arrival we saw no collection of people, the island appearing favourably, we determined to attempt it, and eleven of us landed. We found a path, in which we walked nearly two leagues inland, and came to a village of about twelve houses, in which there were only seven women, who were so large, that there was not one among them who was not a span and a half taller than myself. When they saw us, they were very much frightened, and the principal one among them, who was certainly a discreet woman, led us by signs into a house, and had refreshments prepared for us.

We saw such large women, that were about determining to carry off two young ones, about fifteen years of age, and make a present of them to this king, as they were, without doubt, creatures whose stature was above that of common men. While we were debating this subject, thirty-six men entered the house where we were drinking; they were of such large stature, that

CHAPTER IX.

each one was taller when upon his knees than I when standing erect. In fact, they were of the stature of giants in their size, and in the proportion of their bodies, which corresponded well with their height. Each of the women appeared a *Pantasilea*, and the men *Antei*. When they came in, some of our own number were so frightened that they did not consider themselves safe. They had bows and arrows, and very large clubs, made in the form of swords. Seeing that we were of small stature, they began to converse with us, in order to learn who we were, and from what parts we came. We gave them fair words, for the sake of peace, and answered them, by signs, that we were men of peace, and that we were going to see the world. Finally, we held it to be our wisest course to part from them without questioning in our turn; so we returned by the same path in which we had come—they accompanying us quite to the sea, till we went on board the ships.

Arrive at a place afterwards called Venezuela.

Nearly half the trees of this island are of dye-wood, as good as that of the East. We went from this island to another, in the vicinity, at ten leagues distance, and found a very large village—the houses of which were built over the sea, like Venice, with much ingenuity. While we were struck with admiration at this circumstance, we determined to go and see them; and as we went to their houses, they attempted to prevent our entering. They found out at last the manner in which the sword cuts, and thought it best to let us

CHAPTER IX.

enter. We found their houses filled with the finest cotton, and the beams of their dwellings were made of dye-wood. We took a quantity of their cotton and some dye-wood, and returned to the ships.

Your Excellency must know, that in all parts where we landed, we found a great quantity of cotton, and the country filled with cotton trees. So that all the vessels in the world might be loaded in these parts with cotton and dye-wood.

At length we sailed three hundred leagues farther along the coast, constantly finding savage but brave people, and very often fighting with them, and vanquishing them. We found seven different languages among them, each of which was not understood by those who spoke the others. It is said there are not more than seventy-seven languages in the world, but I say that there are more than a thousand, as there are more than forty which I have heard myself.

Determine to go to Hispaniola.

After having sailed along this coast seven hundred leagues or more, besides visiting numerous islands, our ships became greatly sea-worn, and leaked badly, so that we could hardly keep them free with two pumps going. The men also were much fatigued, and the provisions growing short. We were then, according to the decision of the pilots, within a hundred and twenty leagues of an island called Hispaniola, discovered by the Admiral Columbus six years before. We determined to proceed to it, and as it was inhabited by Christians, to repair our ships there, allow the men a little repose, and recruit our stock of provisions; because from this island to Castile there are three hundred leagues of ocean, without any land intervening.

CHAPTER IX.

Return Voyage.

In seven days we arrived at this island, where we staid two months. Here we refitted our ships and obtained our supply of provisions. We afterwards concluded to go to northern parts, where we discoverd more than a thousand islands, the greater part of them inhabited. The people were without clothing, timid and ignorant, and we did whatever we wished to do with them. This last portion of our discoveries was very dangerous to our navigation, on account of the shoals which we found thereabouts. In several instances we came near being lost. We sailed in this sea two hundred leagues directly north, until our people had become worn down with fatigue, through having been already nearly a year at sea. Their allowance was only six ounces of bread for eating, and but three small measures of water for drinking, per diem. And as the ships became dangerous to navigate with much longer, they remonstrated, saying that they wished to return to their homes in Castile, and not to tempt fortune and the sea any more. Whereupon we concluded to take some prisoners, as slaves, and loading the ships with them, to return at once to Spain. Going, therefore, to certain islands, we possessed ourselves by force of two hundred and thirty-two, and steered our course for Castile. In sixty-seven days we crossed the ocean, and arrived at the islands of the Azores, which be-

CHAPTER IX.

long to the King of Portugal, and are three hundred leagues distant from Cadiz. Here having taken in our refreshments, we sailed for Castile, but the wind was contrary, and we were obliged to go to the Canary Islands, from there to the island of Madeira, and thence to Cadiz.

Abstract of the Voyage.

We were absent thirteen months on this voyage, exposing ourselves to awful dangers, and discovering a very large country of Asia, and a great many islands, the largest part of them inhabited. According to the calculations I have several times made with the compass, we have sailed about five thousand leagues. To conclude—we passed the equinoctial line six and a half degrees to the south, and afterwards turned to the north, which we penetrated so far, that the north star was at an elevation of thirty-five degrees and a half above our horizon. To the west, we sailed eighty-four degrees distant from the meridian of the city and port of Cadiz. We discovered immense regions, saw a vast number of people, all naked, and speaking various languages. On the land we saw numerous wild animals, various kinds of birds, and an infinite quantity of trees, all aromatic. We brought home pearls in their growing state, and gold in the grain; we brought two stones, one of emerald colour, and the other of amethyst, which was very hard, and at least half a span long, and three fingers thick. The sovereigns esteem them most highly, and have preserved them among their jewels. We brought also a piece of crystal, which some jewellers say is beryl, and, ac-

CHAPTER IX.

cording to what the Indians told us, they had a great quantity of the same; we brought fourteen flesh-coloured pearls, with which the queen was highly delighted; we brought many other stones which appeared beautiful to us, but of all these we did not bring a large quantity, as we were continually busied in our navigation, and did not tarry long in any place.

Arrival at Cadiz and sale of slaves.

When we arrived at Cadiz, we sold many slaves, finding two hundred remaining to us, the others, completing the number of two hundred and thirty-two, having died at sea. After deducting the expense of transportation, we gained only about five hundred ducats, which, having to be divided into fifty-five parts, made the share of each very small. However, we contented ourselves with life, and rendered thanks to God, that during the whole voyage, out of fifty-seven Christian men, which was our number, only two had died, they having been killed by the Indians.

I have had two quartan agues since my return, but I hope, by the favour of God, to be well soon, as they do not continue long now, and are without chills. I have passed over many things worthy of being remembered, in order not to be more tedious than I can help, all which are reserved for the pen and in the memory.

They are fitting out three ships for me here, that I may go on a new voyage of discovery; and I think they will be ready by the middle of September. May it please our Lord to give me health and

CHAPTER IX.

a good voyage, as I hope again to bring very great news and discover the island of Trapobana, which is between the Indian Ocean and the Sea of Ganges. Afterwards I intend to return to my country, and seek repose in the days of my old age.

I shall not enlarge any more at present, though many things have been omitted, in part from their not being remembered at all, and in part that I might not be more prolix than I have been.

Sends a globe and a map to Lorenzo de' Medici.

I have resolved, most excellent Lorenzo, that as I have thus given you an account by letter of what has occurred to me, to send you two plans and descriptions of the world, made and arranged by my own hand and skill. There will be a map on a plane surface, and the other a view of the world in spherical form, which I intend to send you by sea, in the care of one Francesco Lotti, a Florentine, who is here. I think you will be pleased with them, particularly with the globe, as I made one not long since for these sovereigns, and they esteem it highly. I could have wished to have come with them personally, but my new departure, for making other discoveries, will not allow me that pleasure. There are not wanting in your city persons who understand the figure of the world, and who may, perhaps, correct something in it. Nevertheless, whatever may be pointed out for me to correct, let them wait till I come, as it may be that I shall defend myself and prove my accuracy.

I suppose your Excellency has learned the news brought by the fleet which the King of Portugal sent two years ago to make discoveries on the coast of Guinea. I do not call such a voyage as that a voyage of discovery, but only a visit to discovered lands; because, as you will see by the map, their navigation was continually within sight of land, and they sailed round the whole southern part of the continent of Africa, which is proceeding by a way spoken of by all cosmographical authors. It is true that the navigation has been very profitable, which is a matter of great consideration here in this kingdom, where inordinate covetousness reigns. I understand that they passed from the Red Sea, and extended their voyage into the Persian Gulf, to a city called Calicut, which is situated between the Persian Gulf and the river Indus. More lately the King of Portugal has received from sea twelve ships very richly laden, and he has sent them again to those parts, where they will certainly do a profitable business if they arrive safely.

May our Lord preserve and increase the exalted state of your noble Excellency as I desire. July 18th, 1500.

Your Excellency's humble servant,

AMERICUS VESPUCIUS.

Respecting the above letter to De Medici, an intelligent Italian critic remarks, that "it is the most ancient known writing of Americus, relating to his voyages to the New World, having been composed within a month after his return from his second voyage, and remaining buried in our archives for a long time. It is a precious monument, for without it we should have been left in ignorance of the great additions which he made to astronomical science. The most rigorous examination of this letter cannot bring to light the least circumstance proving any thing for or against the accuracy of his first voyage. The indifference with which he commences the matter is, however, a strong indication that he had previously written an account of his first voyage to the same Lorenzo de' Medici, to whom he addressed this communication.[1]

[1] Bartolozzi, Ricerche Historico-Critiche circa alle Scoperte D'Amerigo Vespucci, p. 62, 63.

CHAPTER X.

CONTINUATION OF THE LETTER OF AMERICUS TO PIERO SODERINI, GIVING AN ACCOUNT OF HIS SECOND VOYAGE.

Departure from Cadiz, May, 1499.—Arrival in the New World.—Signs of Inhabitants.—Coasting the Shores.—San Luis de Maranham.—Chase and Capture a Canoe.—Cannibalism.—Pearls and Gold.—Inimical Natives.—Chewing the Cud.—Want of Water.—Immense Leaves.—Island of Curacoa.—Large Islanders.—Visit to their Village.—Returning to Castile.—Trade with the Indians.—Large Quantity of Pearls.—Visit Antilla.—Take in Provisions.—Sail for Spain.—Arrival at Cadiz, June 8th, 1500.

THE Second Voyage, and what I saw in it most worthy of being remembered, here follow. We set out from the port of Cadiz, three ships in company, on the 18th of May, 1499, and steered our course directly to the Cape Verd Islands, passing within sight of the Grand Canary. We soon arrived at an island which is called Del Fuego or Fire Island, and having taken in wood and water, we proceeded on our voyage to the southwest. In forty-four days we arrived at a new land, which we judged to be a continent, and a continuation of that mentioned in my former voyage.[1] It was situated

[1] He was twenty days in making the Canaries, and twenty-four more in crossing the Atlantic. Some editions make the reading of this passage, "opposite to that mentioned in my former voyage." The mistake originated in a misprint of the Latin edition, the word "contraria" being substituted for "continua."—*Can.*, tom. i. p. 132.

CHAPTER X.

within the torrid zone, south of the equinoctial line, where the south pole is elevated five degrees, and distant from said island, bearing south, about five hundred leagues.[1] Here we found the days and nights equal on the 27th of June, when the sun is near the tropic of Cancer.

We did not see any people here, and having anchored our ships and cast off our boats, we proceeded to the land, which we found to be inundated by very large rivers. We came to anchor, and having got out the boats, attempted to enter these at many points, but from the immense quantity of water brought down by them, we could find no place, after hard toiling, that was not overflowed. We saw many signs of the country's being inhabited, but, as we were unable to enter it, we concluded to return to the ships, and make the attempt on some other part of the coast.

Coast the shore for about forty leagues.

We raised our anchors accordingly, and sailed along southeast by east, continually coasting the land, which ran in that direction. We attempted to enter at many points within the space of forty leagues, but all our labour was labour lost. We found the currents so strong on this coast that they absolutely obstructed our sailing, and they all ran from the southeast to the northwest. Seeing our navigation was attended with so many inconvien-

[1] The work of Bandini contains a series of singular errors in regard to this letter. The figure 5, wherever it occurs, is printed 8—though in many instances manifestly at variance with the sense.—*Canovai*, tom. i. p. 132.

INLAND SCENE.

They are very excellent marksmen. In fine, we held much intercourse with them, and they took us to one of their villages, about two leagues inland, and gave us our breakfast. (See P. 162.)

CHAPTER X.

ences, we concluded to turn our course to the north-west. Having sailed some time in this direction, we arrived at a very beautiful harbour, which was made by a large island at the entrance, inside of which was a very large bay.[1]

Chase and capture of a canoe.

While sailing along parallel with the island, with a view of entering the harbour, we saw many people on the shore, and, being much cheered, we manœuvred our ships for the purpose of anchoring and landing where they appeared. We might have been then about four leagues at sea. While proceeding on our course for this purpose, we saw a canoe quite out at sea, in which there were several people, and made sail on our ships in order to come up with and take possession of them, steering so as not to run them down; we saw that they stood with their oars raised, I think either through astonishment at beholding our ships, or by way of giving us to understand that they meant to wait for us and resist us; but as they perceived us approaching, they dropped their oars into the water, and began to row towards the land. Having in our company a small vessel of forty-five tons, a very fast sailer, she took a favourable wind, and bore down for the canoe. Coming close up with it, they bore away and came round, and we followed in her wake. In order that the schooner might appear as if she did not wish to board the canoe, she passed it, and then hove up in the wind. Seeing that by this manœuvre they had the advantage, they plied their oars with main

[1] This was San Luis de Maranham.—*Navarrête*, tom. iii. p. 259.

CHAPTER X.

strength, in order to escape; but having our boats at the stern filled with good men, we thought they would take them, which they laboured hard to do for more than two hours, without success. If the schooner had not borne down upon them once more, we should have lost them. When they found themselves embarrassed between the schooner and the boats, they all jumped into the sea, being about twenty men,[1] and at the distance of two leagues from the shore. We followed them the whole day with our boats, and could only take two, which was an extraordinary feat; all the rest escaped to the shore. Four boys remained in the canoe, who were not of their tribe, but had been taken prisoners by them, and brought from another country. We were much surprised at the gross injuries they had inflicted upon these boys, and having been taken on board the ships, they told us they had been captured in order to be eaten. Accordingly we knew that those people were cannibals, who eat human flesh.

We proceeded with the ships, taking the canoe with us at the stern, and following the course which they pursued, anchored at half a league from the shore. As we saw many people on the shore, we landed in the boats, carrying with us the two men we had taken. When we reached the beach, all the people fled into the woods, and

[1] Bandini gives the number of men in this canoe as seventy. A canoe must have been tolerably large to have held even twenty men, although larger ones have been met with, made, like this, out of the trunk of a tree. Ferdinand Columbus speaks of some holding as many as fifty men.—*Canovai*, tom. i. p. 136, note.

we sent one of the two men to negotiate with them, giving them several trifles, as tokens of friendship, such as little bells, buttons, and looking-glasses, and telling them that we wished to be their friends. He brought the people all back with him, of whom there were about four hundred men, and many women, who came unarmed to the place where we laid with the boats. Having established friendship with them, we surrendered the other prisoner, and sent to the ships for the canoe, which we restored. This canoe was twenty-six yards long, and six feet wide, made out of a single tree, and very well wrought. When they had carried it into a river near by, and put it in a secure place, they all fled, and would have nothing more to do with us, which appeared to us a very barbarous act, and we judged them to be a faithless and evil-disposed people. We saw among them a little gold, which they wore in their ears.

Meet friendly natives and procure pearls.

Leaving this place, we sailed about eighty leagues along the coast, and entered a bay, where we found a surprising number of people, with whom we formed a friendship. Many of us went to their villages, in great safety, and were received with much courtesy and confidence. In this place we procured a hundred and fifty pearls (as they sold them to us for a trifle), and some little gold, which they gave us gratuitously.[1] We noticed

[1] The edition of Gruniger says, "five hundred pearls."—*Navarréte*, tom. iii. p. 250.

CHAPTER X.

that in this country they drank wine made of their fruits and seeds, which looked like beer, both white and red; the best was made of acorns, and was very good. We ate a great many of these acorns, as it was the season of them. They are a very good fruit, savoury to the taste, and healthful to the body. The country abounded with the means of nourishment, and the people were well-disposed, being the most pacific of any we had seen.

Remain seventeen days in port.

We remained in this port seventeen days with great pleasure, and every day some new tribe of people came to see us from inland parts of the country, who were greatly surprised at our figures, at the whiteness of our skins, at our clothes, our arms, and the form and size of our ships. We were informed by these people of the existence of another tribe still farther west, who were their enemies, and that they had a great quantity of pearls. They said that those which we discovered in their possession were some they had taken from this other tribe in war. They told us how they fished for pearls, and in what manner they grew; and we found that they told us the truth, as your Excellency shall hear.

We left this harbour, and sailed along the coast, on which we continually saw smoke, and many people on the shore, as we passed. After many days we entered a harbour, for the purpose of repairing one of our ships, as she leaked badly. Here we found many people, with whom, neither by force nor entreaty, could we have any intercourse. When we went ashore, they fiercely disputed our landing, and after they found it impossible to resist us any longer, fled to the woods. Having discovered them to be so barbarous, we sailed away from the place, and finding an island about fifteen leagues distant from the coast, resolved to see whether it was inhabited. We found on this island the most bestial and filthy people that were ever seen, but, at the same time, extremely pacific, so that I am able to describe their habits and customs. Their manners and their faces were filthy, and they all had their cheeks stuffed full of a green herb, which they were continually chewing, as beasts chew the cud, so that they were scarcely able to speak. Each one of them wore, hanging at the neck, two dried gourd-shells, one of which was filled with the same kind of herb they had in their mouths, and the other with a white meal, which appeared to be chalk-dust. They also carried with them a small stick, which they wetted in their mouths from time to time, and then put into the meal, afterwards putting it into the herb, with which both cheeks were filled, and mixing the meal with it.[1]

[1] This herb was either the Betel, or something similar to it. It is very much esteemed in the East Indies. The white mealy substance which he speaks of, was calcined oyster shells. The natives used it for the purpose of quenching their thirst, as Americus supposed, and made use of it also as a medicine.—See *Ramusio*, tom. i. p. 298. *Cook's Voyages*, vol. i. p. 112–434–436. Ferdinand Columbus also speaks of it, and says, "The chiefs continued to put

CHAPTER X.

We were surprised at their conduct, and could not understand for what purpose they indulged in the filthy practice.

Substitute for water used by the natives.

As soon as these people saw us, they came to us with as much familiarity as if we had been old friends. As we were walking with them along the shore, and wished to find some fresh water to drink, they made us understand by signs that they had none, and offered us some of their herbs and meal; hence we concluded that water was very scarce in this island, and that they kept these herbs in their mouths in order to allay their thirst. We walked about the island a day and a half without finding any living water, and noticed that all the water which they drank, was the dew which fell in the night upon certain leaves which looked like asses' ears. These leaves being filled with dew water, the islanders used it for their drink, and most excellent water it was, but there were many places where the leaves were not to be found.

They had no kind of victuals or roots such as we found on the mainland, but lived on fish which they caught in the sea, of which there was an abundance, and they were great fishermen. They presented us with many turtles, and many large and very good fish. The women did not chew the herb as the men did, but carried a gourd with water in

a dry herb in their mouths, and also a certain powder.—*Canovai*, tom. i. p. 141.

Alonzo Nino and Christobal Guerra observed upon the coast of Cumana, that the Indians chewed an herb continually to keep their teeth white.—*Navarrête*, tom iii. p. 15.

it, of which they drank. They had no villages, houses, or cottages, except some arbours which defended them from the sun, but not from the rain; this appearing needless, for I think it very seldom rained on this island. When they were fishing out at sea, they each wore on the head a very large leaf, so broad that they were covered by its shade.[1] They fixed these leaves also in the ground on shore, and as the sun moved, turned them about, so as to keep within the shadow, and defend themselves from the sun's rays. The island contained many animals of various kinds, all of which drank the muddy water of the marshes.

A race of gigantic size.

Seeing there was no utility in staying here, we left and went to another island, which we found inhabited by people of very large stature. Going into the country in search of fresh water, without thinking the island inhabited (as we saw no people), as we were passing along the shore, we remarked very large footprints in the sand. We concluded that if the other members corresponded with the feet, they must belong to very large men. While occupied with these conjectures, we struck a path which led us inland, and imagining that as the island was small, there could not be many people on

[1] Ramusio speaks of a tree or plant growing in the East Indies, which produces four or five leaves, each of which will shelter a man from the sun and rain.—*Ram.* tom. i. p. 161, D.

Conti also speaks of a tree, the leaves of which are six yards long, and nearly the same width. "When it rains they are carried over the head to prevent the people from being wet, and three or four persons stretching it out may be covered."—*Ibid.* p. 339, C. *Canovai*, tom. i. p. 144.

it, we passed on to find out of what description they might be. After we had gone about a league, we saw in a valley five of their cottages, which appeared to be uninhabited, and, on going to them, we found only five women, two quite old, and three girls, all so tall in stature, that we regarded them with astonishment. When they saw us, they became so frightened that they had not even courage to flee, and the two old women began to invite us into their houses, and to bring us many things to eat, with many caresses. They were taller than a tall man, and as large-bodied as Francisco of Albizzi, but better proportioned than we are.

While we were all consulting as to the expediency of taking the three girls by force, and bringing them to Castile, to exhibit the wonder, there entered the door of the cottage thirty-six men much larger than the women, and so well made that it was a pleasure to look at them. They put us in such perturbation, however, that we would much rather have been in our ships, than have found ourselves with such people. They carried immense bows and arrows, and large-headed clubs, and talked among themselves in a tone which led us to think they were deliberating about attacking us.

Seeing we were in such danger, we formed various opinions on the subject. Some were for falling upon them in the house, others thought it would be better to attack them in the field, and others that we should not commence the strife until we saw what they wished to do. We agreed at length to go out of the cottage, and take our way quietly towards the ships. As soon as we did this, they followed at a stone's throw behind us, talking earnestly among themselves, and I think no less afraid of us than we were of them; for whenever we stopped, they did the same, never coming nearer to us. In this way we at length arrived at the shore, where the boats were waiting for us—we entered them, and as we were going off in the distance, they leaped forward and shot many arrows after us, but we had little fear of them now. We discharged two guns at them, more to frighten than to injure, and on hearing the report, they all fled to the mountain. Thus we parted from them, and it appeared to us that we had escaped from a perilous day's work. These people were quite naked, like the others we had seen, and on account of their large stature, I call this island the Island of Giants.[1] We proceeded onward in a direction parallel with the land, on which it often happened that we were obliged to fight with the people, who were not willing to let us take any thing away.

Thoughts of returning to Spain.

Our minds were fully prepared by this time for returning to Castile. We had been at sea about a year, and had but little provision left, and that little damaged, in consequence of the great heat through which we had passed. From the time we left the Island of Cape Verd until then, we had been sailing continually in the torrid zone, having twice

[1] This was probably the island of Curacoa.—*Navarrête*, tom. iii. p. 259.

CHAPTER X.

crossed the equinoctial line, as before stated; having been five degrees beyond it to the south, and then being fifteen degrees north of it.

Being thus disposed for our return, it pleased the Holy Spirit to give us some repose from our great labours. Going in search of a harbour, in order to repair our ships, we fell in with a people who received us with much friendship, and we found that they had a great quantity of oriental pearls, which were very good. We remained with them forty-seven days, and procured from them a hundred and nineteen marks of pearls in exchange for a mere trifle of our merchandise, which I think did not cost us the value of forty ducats. We gave them nothing whatever but bells, looking-glasses, beads, and brass plates; for a bell, one would give all the pearls he had. We learned from them how and where they fished for these pearls, and they gave us many oysters in which they grew. We procured one oyster in which a hundred and thirty pearls were growing, but in others there were a less number. The one with the hundred and thirty the queen took from me, but the others I kept to myself, that she might not see them.

Your Excellency must know, that if the pearls are not ripe and not loose in the shell, they do not last, because they are soon spoiled. Of this I have seen many examples. When they are ripe, they are loose in the oyster, and mingle with the flesh, and then they are good. Even the bad ones which they had, which for the most part were rough, and disfigured with holes, were nevertheless worth a considerable sum.

At the end of forty-seven days, we left these people in great friendship with us, and from the want of provisions went to the Island of Antilla, which was discovered some years before by Christopher Columbus. Here we obtained many supplies, and staid two months and seventeen days. We passed through many dangers and troubles with the Christians who were settled in this island with Columbus (I think through their envy), the relation of which, in order not to be tedious, I omit. We left there on the twenty-second of April, and after sailing a month and a half, entered the port of Cadiz, where we were received with much honour, on the eighth day of June.[1] Thus terminated, by the favour of God, my second voyage.

[1] The months of April and June are adopted by Canovai, and very properly, instead of the months of September and April, which are used in some other editions. This reading makes the letter correspond with that to De' Medici, describing the same voyage, and besides, gives the correct date of the termination of the voyage. Americus says that it lasted thirteen months; if it ended in September, it would have been seventeen.—See *First Letter of Americus to De' Medici. Canovai*, tom. i. p. 151.

CHAPTER XI.

Unjustifiable Perversion of the Words of Americus.—Attack of Sickness.—New Spanish Fleet for him.—His Position in Spain.—Motives of the King of Portugal in attempting to gain the Services of Americus.—First Attempt by Letter.—Second Attempt by a Messenger.—Juliano Giocondo.—He leaves Spain secretly.—Goes to Lisbon.—Reception at the Court of Emmanuel.—Importance of his Voyage to the Kingdom of Portugal.—Extract from Thomson's Seasons.—A Word respecting the Date of the Voyage.—Inaccuracy of Herrera.

It was during the month of July, in the year 1500, that Americus wrote his letter to Lorenzo de' Medici, giving a description of the voyage which had just been brought to a conclusion. He apologizes, as has been seen, for his long silence, and gives as an excuse for it, the reason, that nothing had occurred to him worthy of being commemorated, excepting that which he proceeded to narrate. A most unjustifiable use has been made of this expression of the navigator, by those who are desirous of discrediting his account of his first voyage. They argue that it is equivalent to saying that he had not made a previous voyage, for it would have been a remarkable forgetfulness to have said that nothing of importance had occurred, if he had made a previous voyage, of eighteen months duration, in 1497–8. How much more ingenuous would it be to suppose that he had previously written De' Medician account of that first voyage, in letters which have been lost in the lapse of time, and that the interval between those communications and the one under consideration, a period of more than fourteen months at the least, compelled him to speak of his long silence and make excuses for it. The weakness of the argument made use of to discredit him, is of itself an evidence of the want of cogent proof in support of their position.[1]

Preparation for a third voyage from Spain.

Notwithstanding the severe attack of sickness which Americus experienced immediately after his return, (the quartan ague, contracted probably by exposure to the unhealthy climate of the West Indies,) he devoted himself at once to preparation for a third voyage. It would seem that the merchants of Seville were not easily disheartened by the unprofitable result, in a pecuniary point of view, of the voyage of Ojeda and Americus; or that the government itself had taken his fortunes under its special charge. While, however, a new fleet was being made ready, which he expected would be in complete order for sea as early as the month of September, some circumstances occurred which led him to abandon the service of Spain and try his fortune under the auspices of a new monarch.

What these circumstances were can now only be conjectured. Americus himself subsequently speaks of the course which he had adopted in terms which show that he did not leave Spain without doubting

[1] Irving, vol. ii. p. 885.

CHAPTER XI

in his own mind the propriety of the proceeding. He stood deservedly high in the estimation of the Court, and the amenity and modesty of his manners had attached to him a great number of warm friends and admirers. It is probable that he accepted the offers, which were made to him by the King of Portugal, in a momentary feeling of pique at some fancied neglect, or in disgust at the measures brought about by persons envious of his well-earned fame.[1]

Reasons which led King Emmanuel to make offers to Americus.

The motives of the King of Portugal in endeavouring to secure the services of Americus are very apparent. The accidental discovery made by Cabral, about a year before this time, who, while attempting to double the Cape of Good Hope, on his way to the East Indies, had been driven across the South Atlantic to the shores of Brazil by adverse winds, had given rise to disputes and dissensions between the governments of Spain and Portugal. These disputes had just been settled by a compromise. The line of demarcation between their respective dominions was changed, and removed three hundred and seventy leagues west of its former position. Cabral saw but very little of the country which he had fallen in with so unexpectedly. He took formal possession of it, however, in the name of his sovereign, and despatched one of the ships of his fleet to give information of his discovery, while in the meantime he pursued his original voyage.[2]

[1] See chap. xiii.

[2] Canovai, tom. ii. p. 79.

CHAPTER XI.

The accounts of Americus respecting this newly-acquired region could not have failed to reach the ears of King Emmanuel. He found himself, by the recent agreement, put into possession of a country far more extensive than the meagre reports of Cabral could have warranted him to hope for. Unable to avail himself of the services of that navigator, and duly estimating the distinguished reputation and skill of Americus, he spared no pains to detach him from the service of Spain, and entice him to Portugal. It was then that the Portuguese government bitterly repented its repulse of Columbus, and regretting deeply its ill-timed economy, King Emmanuel resolved to tempt Americus with the prospect of splendid rewards.

Letters from the King of Portugal and a messenger sent to Americus.

The first attempt which was made to induce him to accompany an expedition from Lisbon, was by letter from the king himself, and was unsuccessful. Americus, unprepared for the proposition, delayed the bearer of the letter, and gave him at last an answer in the negative. It was not, however, couched in such decided terms as to discourage the king, or preclude the possibility of gaining him over at last. He pleaded ill-health, and said, indefinitely, that when he recovered he might be induced to go.

The second attempt was more favourably received. Juliano Giocondo, an Italian, then resident at Lisbon, was despatched soon after, to entreat Americus with greater urgency. He came at once to Seville, where Americus was residing, and, by dint of earnest persuasion, induced him at last to enter the service of Emmanuel. Americus yielded, against the advice of his friends, who, according to his own account, all looked with ill-favour upon the project. Fearing that some attempt might be made to detain him, he left the kingdom privately, in company with Giocondo and proceeded at once to Lisbon.

"It does not appear," says Canovai, "that King Ferdinand considered himself wronged, by the sudden flight, and, to say the least, apparent discourtesy of Americus, in leaving the kingdom and the king, his patron, without salutation or leave-taking. It was probably looked upon as a trait of his reserved character, or an evidence of his aversion to idle and slanderous rumours, which he was unwilling to take the pains to contradict. Rumours and whisperings soon die away, when they have nothing to feed upon, and when Americus returned, as though from a journey, the slight was forgotten, and he was treated with greater honour than before."[1]

Americus was received with open arms at the court of Emmanuel, and commenced with ardour the preparation of the fleet. It is impossible to say who had the command of this expedition, but it is apparent that its nautical management was under the control of Americus, from the letters to De' Medici and Soderini which follow. The navigator wrote three accounts of this his first voyage in the Portuguese service, two of them directed to

[1] Canovai, tom. ii. p. 80.

BATTLE WITH THE NATIVES.

While thus disheartened and flying, one of our sailors, a Portuguese, a man fifty years of age, jumped on shore, and with a loud voice called out to us, "Children! turn your faces to your enemies, and God will give you the victory." (SEE P. 165.)

De' Medici, of which the most elaborate is given, and the other to Soderini. He evidently looked upon it as the most important in its discoveries that he had ever made, and he regarded it correctly. Unfortunately, it was equally signalized by the tempestuous weather he experienced in the course of it. Had it not been for this, there is little doubt that he would have realized all his hopes of a southwestern passage to India, but the violent storms he encountered compelled him to desist and return to Portugal.

Great importance of his voyage to Portugal.

Notwithstanding, the results of the voyage were of vast importance to Portugal. An immensely wealthy country was added to her dominions, whose mines of gold and diamonds furnished her most opportunely with resources for prosecuting her conquests and discoveries in the East. Then, to make use of the graphic words in which the poet Thomson describes the effect of the voyages of De Gama, originally suggested by Prince Henry, and which may be applied with equal justice to this voyage of Americus :

> Then from ancient gloom emerged
> The rising world of trade : the genius, then,
> Of Navigation, that in hopeless sloth
> Had slumbered on the vast Atlantic deep
> For idle ages, starting, heard at last
> The Lusitanian prince, who, Heaven-inspired,
> To love of useful glory roused mankind,
> And an unbounded commerce mixed the world.[1]

One word respecting the authenticity of the voy-

[1] Thomson's Seasons—Summer.

CHAPTER XI.

age which is described in the two following chapters. The Spanish historian Herrera, as has been seen, with the view of sustaining the position that the first voyage of Americus was altogether supposititious, pretends that he was sailing in 1501, in the company of Ojeda, in the Gulf of Darien.[1] Most unfortunately for the accurary of this historian, there exists undoubted evidence to the contrary. Peter Martyr, whose veracity is unquestionable, states that Americus sailed many degrees south of the line, in the Portuguese service.[2] Numerous other writers assert the same, though they differ respecting the exact date of the voyage. Gomara, however, fixes the date unequivocally, and expressly declares that Americus was despatched by King Emmanuel on a voyage of discovery in the year 1501.[3] No reasonable doubt can then be entertained that the voyage actually took place, and the reader may safely peruse the accounts of the navigator in spite of the unmanly attempts of partisan critics to injure his credibility.

1 Herrera, Historia, &c., Decad. i. l. 4, c. 11.

2 Martyr, Ocean. D. ii. l. 1, p. 199.

3 Gomara, Hist. of the Indies, chap. ciii. in Barcia's Historiadores.

CHAPTER XII.

SECOND LETTER OF AMERICUS TO LORENZO DI PIER-FRANCESCO DE' MEDICI, GIVING A BRIEF ACCOUNT OF HIS THIRD VOYAGE, MADE FOR THE KING OF PORTUGAL.[1]

Departure from Cape Verd.—Arrival at the Continent.—Heavenly Bodies.—Beauty of the Country.—Numerous Animals.—The Natives destitute of Laws and Religion.—Their Food and Ornaments.—Longevity.—Mode of Reckoning Time.—Their Wars and Cannibalism.—Climate.—Products of the Country.

CHAPTER XII.

MY MOST EXCELLENT PATRON, LORENZO:

(After due commendation), My last letter to your Excellency was written from a place on the coast of Guinea, called Cape Verd, and in it you were informed of the commencement of my voyage. This present letter will advise you of its continuation and termination.

Departure from Cape Verd and arrival at the continent.

We started from the above-mentioned Cape, having first taken in all necessary supplies of wood and water, to discover new lands in the ocean. We sailed on a southwesterly course, until, at the end of sixty-four days, we discovered land, which, on many accounts, we concluded to be Terra Firma. We coasted this land about eight hundred leagues

[1] This letter was published for the first time in the year 1789, by Bartolozzi, at the close of his work entitled "Ricerche Istorico Critiche circa alle Scoperle d'Amerigo Vespucci."

CHAPTER XII.

in a direction west by south. It was full of inhabitants, and I noticed many remarkable things, which I determined to narrate to your Excellency.

Heavenly bodies of the Southern Hemisphere.

We sailed in these seas until we entered the Torrid Zone and passed to the south of the equinoctial line and the Tropic of Capricorn, so that we were fifty degrees to the south of the line. We navigated here four mouths and twenty-seven days, seeing neither the Arctic Pole, nor Ursa Major or Minor. We discovered here many beautiful constellations, invisible in the Northern Hemisphere, and noted their marvellous movements and grandeur. We marked the course of their revolutions, and with geometrical calculations determined the position of these heavenly bodies. The most notable of the things which occurred in this voyage I have collated for a small work, which, when I am at leisure, I shall find occupation in completing, and which will acquire for me some fame after my death. I had in readiness a sketch of this to send to you, but the King's Highness retains it, and when he returns it, I will forward it as I proposed. In effect, my navigation extended to a fourth part of the world, and a line to my zenith there, made a right angle, at the centre of the earth, with that of the inhabitants of the Northern Hemisphere, forty degrees above the equator.

Numerous wild animals, but none that are domestic.

To proceed now to a description of the country, of the plants therein, and of the customs of the inhabitants, I would observe, that this region is most delightful, and covered with immense forests, which never lose their foliage, and throughout the year yield the sweetest aromatic odours, and produce an infinite variety of fruit, grateful to the taste, and healthful for the body. In the fields flourish so many sweet flowers and herbs, and the fruits are so delicious in their fragrance, that I fancied myself near the terrestrial paradise. What shall I tell you of the birds, and of the brilliant colours of their plumage? What of their variety, their sweet songs, and their beauty? I dare not enlarge upon this theme, for I fear that I should not be believed. How shall I enumerate the infinite variety of sylvan animals, lions, panthers, and catamounts, though not not like those of our regions, wolves, stags, and baboons of all kinds? We saw more wild animals, such as wild hogs, kids, deer, hares, and rabbits, than could ever have entered the ark of Noah, but we saw no domestic animals whatever.

Now consider reasoning animals. We found the whole region inhabited by a race of people who were entirely naked, both men and women. They are well-proportioned in body, with black hair, and little or no beard. I laboured much to investigate their customs—remaining twenty-seven days for that purpose—and the following is the information I acquired.

Customs of the natives.

They have no laws, and no religious belief, but live according to the dictates of nature alone. They know nothing of the immortality of the soul; they have no private property, but every thing in common; they have no boundaries of kingdom or province; they obey no king or lord, for it is wholly unnecessary, as they have no laws, and each one is his own master. They dwell together in houses made like bells—in the construction of which they use neither iron nor any other metal. This is very remarkable, for I have seen houses two hundred and twenty feet long, and thirty feet wide, built with much skill, and containing five or six hundred people. They sleep in hammocks of cotton, suspended in the air, without any covering; they eat seated upon the ground, and their food consists of the roots of herbs, of fruits and fish. They eat, also, lobsters, crabs, and oysters, and many other kinds of muscles and shell-fish, which are found in the sea. As to their meat, it is principally human flesh. It is true that they devour the flesh of animals and birds; but they do not catch many, because they have no dogs, and the woods are so thick, and so filled with wild beasts, that they do not care to go into them, without going in large bodies.

The men are in the habit of decorating their lips and cheeks with bones and stones, which they suspend from holes which they bore in them. I have seen some of them with three, seven, and even as many as nine holes, filled with white or green alabaster—a most barbarous custom, which they follow, in order, as they say, to make themselves appear fierce and ferocious.

*   *   *   *   *   *   *   *
*   *   *   *   *   *   *   *

CHAPTER XII.

They are a people of great longevity. We met with many who had descendants of the fourth degree. Not knowing how to compute time, and counting neither days, months, or years, excepting in so far as they count the lunar months, when they wanted to signify to us any particular duration of time, they did it by showing us a stone for each moon; and, computing in this manner, we discovered that the age of one man that we saw was seventeen hundred moons, or about one hundred and thirty-two years, reckoning thirteen moons to the year.

Their longevity and mode of computing time.

They are a warlike race, and extremely cruel. All their arms and bows are, as Petrarch says, "committed to the winds;" for they consist only of spears, arrows, and stones. They use no shields for the body—going to battle wholly naked. There is no order or discipline in their fights, except that they follow the counsels of the old men. Most cruelly do they combat, and those who conquer in the field bury their own dead, but cut up and eat the dead of their enemies. Some, who are taken prisoners, are carried to their villages for slaves. Females taken in war, they frequently marry; and sometimes the male prisoners are allowed to marry the daughters of the tribe; but occasionally a diabolical fury seems to come over them, and, calling together their relations and all the people, they sacrifice these slaves, the children with their parents, with many barbarous ceremonies. This we know of a cer-

Their wars and savage cruelty.

CHAPTER XII.

tainty; for we found much human flesh in their houses, hung up to smoke, and we purchased ten poor creatures from them, both men and women, whom they were about to sacrifice, to save them from such a fate.

Much as we reproached them on this account, I cannot say whether they amended at all. The most astonishing thing in all their wars and cruelty was, that we could not find out any reason for them. They made wars against each other, although they had neither kings, kingdoms, nor property of any kind, without any apparent desire to plunder, and without any lust for power, which always appeared to me to be the moving causes of wars and anarchy. When we asked them about this, they gave us no other reason than that they did so to avenge the murder of their ancestors. To conclude this disgusting subject, one man confessed to me that he had eaten of the flesh of over two hundred bodies, and I believe it was the truth.

Climate and health of the country.

In regard to the climate of this region, I should say that it was extremely pleasant and healthful; for, in all the time that we were there, which was ten months, not one of us died, and only a few were sick. They suffer from no infirmity, pestilence, or corruption of the atmosphere, and die only natural deaths, unless they fall by their own hands, or in consequence of some accident. In fact, physicians would have a bad time in such a place.

CHAPTER XII.

Productions of the country.

As we went there solely to make discoveries, and started with that view from Lisbon, without intending to look for any profit, we did not trouble ourselves to explore the country much, and found nothing of much value; not that I do not believe that it is capable, from its climate and general appearance, of containing every kind of wealth. It is not to be wondered at, that we did not discover at once every thing that might be turned to profit there, for the inhabitants think nothing of gold, silver, or precious stones, and value only feathers and bones. But I hope that I shall be sent again by the King to visit these regions, and that many years will not elapse, before they will bring immense profit and revenue to the kingdom of Portugal. We found great quantities of dye-wood, enough to load all the ships that float, and costing nothing. The same may be said of cassia. We saw also crystals, spices, and drugs, but the qualities of the last are unknown.

The inhabitants of the country tell of gold and other metals, but I am one of those, who, like St. Thomas, are slow to believe. Time will show all.

Most of the time of our stay, the heavens were serene, and adorned with numerous bright and beautiful stars, many of which I observed, with their revolutions. This may be considered a schedule, or, as it were, a *capita rerum*, of the things which I have seen in these parts. Many things are omitted, which are worthy of being mentioned, in order to avoid prolixity, and because they are

CHAPTER XII.

found in my account of the voyage. As yet I tarry in Lisbon, waiting the pleasure of the King, to determine what I shall do. May it please God that I do whatever is most to his glory and the salvation of my soul.

Your Excellency's servant,
AMERICUS VESPUCIUS.

CHAPTER XIII.

SECOND LETTER OF AMERICUS TO LORENZO DI PIER-FRANCESCO DE' MEDICI, GIVING A FULLER ACCOUNT OF HIS THIRD VOYAGE, MADE FOR THE KING OF PORTUGAL.[1]

Preamble respecting the First Letter of Americus to De Medici.—Sails from Lisbon May 13th, 1501.—Arrives at the Canaries.—Coasts the Shores of Africa.—Experiences violent Gales.—Provisions fall short.—Long Passage.—Despair at their Situation.—Arrive at last at the Continent.—Ignorance of the Pilots.—Astronomical Observations of Americus.—Coast along the Shores of South America.—Intercourse with the Natives.—Thickly-inhabited Country.—Singular Customs of the Natives.—Their Mode of Life.—Cannibalism again.—Climate and Fruits.—Stars of the Antarctic Pole.—Beautiful Iris or Rainbow.—Geometrical Calculations of Americus.—Gratitude to the Supreme Being.—Arrival at Lisbon.—Another Voyage in Contemplation.

In days past, I gave your Excellency a full account of my return, and if I remember aright, wrote you a description of all those parts of the New World which I had visited in the vessels of his serene highness the King of Portugal. Carefully considered, they appear truly to form another world, and therefore we have, not without reason, called it the New World. Not one of all the ancients had

[1] One circumstance distinguishes this letter from the others of Americus. It is not in the Italian versions, filled, as all the rest are, with Italianized Spanish words, or rather with corrupt Spanish. The text of Ramusio is purely Tuscan, and is copied by Canovai, from whom this translation is made.—*Canovai*, tom. i. p. 153, 154.

CHAPTER XIII.

any knowledge of it, and the things which have been lately ascertained by us, transcend all their ideas. They thought there was nothing south of the equinoctial line but an immense sea, and some poor and barren islands. The sea they called the Atlantic, and if sometimes they confessed that there might be land in that region, they contended that it must be sterile, and could not be otherwise than uninhabitable.

The present navigation has controverted their opinions, and openly demonstrated to all, that they were very far from the truth. Beyond the equinoctial line, I found countries more fertile and more thickly inhabited, than I have ever found any where else, even in Asia, Africa, and Europe, as will be more fully manifested by duly attending to the following relation. Setting aside all minor matters, I shall relate only those of the greatest importance, which are well worthy of commemoration, and those which I have personally seen or heard of from men of credibility. I shall now speak with much care concerning those parts most recently discovered, and without any romantic addition to the truth.

Departure from Lisbon May 13th, 1501.

With happy omens of success, we sailed from Lisbon, with three armed caravels, on the thirteenth day of May, 1501, to explore, by command of the king, the regions of the New World. Steering a southwest course, we sailed twenty months, in the manner which I shall now relate. In the first place, we went to the Fortunate Islands, which are now called the Grand Canaries. They are in the third climate, in the farthest part of the West which is inhabited. After navigating the ocean, we ran along the coast of Africa and the country of the blacks, as far as the promontory which is called by Ptolemy, Etiopo, by our people, Cape Verd, and by the negroes, Biseneghe, while the inhabitants themselves call it Madanghan. The country is situated within the Torrid Zone, in about fourteen degrees north latitude, and is inhabited by the blacks. Here having refreshed ourselves, and reposed awhile, we took in every kind of provision, and set sail, directing our course towards the Antarctic Pole.

Sail on a southwesterly course and experience severe storms.

We bore a little to the west, as the wind was easterly, and we never saw land until after we had sailed three months and three days consecutively. What great toils and dangers we were exposed to in this navigation, what troubles and vexations we suffered, and how often we were disgusted with life, I shall leave those to judge who have had similar experience—those particularly who know what great difficulties are met with, while looking for uncertain things, and attempting discoveries in places where man has never before been; but I would not wish any one to be our judge who has had no experience in these things.

To shorten my relation as much as possible, your Excellency must know, that we sailed ninety-seven days, experiencing harsh and cruel fortune. During forty-four days, the heavens were in great commo-

CHAPTER XIII.

tion, and we had nothing but thunder and lightning and drenching rain. Dark clouds covered the sky, so that by day we could see but little better than we could in ordinary nights, without moonshine. Our nights were of the blackest darkness. The fear of death came over us, and the hope of life almost deserted us. After all these heavy afflictions, at last it pleased God, in his mercy, to have compassion on us and to save our lives. On a sudden, the land appeared in view, and at the sight of it our courage, which had fallen very low, and our strength, which had become weakness, immediately revived. Thus it usually happens to those who have passed through great affliction, and especially to those who have been preserved from the rage of evil fortune.

Come to anchor August 17th, 1501.

On the seventeenth day of August, in the year 1501, we anchored by the shore of that country, and rendered to the Supreme Being our most sincere thanks, according to the Christian custom, in a solemn celebration of mass.[1] The land we discovered did not appear to be an island, but a continent, as it extended far away in the distance, without any appearance of termination.[2] It was

[1] Bandini makes a mistake in this date, giving it as the first day of August; other editions have it the 17th of August, which is correct, as Americus started on the 13th of May, and sailed three months and three days.—*Canovai*, tom. i. p. 158.

[2] It may seem strange that Americus should not at once have recognized the continent which he had visited before in his second voyage, and have mentioned the fact; but it must not be forgotten that his vessels had been buffeting with severe gales, and driven for some time almost at the mercy of the waves—that he reached land, sit-

beautifully fertile, and very thickly inhabited. All sorts of wild animals, which are wholly unknown in our parts, were there found in abundance. Many other things I would describe, but have studiously avoided mentioning, in order that my work might not become large beyond measure. One thing only I feel that I should not omit: it is, that, aided by the goodness of God, in due time, and according to our need, we saw land; for we were not able to sustain ourselves any longer; all our provisions having failed us; our wood, water, biscuit, salt meat, cheese, wine, oil, and, what is more, our vigour of mind, all gone. By God's mercy, therefore, our lives were spared, and to him we ought to render thanks, honour, and glory.

We were unanimously of opinion that our navigation should be continued along this coast, and that we should not lose sight of it. We sailed, therefore, in accordance with this conclusion, till we arrived at a certain cape, which makes a turn to the south. This cape is, perhaps, three hundred leagues distant from the place where we first saw land. In sailing this distance we often landed, and had intercourse with the inhabitants, as will be more elaborately mentioned hereafter. I have omitted to state that this newly-discovered

uated at least fifty leagues farther south than he did before, in a different season, and when the country was not overflowed. After all he might have recognized it without thinking it important to say that he did so.—*Canovai*, tom. i. p. 158.

CHAPTER XIII.

land is about seven hundred leagues distant from Cape Verd, though I was persuaded that we had sailed more than eight hundred. This was partly owing to the severe storm and our frequent accidents, and partly to the ignorance of the pilot; both of which causes had a tendency to lengthen the voyage.

Ignorance of the pilots.

We had arrived at a place which, if I had not possessed some knowledge of cosmography, by the negligence of the pilot, would have finished the course of our lives. There was no pilot who knew our situation within fifty leagues, and we went rambling about, and should not have known whither we were going, if I had not provided in season for my own safety and that of my companions, with the astrolabe and quadrant, my astrological instruments. On this occasion I acquired no little glory for myself; so that, from that time forward, I was held in such estimation by my companions, as the learned are held in by people of quality. I explained the sea-charts to them, and made them confess that the ordinary pilots were ignorant of cosmography, and knew nothing in comparison with myself.

The cape of this newly-discovered land, which turned towards the south, was an object which excited in us a great desire to arrive at it, and examine it attentively. It was determined, by common consent, to make an investigation, and understand the customs and disposition of the people of the country. We sailed, accordingly, near the coast for about six hundred leagues. We landed often, and often came to a parley with the inhabitants, who received us with honour, and in a very friendly manner. Having discovered their kindness, and very innocent nature, we staid with them, not without receiving much honour, for fifteen or twenty days at a time. They are extremely courteous in entertaining strangers, which will be more clearly shown hereafter. This continent commences at eight degrees south of the equinoctial line, and we sailed so far along the coast, that we passed seventeen degrees beyond the winter tropic, towards the Antarctic Pole, which was here elevated fifty degrees above the horizon.

The things which I saw there are unknown to the men of our times. That is, the people, their customs, their humanity, the fertility of the soil, the mildness of the atmosphere, the salubrious sky, the celestial bodies, and above all the fixed stars of the eighth sphere, of which no mention has ever been made. In fact, until now they have never been known, even by the most learned of the ancients, and I shall speak of them therefore more particularly.

A thickly-inhabited country. Singular customs.

This country is more numerously inhabited than any I had seen for some time, and the people are very mild and familiar. They do not offend any one; they go entirely as nature has brought them forth; naked they are born, and naked they die. Their bodies are very well formed, and may be

CHAPTER XIII.

said to be fairly proportioned; their colour is of a reddish cast, which is owing partly to their being naked, and therefore easily sunburnt; their hair is black, but long and straight. In walking and in their games they display superior dexterity. They have handsome faces and a noble aspect, but they deform them in an incredible manner by perforation. Their cheeks, their jaws, their noses, lips and ears have not one little hole only, but many large ones in them; so that I have often seen one have seven holes in his face, each of the size of a damson plum. Having dug out the flesh, they fill the holes with certain blue pebbles, of bright marble, or beautiful alabaster, or ivory, or of very white bones, made according to their fashion, and very conveniently wrought. This thing appears so uncouth, disgusting, and barbarous, that at the first sight, a man having his face filled with stones and pierced with many holes, appeared like a monster. It will hardly be believed, that one man had seven stones in his face, each one more than half a span in size; there is no one, indeed, who would not be astonished by an attentive examination of things so monstrous. Nevertheless they are true, for I myself have often seen seven stones placed in this fashion, and nearly sixteen ounces in weight.

In the ears they wear more precious ornaments, such as rings fastened in, and pendant pearls after the fashion of the Egyptians and Indians. The custom of wearing stones is observed by the men alone. The women only wear ornaments in the ears. They have neither wool nor flax, consequently they have no cloth at all, neither do they use cotton clothing, as by going entirely naked they have no need of any garments.

Domestic habits of the natives.

There is no patrimony among them, but every thing is common. They have neither king nor empire; each one is a king by himself. They take as many wives as they please. In the intercourse of the sexes they have no regard to kindred, intermarrying the son with the mother, and the brother with the sister, and dissolving these connections whenever it pleases them, for they are wholly without laws, and live ungoverned by reason. They have neither temples nor religion, and do not even worship idols. What more shall I say? They have a wicked and licentious manner of living, more like the style of the Epicureans than that of the Stoics. They carry on no commerce, and have no knowledge of money. Still they have strife among them, and fight cruelly, and without any order. The old men, by their speeches, stir up the young men, draw them into their opinions whenever they please, and inflame them for war, in which they kill their enemies. If they overcome and subdue them, they eat them, and consider them very delicious food. They feed on human flesh to such a degree, that the father may eat the son, or the son may eat the father, as the chance may be. I saw one very wicked wretch who boasted, and held it as no small glory to himself, that he had

CHAPTER XIII.

eaten more than three hundred men. I saw also a certain town, in which I remained perhaps twenty-seven days, where human flesh, having been salted, was suspended from the beams of the dwellings, as we suspend the flesh of the wild boar from the beams of the kitchen, after having dried it in the sun or smoked it, or as we suspend sausages and other similar things. They were greatly astonished that we did not eat our enemies, whose flesh, they say, excites the appetite, and has an extraordinary relish, and is of a most sweet and delicate flavour.

Their arms. Their longevity.

Their arms are bows and arrows, and the latter being pointed with iron, they fight most cruelly with them, as those who are naked are assaulted and wounded like brute animals. We endeavoured many times to convert them to our opinions, and often admonished them, for the purpose of inducing them finally to abandon such an infamous custom as an abomination. Many times they promised us to refrain from practising such cruelty.

* * * * * * * *
* * * * * * * *

They live a hundred and fifty years, according to what I could learn, and are very seldom sick.[1] If

[1] "I found such a very perfect and singular atmosphere in this country (Arabia Felix), that I spoke with many persons who had lived more than a hundred and twenty-five years, and they were yet in good health and hearty."—*Ramusio*, tom. i. p. 155. Some writers have attributed the long life of the Indians to the habit of anointing their bodies with oily substances, "At this day," says a writer, "the natives of Brazil anoint themselves, and are very long lived, so much so, that five years ago, some French friars met some natives, who remembered the building of Pernambuco, a hun-

they chance to fall into any infirmity, they cure themselves immediately with the juice of herbs. These are the things I have discovered among them, which are worthy of esteem: the temperate atmosphere, the favourable sky, and long life; and this arises, perhaps, from the east wind, which blows there continually, and has the same effect on them that the north wind has on us. They take great pleasure in fishing, and for the most part live by it, nature aiding them to that effect, as the sea abounds there with all sorts of fish. With hunting they are little delighted, on account of the great multitude of wild animals, through fear of which they do not pursue their game in the forests. All sorts of lions, bears, and other animals are seen there. The trees grow to an almost incredible height, and they refrain, therefore, from going into the forests, because, being naked and unarmed, they would not be able safely to contend with the wild beasts.

The climate is very temperate, and the country fruitful, and supremely delightful. Although it has many hills, yet it is watered by a great number of springs and rivers, and the forests are so closely studded that one cannot pass through them, on account of the thickly-standing trees. Among these ramble ferocious animals of various kinds. The trees and fruits grow without the labour of cultivation, and indeed their fruits are most excellent, and are found in great abundance. Yet they are not

dred and twenty years since, and they had then arrived at the age of manhood."—*Hist. Vit. et Mort.* p. 536. *Canovai*, tom. i. p. 169.

CHAPTER XIII.

pernicious to the system, though very unlike our own. In like manner, the earth produces great quantities of herbs, and roots of which they make bread and other eatables. There are many kinds of grain, but they are not exactly similar to ours. The country produces no metal except gold, of which there is a great abundance. Though we in this first voyage have brought home none, yet all the people of the country certified to the fact, affirming that the region abounded in gold, and saying that among them it was little esteemed, and nearly valueless. They have many pearls and precious stones, as we have recorded before. Now though I should be willing to describe all these things particularly, from the great number of them, and their diverse nature, this history would become too extensive a work. Pliny, a most learned man, who compiled histories of many things, did not imagine the thousandth part of these. If he had treated of each one of them, he would have made a much larger, but in truth a very perfect work.

The climate and the beauty of the country suggest the idea of a terrestrial paradise.

The various species of parrots, and their variegated colours, afford particularly no small matter of astonishment. The trees all yield an odour of unimaginable sweetness, and from all of them issue gums, liquors, and juices. If we knew their virtues, I think there would be nothing wanting to us, not only in regard to our pleasures, but in regard to the maintenance of our health, or to the recovering of it when lost. If there is a terrestrial paradise in the world, it cannot be far from this region. The country, as I have said before, facing the south has such a temperate climate, that in winter they have no cold, and in summer they are not troubled with heat.

Astronomical observations.

The sky and the atmosphere are seldom overshadowed with clouds, and the days are almost always serene. Dew sometimes falls, but very lightly, and only for the space of three or four hours, and then vanishes like mist. They have scarcely any vapours, and the sky is splendidly adorned with stars unknown to us; of which I have retained a particular remembrance, and have enumerated as many as twenty, whose brightness is equal to that of Venus and Jupiter. I considered also their circuit and their various motions, and having a knowledge of geometry, I easily measured their circumference and diameter, and I am certain, therefore, they are of much greater magnitude than men imagine. Among the others, I saw three *Canopi*. Two were very bright; the third was dim, and unlike the others.[1]

[1] The splendour and beauty of these stars probably induced Americus to give them the name of Canopus, which is the most brilliant star in the constellation Argo. Corsali, an ancient Florentine navigator, speaks thus of the Antarctic stars which occupied the attention of Americus: "Here we saw an admirable order of stars, which in that part of the heavens which is opposite to our North Star were exhibited in endless revolving."—*Ramusio*, tom. i. p. 177, E.

Cadamosto, speaks of observations taken by him of these stars, and describing the situation of them, says, "The North Star appeared very low upon the sea, being not more than the length of a lance above it. We saw six stars low upon the sea, clear, bright, and large, and ranging them by the compass, we concluded that they were the Ursa Major of the

CHAPTER XIII.

The stars of the Southern Hemisphere.

The Antarctic Pole has not the Ursa Major and Minor, which may be seen at our Arctic Pole; neither are there any bright stars touching the pole, but of those which revolve round it, there are four in the form of a quadrangle. While these are rising, there is seen at the left a brilliant *Canopus*, of admirable magnitude, which, having reached mid-sky, forms the figure of a triangle. To these succeed three other brilliant stars, of which the one placed in the centre has twelve degrees of circumference. In the midst of them is another brilliant *Canopus*. After these follow six other bright stars, whose splendour surpasses that of all others in the eighth sphere. The middle one is thirty-two degrees in circumference. After these figures follows a large *Canopus*, but it is dim. These are all to be seen in the milky way, and when they arrive at the meridian, show the figure of a triangle, but have two sides longer than the other.

I saw there many other stars, and carefully observing their various motions, composed a book, which treats of them particularly. In this book I

South, but the principal star we did not see."—*Ramusio*, tom. i. p. 107, B.

Giuntini writes, "Those, who in this age, have taken a voyage from Spain towards the South, relate that many bright stars are to be seen about the Southern Pole, of which Americus Vespucius, our Florentine, is said to have enumerated twenty."

The reasoning of Americus concerning the Southern Stars, the rainbow, and the falling stars, is in accordance with the taste and phraseology of the age in which he lived, and is, consequently, very slightly conformable to the ideas of philosophers and astronomers of the present day. This note is inserted to illustrate the views of cotemporaneous navigators, and of writers who flourished at about the same time.—*Canovai*, tom. i. p. 173–176.

CHAPTER XIII.

have related almost all the remarkable things which I encountered in the course of my navigation, and with which I have become acquainted.

Work of Americus on the subject of astronomy.

This book is at present in the possession of his Most Serene Highness, the King, and I hope he will return it soon into my hands. I examined some things in that hemisphere very diligently, which enable me to contradict the opinions of philosophers, being altogether repugnant to them. Among other things, I saw the rainbow, that is, the celestial arch, which is white near midnight.[1] Now in the opinion of some, it takes the colour of the four elements—the red, from fire; the green, from the earth; the white, from the air; and the blue, from the water. Aristotle, in his book entitled "Meteors," is of a very different opinion. He says, "The celestial arch is a repercussion of the sun's rays, in the va-

[1] "By this white rainbow, he means, perhaps, that he had seen some of those crowns which astronomers call 'Halos,' and which appear round the moon, and other planets and fixed stars, and are often of whitish colour," &c. Thus writes Bandini, commenting on this passage, in the letter of Americus. A Portuguese pilot speaks of such a rainbow in the work of Ramusio: "It has been noticed," says he, "after a rain, that the moon, by night, makes that appearance of the Iris called the bow, such as is made by the sun in the daytime. But the colours made by the moon are like white mist."—Tom. i. p. 116, D. Now the Halo does not form an "arch," but an entire circle, and is not very rare among us, having been often particularly mentioned by navigators. "They saw," says Cook, "almost every morning a rainbow, until one night in the forepart of July, they saw one astonishingly beautiful, occasioned by the refraction of the light of the moon."—*Cook's Voyages*, vol. v. p. 287. "The palest light of the moon produces in like manner a rainbow, which is less observed on account of its faint and fading colours, but I observed one with very lively colours, on the twenty-ninth of June, 1773," &c.—*Ibid.* vol. ix. p. 134. *Canovai*, tom i. p. 177, 178.

CHAPTER XIII.

pours of the clouds where they meet, as brightness, reflected from the water upon the wall, returns to itself. By its interposition it tempers the heat of the sun; by resolving itself into rain, it fertilizes the earth, and by its splendour beautifies the heavens. It demonstrates that the atmosphere is filled with humidity, which will disappear forty years before the end of the world, which will be an indication of the dryness of the elements. It announces peace between God and men, is always opposite the sun, is never seen at noon, because the sun is never in the north." But Pliny says, that after the autumnal equinox, it appears at every hour. This I have extracted from the Comments of Landino on the fourth book of the Æneiad, and I mention it that no one may be deprived of the fruit of his labours, and that appropriate honours may be rendered to every one.

I saw this bow two or three times; neither am I alone in my reflections upon this subject. Many mariners are also of my opinion. We saw, also, the new moon at mid-day, as it came into conjunction with the sun. There were seen, also, every night, vapours and burning flames flashing across the sky. A little above, I called this region by the name of hemisphere, which, if we would not speak improperly, cannot be so called, when comparing it with our own. It appeared only to present that form partially, and it seemed to us speaking improperly to call it a hemisphere.

Illustration of the Antipodes.

As I have before stated, we sailed from Lisbon,

which is nearly forty degrees distant from the equinoctial line towards the north, to this country, which is fifty degrees on the other side of the line; the sum of these degrees is ninety, and is the fourth part of the circumference of the globe, according to the true reckoning of the ancients. It is therefore manifest to all, that we measured the fourth part of the Earth. We, who reside in Lisbon, nearly forty degrees north of the equinoctial line, are distant from those who reside on the other side of the line, in angular meridional length, ninety degrees; that is, obliquely. In order that the case may be more plainly understood, I would observe, that a perpendicular line starting from that point in the heavens which is our zenith, strikes those obliquely who are fifty degrees beyond the equinoctial line; whence it appears that we are in the direct line, and they, in comparison with us, are in the oblique one, and this situation forms the figure of a right-angled triangle, of which we have the direct lines, as the figure more clearly demonstrates.[1] I have thus spoken with sufficient prolixity as to cosmography.

Such are the things which in this, my last navigation, I have considered worthy of being made known; nor have I, without reason, called this

[1] The figure spoken of consists, as will be seen on the next page, of two straight lines extending from the centre of the earth to the sky. If the first line strikes the point in the heavens, which is at our zenith, the second, drawn at right angles with it, will strike the zenith of a person standing at ninety degrees distance from us.—*Canovai*, tom. i. p. 182.

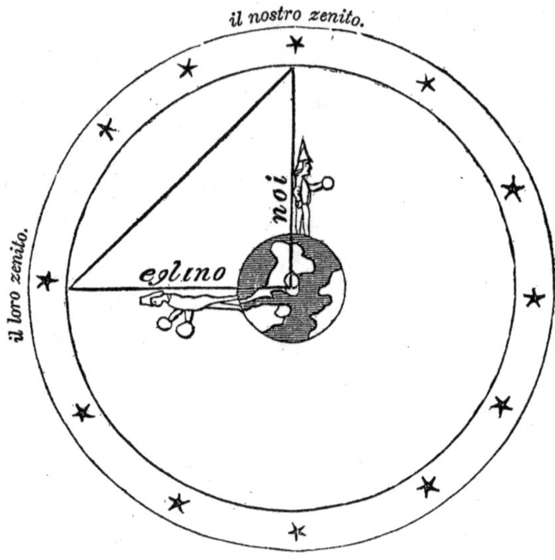

work the "Third Journey." I have before composed two other books on navigation which, by command of Ferdinand, King of Castile, I performed in the West, in which many things not unworthy of being made known are particularly described; especially those which appertain to the glory of our Saviour, who, with marvellous skill, built this machine, the world. And, in truth, who can ever sufficiently praise God? I have related marvellous things concerning him in the aforesaid work. I have stated briefly that which relates to the position and ornaments of the globe; so that when I shall be more at leisure, I may be able to write out, with greater care, a work upon cosmography, in order that future ages may bear me in remembrance. Such works teach me more fully, from day to day, to honour the

Supreme God, and finally to arrive at the knowledge of those things which our ancestors and the ancient fathers had no acquaintance with. With most humble prayers I supplicate our Saviour, whose province it is to have compassion upon mortals, that he will prolong my life sufficiently, that I may perform what I have purposed to do. My three journeys I think I shall defer writing about in full till another time. Probably when I have returned safe and sound to my native country, with the aid and counsel of learned men, and with the encouragement of friends, I shall write with greater care a larger work.

Apology for not sending the journals of the voyage.

Your Excellency will pardon me for not having sent you the journals which I kept from day to day in this my last navigation, as I had promised to do. The king has been the cause of it, and he still retains my pamphlets. But since I have delayed performing this work until the present day, perhaps I shall add the fourth "Journey." I contemplate going again to explore that southern part of the New World; and for the purpose of carrying out such intention, two vessels are already armed and equipped, and abundantly supplied with provisions. I shall first go eastward, before making the voyage south; I shall then sail to the southwest, and when I shall have arrived there, I shall do many things for the praise and glory of God, the benefit of my native country, the perpetual memory of my name, and particu-

CHAPTER XIII.

larly for the honour and solace of my old age, which has already nearly come upon me.

There is nothing wanting in this affair but the leave of the king; and when this is obtained, as it soon will be, we shall sail on a long voyage, and may it please God to give it a happy termination.

Your Excellency's servant,

AMERICUS VESPUCIUS.

CHAPTER XIV.

CONTINUATION OF THE LETTER TO PIERO SODERINI, GIVING A DESCRIPTION OF THE THIRD VOYAGE OF AMERICUS.

Stay at Lisbon after Second Voyage.—Letters from the King of Portugal.—Juliano Bartolomeo del Giocondo sent from Lisbon to urge Americus to sail in the Portuguese Service.—His Consent and Departure for Lisbon.—Sails from Lisbon, 13th of May, 1501.—Encounters severe Storms.—Arrives at the Continent.—Sails along the Shores.—Attempts to treat with the Natives.—Two of the Crew proceed Inland.—Treachery of the Natives.—One of the Crew killed and eaten.—Learn the Death of the other two.—At length meet with Friendly Natives.—Continue the Voyage to the North.—April 7th, discover New Land.—More severe Storms.—Return to Lisbon.—Arrive on the Seventh of September, 1502.

I WAS reposing myself in Seville, after the many toils I had undergone in the two voyages made for His Serene Highness Ferdinand, King of Castile, in the Indies, yet indulging a willingness to return to the land of pearls, when fortune, not seeming to be satisfied with my former labours, inspired the mind of his Serene Majesty, Don Emmanuel, King of Portugal (I know not through what circumstances), to attempt to avail himself of my services. There came to me a royal letter from his Majesty, containing a solicitation that I would come to Lisbon and speak with his highness, he promising to show me many favours. I did not at once determine to go, and argued with the messenger, telling him I was

CHAPTER XIV.

ill, and indisposed for the undertaking, but that when I recovered, if his Highness wished me to serve him, I would do whatever he might command me.

Persuasions to induce Americus to go to Lisbon.

Seeing that he could not obtain me, he sent Juliano di Bartolomeo del Giocondo, who at that time resided in Lisbon, with commission to use every possible means to bring me back with him.[1] Juliano came to Seville, and on his arrival, and induced by his urgent entreaties, I was persuaded to go, though my going was looked upon with ill-favour by all who knew me. It was thus regarded by my friends, because I abandoned Castile, where I had been honoured, and because they thought that the king had rightful possession of me, and it was considered still worse that I departed without taking leave of my host.

Having presented myself at the court of King Emmanuel, he appeared to be highly pleased with my coming, and requested that I would accompany his three ships which were ready to set out for the discovery of new lands. Thus, esteeming a request from a king as equivalent to a command, I was obliged to consent to whatever he asked of me.

Departure from Lisbon May 13, 1501.

We set sail from the port of Lisbon with three ships in company, on the thirteenth[2] day of May,

1 This Juliano was the same individual who translated, from Spanish to Italian, and from Italian to Latin, this relation of the voyage of Americus, as appears in the Latin edition which Munoz speaks of, and in the Italian editions printed in Milan in 1508 and 1519.—*Navarrête*, tom. iii. p. 263.

2 Respecting the date of the commencement of this voyage, see notes of the preceding chapter; see also the Dissertazione Giustificativa, No. 19.

GIGANTIC SAVAGES.

They carried immense bows and arrows, and large headed clubs, and talked among themselves in a tone which led us to think they were deliberating about attacking us. (See P. 184.)

CHAPTER XIV.

1501, and steered our course directly for the Grand Canary Islands, which we passed without stopping, and coasted along the western shores of Africa. On this coast we found excellent fishing, taking a kind of fish called porghies, and were detained there three days. From there we went to the coast of Ethiopia, arriving at a port called Beseneghe, within the Torrid Zone, and situated in the fourteenth degree of north latitude, in the first climate. Here we remained eleven days taking in wood and water —as it was my intention to sail for the South through the great Atlantic Ocean.

Arrival at the continent, after severe storms, on the 17th of August.

We left this port of Ethiopia, and sailed on our course, bearing a quarter south, and in ninety-seven days we made the land at a distance of seven hundred leagues from said port. In those ninety-seven days we had the worst weather that ever man experienced who navigated the ocean; a succession of drenching rains, showers, and tempests. The season was very unpropitious, as our navigation was continually drawing us nearer the equinoctial line, where, in the month of June, it is winter, and where we found the days and nights of equal length, and our shadows falling continually towards the south. It pleased God, however, to show us new land, on the seventeenth day of August, at a half a league distance from which, we anchored. We launched our boats and went ashore, to see if the country was inhabited, and if so, by what kind of people, and we found at length a population far more degraded than brutes.

CHAPTER XIV.

Take possession of the country in the name of the king.

Your Excellency will understand that at first we did not see any inhabitants, though we knew very well, by the many signs we saw, that the country was peopled. We took possession of it in the name of his most Serene Majesty, and found it to be pleasant and verdant, and of good surface, and situated five degrees south of the equinoctial line; thus much we ascertained, and then returned to the ships. On the next day, as we were in great need of wood and water, we determined to go on shore and procure the necessary supplies. While we were there, we saw people looking at us from the summit of a mountain, but they did not venture to descend. They were naked, and of the same colour and figure as those heretofore discovered by me for the King of Spain. We made much exertion to persuade them to come and speak with us, but we could not assure them sufficiently to trust us. Seeing their obstinacy and malignity, as it was growing late, we returned to the ships, leaving on shore for them many bells, looking-glasses, and other things, in places where they could find them. When we had gone away, they descended from the mountain, and took possession of the things we had left, appearing to be filled with wonder while viewing them. So on this day we obtained no advantage, save that of procuring some water.

Two of the crew despatched to treat with the natives.

The next morning, we saw from the ships that the people of the country were making many bonfires, and thinking them signals for us to come to them, we went on shore. We found that many people had arrived, but they kept always at a distance, though they made signs that they wished us to accompany them inland.

Whereupon two of our Christians were induced to ask the captain's permission to brave the danger and go with them, in order to see what kind of people they were, and whether they had any riches, spices, or drugs. They importuned him so much, that he finally consented. After having been fitted out with many articles of trade, they left us, with orders not to be absent more than five days, as we should expect them with great anxiety. So they took their way into the country, and we returned to the ships to wait for them, which we did for the space of six days. Nearly every day there came people to the shore, but they would never speak with us.

One of the crew killed and eaten.

On the seventh day we landed, and found that they had brought their wives with them. As we reached the shore, the men of the country commanded their women to speak with us. We observed that they hesitated to obey the order, and accordingly determined to send one of our people, a very courageous young man, to address them. In order to encourage them, we entered the boats while he went to speak with the women. When he arrived, they formed themselves into a great circle around him, touching him and looking at him as with astonishment. While all this was going on, we saw a woman coming from the mountain, carrying a large club in her hand; when she ar-

CHAPTER XIV. rived where the young Christian stood, she came up behind him, and raising the bludgeon, gave him such a blow with it, that she laid him dead on the spot, and immediately the other women took him by the feet and dragged him away towards the mountain.

Fate of the two messengers. The men ran towards the shore forthwith, and began to assail us with their bows and arrows, throwing our people into great fright, owing to the many arrows that reached them, in consequence of the boats having grounded. No one resorted to arms, but for a time all was terror and panic. After a while, however, we discharged four swivels at them, which had no other effect than to make them flee towards the mountain, when they heard the report. There we saw that the women had already cut the young Christian in pieces, and at a great fire which they had made, were roasting him in our sight, showing us the several pieces as they eat them. The men also made signs to us, indicating that they had killed the other two Christians and eaten them in the same manner, which grieved us very much.

Seeing with our own eyes the cruelty they practised towards the dead, and the most intolerable injury they had done to us, more than forty of us adopted the determination to rush on shore, avenge such cruel murders, and punish such bestial and inhuman conduct. The Superior Captain, however, would not consent to it, and thus they remained satiated with the great injury they had done us;

and we left them most reluctantly, highly chagrined at the course of our Captain.

We departed from this place and sailed along in a southeastern direction, on a line parallel with the coast, making many landings, but never finding any people who would converse with us. Continuing in this manner, we found at length that the line of the coast made a turn to the south, and after doubling a cape which we called Cape St. Augustin, we began to sail in a southerly direction. This cape is a hundred and fifty leagues distant easterly from the aforementioned land where the three Christians were murdered, and eight degrees south of the equinoctial line. While sailing on this course, we one day saw many people standing on the shore, apparently in great wonder at the sight of our ships. We directed our course towards them, and having anchored in a good place, proceeded to land in the boats, and found the people better disposed than those we had passed. Though it cost us some exertion to tame them, we nevertheless made them our friends, and treated with them.

In this place we staid five days, and here we found cassia stems very large and green, and some already dry on the tops of the trees. We determined to take a couple of men from this place, in order that they might teach us the language. Three of them came voluntarily with us, in order to visit Portugal.

Being already wearied with so much writing, I will delay no longer to inform your Excellency that

CHAPTER XIV.

we left this port and sailed continually in a southerly direction in sight of the shore, making frequent landings, and treating with a great number of people. We went so far to the south that we were beyond the tropic of Capricorn, where the south pole is elevated thirty-two degrees above the horizon. We had then entirely lost sight of *Ursa Minor*, and even *Ursa Major* was very low, nearly on the edge of the horizon; so we steered by the stars of the south pole, which are many, and much larger and brighter than those of the north. I drew the figures of the greater part of them, particularly of those of the first and second magnitude, with a description of the circles which they made around the pole, and an account of their diameters and semi-diameters, as may be seen in my "*Quattro Giornate*" (Four Journeys).

Voyage along the coast seven hundred and fifty leagues.

We ran on this coast about seven hundred and fifty leagues; one hundred and fifty from Cape St. Augustin towards the west, and six hundred towards the south. If I were to relate all the things that I saw on this coast, and others that we passed, as many more sheets as I have already written upon, would not be sufficient for the purpose. We saw nothing of utility on this coast, save a great number of dye-wood and cassia trees, and also of those trees which produce myrrh. There were, however, many natural curiosities which cannot be recounted.

Having been already full ten months on the voyage, and seeing that we had found no minerals in the country, we concluded to take our leave of it, and attempt the ocean in some other part. It was determined in council to pursue whatever course of navigation appeared best to me, and I was invested with full command of the fleet. I ordered that all the people and the fleet should be provided with wood and water for six months; as much as the officers of the ships should judge it prudent to sail with. Having laid in our provisions, we commenced our navigation with a southeasterly wind, on the fifteenth day of February, when the sun was already approaching the equinoctial line, and tended towards this, our northern hemisphere. We were in such a high southern latitude at this time that the south pole was elevated fifty-two degrees above the horizon, and we no longer saw the stars, either of Ursa Minor or Ursa Major.

Encounter another violent storm.

On the third of April we had sailed five hundred leagues from the port we left. On this day commenced a storm, which was so violent that we were compelled to take in all our sails, and run under bare poles. The wind was south and very strong, with very high seas, and the air very piercing. The storm was so furious that the whole fleet was in great apprehension. The nights were very long, being fifteen hours in duration on and about the seventh of April, the sun being then in sign of Aries, and winter prevailing in this region.

Your Excellency will please to observe that while driven by this storm on the seventh of April, we came in sight of new land, and ran within twenty leagues of it, finding the whole coast wild, and see-

CHAPTER XIV.

ing neither harbour nor inhabitants. The cold was so severe that no one in the fleet could either withstand or endure it, which I conceive to be the reason of this want of population. Finding ourselves in such great danger, and the storm so violent that we could hardly distinguish one ship from on board another, on account of the high seas that were running, and the misty darkness of the weather, we agreed that the Superior Captain should make signals to the fleet to turn about, and that we should leave the country and steer our course in the direction of Portugal. This proved to be very good counsel, for certain it is, if we had delayed that night, we should all have been lost. We took the wind aft, and during the night and next day the storm increased so much that we were very apprehensive for our safety, and made many vows of pilgrimage and the performance of other ceremonies usual with mariners in such weather.[1]

We ran five days, making about two hundred and fifty leagues, and continually approaching the equinoctial line, and finding the air more mild and the sea less boisterous; till at last it pleased God to deliver us from this our great danger. It was our intention to go and reconnoitre the coast of Ethiopia,

[1] The custom of making vows of pilgrimage, in case of delivery from stormy weather, was very common among the sailors of that day. The Church of St. Mary of Guadaloupe was the favourite resort of the Spanish and Portuguese sailors. "This day," writes Lopez, "many vows were made and lots were cast, to see who should go and visit the Holy Church of St. Mary of Guadaloupe."—*Ramusio*, tom. i. p. 145, C.

which was thirteen hundred leagues distant from us, through the great Atlantic Sea, and by the grace of God we arrived at it, touching at a southern port called Sierra Leone, where we staid fifteen days, obtaining refreshments.

Arrival at Lisbon on the 7th of September, 1502.

From this place we steered for the Azore Islands, about seven hundred and fifty leagues distant, where we arrived in the latter part of July, and staid another fifteen days, taking some recreation. Then we departed for Lisbon, three hundred leagues distant, and situated farther west, which port we entered on the seventh of September, 1502, in good preservation (for which the All Powerful be thanked), with only two ships, having burned the other in Sierra Leone, because it was no longer seaworthy. In this voyage we were absent about fifteen months, and sailed nearly eleven of them without seeing the north star, or either of the constellations Ursa Major and Minor, which are called the horn, steering meanwhile by the star of the other pole. The above is what I saw in this my third voyage, made for his Serene Highness the King of Portugal.

CHAPTER XV.

Reception at Lisbon.—Honours in that City and Florence.—High Reputation of Americus.—His Astronomical Discoveries.—His Method of determining Longitude.—The Southern Cross.—A New Expedition prepared.—Gonzalo Coelho.—Sails from Lisbon with six Ships on the 10th of May, 1503.—Foolish Vanity and Obstinacy of the Commander Coelho.—Loss of Part of the Fleet.—Great Inconvenience occasioned thereby.—Americus pursues his Voyage.—Discovers an Island.—Very tame Birds thereon.—Arrives at the Continent.—Bay of All Saints.—Builds a Fort there.—Leaves a Garrison.—Return Voyage.—Arrival at Lisbon, June 18th, 1504.—Commends his Family to the Notice of Soderini.—Concluding Remarks.

THE return of Americus from his third voyage occasioned great joy in Lisbon. He was received with high honours by King Emmanuel, who celebrated his safe arrival with much magnificence. His ship, which had become unseaworthy, was broken up, and portions of it were carried in solemn procession to a church, where they were suspended as valuable relics. Nor were the rejoicings and celebrations confined to Portugal. His own countrymen received the accounts of his discoveries with exultation. Public ceremonies were ordered, and honours were bestowed upon those members of his family who were then in Florence.

Americus acquired as much, if not more reputation, in consequence of his astronomical and geometrical discoveries in his two last voyages, as in consequence of his exploration of new countries. He was generally admitted to be vastly in advance of all the navigators of the age in his knowledge of these sciences; and though his calculations are undoubtedly defective in many points, yet they are far more accurate than those of any preceding or cotemporary mariner.

"Astronomy," says the Justificatory Dissertation, "had in ancient times comparatively very little influence in nautical affairs. The wisest pilot, in his studies of the planets and stars, was limited to observations of the phases of the moon, in order to foresee the tides—to a calculation, in the daytime of the meridian altitude of the sun, and in the night-time, to the steering of his vessel by the constellations of Ursa Major and Minor. Longitude was calculated by an inexact and precarious method, and no navigator considered it necessary to know much of the movements of the moon or the planets."[1]

Method of computing longitude.

The method of ascertaining longitude at sea, by observing the conjunction of the moon with a planet, was one of his most important discoveries. The fact that these conjunctions were observed to take place, at different hours in different places, had long been known. The astronomer and cosmographer, Ptolomey, the highest authority in those days, reporting, among other things, a con-

[1] Diss. Gius. No. 88.

CHAPTER XV.

junction of the moon with Spiga, gave notice that the phenomenon, which was observed in Rome at five o'clock, appeared in Alexandria at 6.20′; but neither he, nor the many philosophers who, after him, meditated upon the subject, thought of rendering such a conjunction available for the fixing of longitude at sea.[1]

To Americus, therefore, belongs the honour of applying this method for the first time; and it is by no means improbable that, by his writings, as well as by those of the astronomer of Alexandria, Galileo may have been led to apply, to the same purpose, the frequent eclipses of the small planets which he discovered revolving round Jupiter.

Observations of the heavenly bodies. The southern cross.

The observations and enumeration of the stars which Americus made, added greatly to his fame, and were of infinite service to future mariners. The voyagers of that day to the South were greatly alarmed at not finding in the southern heavens a guide like the polar star of the North. Vicente Pinzon, who navigated in the same direction, and at about the same time with Americus, expected to find one, and in his dismay at its absence, attributed it to some swelling of the earth's surface, which hid it from his view. Nothing was then known of the beautiful constellation, which supplies its place, to mariners in the Antarctic seas. The "many sleepless nights" which Americus devoted to the examination of the Southern Cross, and other heavenly

[1] Diss. Gius. No. 92. Almag. L. vii. c. 3.

bodies of the same hemisphere, the many laborious calculations which he entered into, when, in the words of his favourite poet,

CHAPTER XV.

> Each star of the other pole, night now beheld
> And ours so low, that from the ocean floor
> It rose not;—[1]

must have been well repaid by the convictions he arrived at, and the fame which he acquired as an accurate astronomer. It is evident from his writings that he was not insensible to the natural feelings of honourable ambition, and considered not only the benefits he was conferring upon mankind, but looked forward to acquiring a reputation which might be the comfort and consolation of his old age.

Actuated by the belief that Americus would have succeeded in reaching India by the way of the southwest, had not his last voyage been interrupted by the severe storms which he encountered, King Emmanuel lost no time in preparing another expedition. Americus is as silent as usual respecting the commander of the new fleet; but though he does not mention his name, it is a well-ascertained fact that Gonzalo Coelho held the chief command of the six vessels which composed the armament, and that only one of them was commanded by himself. This fleet was ready for sea early in the spring of 1503, and the principal object of the voyage was to discover the island Malacca, then supposed to be the centre of commerce in the East In-

[1] Carey's Dante, Purgatory, Canto xxvi.

CHAPTER XV.

dies. The narration of this voyage occupies the closing portion of the letter of Americus to Soderini. Disgusted with the foolish obstinacy of his commander, and discouraged by the effects of his wilfulness, he evidently wishes to escape from so disagreeable a subject, and is more than usually concise.

CONCLUSION

OF THE LETTER TO PIERO SODERINI, GIVING AN ACCOUNT OF THE FOURTH VOYAGE OF AMERICUS.

It remains for me to relate the things which were seen by me, in my Fourth Voyage; and by reason that I have now become wearied, and also because this voyage did not result according to my wishes (in consequence of a misfortune which happened in the Atlantic Sea, as your Excellency will shortly understand), I shall endeavour to be brief.

Departure from Lisbon six ships in company.

We set sail from this port of Lisbon, six ships in company, for the purpose of making discoveries with regard to an island in the East, called Malacca, which is reported to be very rich.[1] It is, as it were, the warehouse of all the ships which come

[1] "All this period," says Canovai, "is strangely disfigured in the edition of Valori. Instead of East, West is written; the Arctic pole is changed to the Antarctic, and the three degrees by which Malacca is separated from the equator, are there read thirty-three. From this may be inferred the credit to which this edition is entitled, if there was a shadow of criticism in those who regard it as infallible."—*Canovai*, tom. ii. p. 26.

from the Sea of Ganges and the Indian Ocean, as Cadiz is the storehouse for all the ships that pass from East to West and from West to East, by the way of Calcutta. This Malacca is farther east, and much farther south, than Calcutta, because we know that it is situated at the parallel of three degrees north latitude. We set out on the tenth day of May, 1503, and sailed direct for the Cape Verd Islands, where we made up our cargo, taking in every kind of refreshment. After remaining here three days, we departed on our voyage, sailing in a southerly direction.

Obstinacy of the commander and loss of part of the fleet.

Our Superior Captain was a presumptuous and very obstinate man; he would insist upon going to reconnoitre Sierra Leone, a southern country of Ethiopia, without there being any necessity for it, unless to exhibit himself as the captain of six vessels. He acted contrary to the wish of all our other captains in pursuing this course. Sailing in this direction, when we arrived off the coast of this country, we had such bad weather, that though we remained in sight of the coast four days, it did not permit us to attempt a landing. We were compelled at length to leave the country, sailing from there to the south, and bearing southwest.

When we had sailed three hundred leagues through the Great Sea, being then three degrees south of the equinoctial line, land was discovered, which might have been about twenty-two leagues distant from us, and which we found to be an island in the midst of the sea. We were filled with won-

CHAPTER XV.

der at beholding it, considering it a natural curiosity, as it was very high, and not more than two leagues in length and one in width. This island was no inhabited by any people, and was an evil island for the whole fleet; because, as your Excellency will learn, by the evil counsel and bad management of our Superior Captain, he lost his ship here. He ran her upon a rock, and she split open and went to the bottom, on the night of St. Lorenzo, which is the tenth of August, and nothing was saved from her except the crew. She was a ship of three hundred tons, and carried every thing of most importance in the fleet.

As the whole fleet was compelled to labour for the common benefit, the Captain ordered me to go with my ship to the aforesaid island, and look for a good harbour, where all the ships might anchor. As my boat, filled with nine of my mariners, was of service, and helped to keep up a communication between the ships, he did not wish me to take it, telling me they would bring it to me at the island. So I left the fleet, as he ordered me, without a boat, and with less than half my men, and went to the said island, about four leagues distant. There I found a very good harbour, where all the ships might have anchored in perfect safety. I waited for the captain and the fleet full eight days, but they never came; so that we were very much dissatisfied, and the people who remained with me in the ship were in such great fear, that I could not console them. On the eighth day we saw a ship

CHAPTER XV

coming off at sea, and for fear those on board might not see us, we raised anchor and went towards it, thinking they might bring me my boat and men. When we arrived alongside, after the usual salutations, they told us that the Captain had gone to the bottom, that the crew had been saved, and that my boat and men remained with the fleet, which had gone further to sea. This was a very serious grievance to us, as your Excellency may well think. It was no trifle to find ourselves a hundred leagues distant from Lisbon, in mid-ocean, with so few men.

my.

However, we bore up under adverse fortune, and returning to the island, supplied ourselves with wood and water with the boat of my consort. This island we found uninhabited. It had plenty of fresh water, and an abundance of trees filled with countless numbers of land and marine birds, which were so simple, that they suffered themselves to be taken with the hand. We took so many of them that we loaded a boat with them. We saw no other animals, except some very large rats, and lizards with two tails, and some snakes.

Arrival at the Bay of All Saints.

Having taken in our supplies, we departed for the southwest, as we had an order from the king, that if any vessel of the fleet, or its captain, should be lost, I should make for the land of my last voyage. We discovered a harbour which we called the Bay of All Saints, and it pleased God to give us such good weather, that in seventeen days we arrived at it.[1] It was distant three hundred leagues

[1] This bay still retains the name given to it by Americus.

CHAPTER XV.

from the island we had left, and we found neither our captain nor any other ship of the fleet in the course of the voyage. We waited full two months and four days in this harbour, and seeing that no orders came for us, we agreed, my consort and myself, to run along the coast.

Build a fortress on the main land.

We sailed two hundred and sixty leagues further, and arrived at a harbour where we determined to build a fortress. This we accomplished, and left in it the twenty-four men that my consort had received from the captain's ship which was lost.

In this port we staid five months, building the fortress and loading our ships with dye-wood. We could not proceed farther for want of men, and besides, I was destitute of many equipments. Thus, having finished our labours, we determined to return to Portugal, leaving the twenty-four men in the fortress, with provisions for six months, with twelve pieces of cannon, and many other arms. We made peace with all the people of the country, who have not been mentioned in this voyage, but not because we did not see and treat with a great number of them. As many as thirty men of us went forty leagues inland, where we saw so many things, that I omit to relate them, reserving them for my "Four Journeys."

Return to Lisbon June 18th, 1504.

This country is situated eighteen degrees south of the equinoctial line, and fifty-seven degrees farther west than Lisbon, as our instruments showed us. All this being performed, we bid farewell to the Christians we left behind us, and to the country, and commenced our navigation on a north-north-east course, with the intention of sailing directly to this city of Lisbon. In seventy-seven days, after many toils and dangers, we entered this port on the eighteenth day of June, 1504, for which God be praised. We were well received, although altogether unexpected, as the whole city had given us up for lost. All the other ships of the fleet had been lost through the pride and folly of our commander, and thus it is that God rewards haughtiness and vanity.

At present I find myself here in Lisbon again, and I do not know what the king will wish me to do, but I am very desirous of obtaining repose. The bearer of this, who is Benvenuto di Domenico Benvenuti, will tell your Excellency of my condition, and of any other things which have been omitted to avoid prolixity, but which I have seen and experienced. I have abbreviated the letter as much as I could, and omitted to say many things very natural to be told, that I might not be tedious. Your Excellency will pardon me, as I beg you will consider me of the number of your servants. Allow me to commend to you Sr. Antonio Vespucci, my brother, and all my family. I remain, praying God that he may prolong your life, and prosper that exalted republic of Florence, and the honour of your Excellency,

Your very humble servant,

AMERICUS VESPUCIUS.

Dated in Lisbon, the 4*th of September*, 1504.

CHAPTER XV.

Thus ended the last voyage of Americus. Desirous of repose, and perhaps somewhat disheartened by its unfortunate result, he abandoned, for the present, all ideas of again proceeding to sea, and devoted himself to the task of writing full accounts of his discoveries. It is greatly to be regretted that the works to which he makes allusion, have not been preserved for the benefit of the world, for it is evident, by the way in which he speaks of them, that they contained more ample accounts than the letters. The spirit of research may yet lead some industrious antiquarian to the discovery of those documents, the loss of which are most to be deplored, his manuscript journals. There are yet unexplored, large quantities of documents, and records relating to the discovery of America, and each day brings to light some new fact to illustrate the history of that great event.

CHAPTER XVI.

Return of Americus to Spain, 1504.—At Court, February, 1505.—Columbus.—Ill Treatment of him.—Death of Queen Isabella.—Effect on the Fortunes of Americus.—Royal Grants to him.—New Expedition.—Vicente Yañes Pinzon.—The Name of America.—False Assertion and Deduction.—Reasons why the Name was first given.—Ilacomilo's Cosmography.—First Use of the Name.—Extracts from an able Article in the N. A. Review.—Canovai's Opinion.

AMERICUS remained in Portugal but a short time after his unexpected return from his fourth voyage. In the latter part of the year 1504, he returned to Seville, and in February, 1505, he left that city, on his way to the court, which was then held at Segovia, bearing the letter from Columbus to his son, which appears in a previous chapter. The Admiral had arrived from his last voyage, only a few months previously. Worn down by neglect and the infirmities of age, it was difficult to imagine him the same man, who was once treated with such high honour by monarchs and nobles. He afforded a melancholy proof of the ingratitude of kings, and was then pleading for rights, of which he had been iniquitously deprived, like a criminal before his judge—his claims treated with indifference—while the intrigues of his foes led every day to fresh injuries.

CHAPTER XVI.

Death of Queen Isabella.

The death of his ever-kind protectress, the Queen Isabella, which took place a few days after his own arrival, was a severe blow to the Admiral, and completed the long list of disasters which had befallen him in his old age. While she lived, some hope of obtaining justice seemed left to him; but his cause, which had languished during her illness, became hopeless when she was no more. Still Americus, animated by warm feelings of respect and admiration for the great discoverer, zealously offered to render him all the assistance in his power at court, and the proposal was as frankly accepted as it was freely made.[1]

Influence of the queen's death on the fortunes of Americus.

Whether the death of the queen had any effect upon the fortunes of Americus, there are no means of determining. It would appear that it had a favourable influence, if the opinion of his Italian biographers is followed, who hold to the supposition that Americus was more of a favourite with the king, than with his consort. His return, so closely succeeding the death of Isabella, lends a semblance of plausibility to their views; and the favour which was shown him at court is another circumstance tending to corroborate them.[2]

Navarrête inclines to the opinion, that Americus was sent for by King Ferdinand, in order that he might obtain information from him of the plans and projects of the Portuguese government, as well in relation to their expeditions to the shores

[1] Irving, vol. ii. p. 856, 857. [2] Canovai, tom. ii. p. 48–50.

of the New World, as to the progress they were making in their voyages and establishments in the East Indies.[1] So far from noticing with displeasure his clandestine departure from Spain, on the 11th day of April, 1505, the king made him a grant of 12,000 maravedis; and on the 24th of the same month, letters of naturalization in his behalf were issued, in consideration, as they recite, of his fideli-ty and many valuable services to the crown.[2]

Preparations for a new expedition for Americus and Pinzon.

Being thus qualified to serve the king in the capacity of a commander, preparations were commenced, by the orders of government, for a new expedition. Americus and Vicente Ya ez Pinzon were named the commanders. The spirit of discovery was aroused again in the mind of Americus, and he set out for the ports of Palos and Moguer, where he remained through the month of May, to see and consult with his colleague, in relation to the necessary wants of the expedition. There is little doubt that the representations of Americus alone led to this new enterprise, and Pinzon was the most proper person to associate with him in the undertaking; for he had already been upon the coast of Brazil, which was the destination of the fleet.[3] In fact, all the claims of Spain to any part of that region rested upon a previous voyage of Pinzon, who, in 1500, had taken possession of the more northern part, in the name of the Spanish sovereigns.

[1] Navarréte, tom. iii. p. 320.

[2] See Illustrations and Documents. Translation of Documents from Navarréte.

[3] Navarréte, tom. iii. p. 321.

CHAPTER XVI.

The name of America and its origin.

It was about this time that the name of America began to be first used, and was applied to the countries which Americus visited in his last voyages. The assertion has been made, that soon after his return to Spain he prepared a chart, in which the coast of Brazil was delineated and called by the name of America; but it is unsupported by any verifying evidence or authority. If he had done this, however, it would be no sufficient reason to justify his calumniators in their charges against him of dishonourable treatment of Columbus. It was a custom then, and has continued a custom ever since, for discoverers to call after themselves some prominent place, river, or mountain, fallen in with in the course of their explorations. Americus never could have imagined the extended signification which the name was afterwards destined to attain, and the injustice of those who, as has been remarked in a previous chapter, attribute to him the crime of falsifying the date of his first voyage, with this end in view, is apparent to any one who is not ignorant of the limited application of the name in the first instance.[1]

"We may conjecture," says the writer of an able critical article in the North American Review for April, 1821, which has afforded great assistance in the preparation of this work, by its valuable suggestions and references, "we may conjecture, with a great degree of certainty, that

[1] N. A. Review, April, 1821, p. 339.

on Vespucci's return from his last voyage, the coast which he had visited began to pass by his name. Two reasons may be given why this honour should have been conferred on him, rather than on his superior officers. One reason is, that, although he was not first in command, yet his pre-eminence in nautical and geographical knowledge gave him that control over the proceedings of the rest, which men of strong minds inevitably acquire in moments of difficulty and danger. Indeed, we find that he came back from his fourth voyage, when Coelho, with the greater part of the squadron, had perished, and when he himself was no longer expected; in which circumstances it would be perfectly natural for the Portuguese to attribute to him the sole merit of the discovery of Brazil. The second reason is, that, as Vespucci was highly skilled in the construction of charts, and as those which he made were held in great esteem, he may, in depicting the coast of Brazil, have given it the name of America."[1]

First suggestion of the name of America.

The first suggestion of the name which appears in print was probably contained in the Latin work on Cosmography, by Ilacomilo, being the edition of Gruniger, printed in Strasburg in 1509, from which Navarrête makes his translation of the letter to Soderini. Navarrête says, that "in the ninth chapter

[1] "P. Martyr informs us he had seen a Portuguese chart of parts of the New World in the construction of which Vespucci assisted."—*Ocean. Decad.* p. 199. See likewise *Memorias de Litteratura Portugueza*, tom. iii. p. 339.

CHAPTER XVI.

of this work, the author, after describing the situation of the different portions of the world, places first the three which were known to Ptolomey, and proceeds with the following suggestion, alluding to the voyages printed as a continuation of his cosmography. "Nunc vero et hae partes sunt latius lustratæ, et alia quarta pars, per Americum Vesputium, ut in sequentibus audietur, inventa est; quam non video cur quis jure vetet ab Americo inventore, sagacis ingenii viro, Amerigem quasi Americi terram sive Americam dicendam, cum et Europa et Asia a mulieribus sua sortitæ sint nomina."

This passage is not the only one in the work which suggests the same thing. In the seventh chapter, which treats of the different climates of the world, the author speaks of "the fourth part of the world, which may be called Amerige or America, because discovered by Americus."[1]

The article above quoted says that "the earliest mention which the industry of authors has been able to detect, of the word America, is about the year 1514, in a letter written by Joachim Vadianus, a Swiss scholar, known by his Commentary on Pomponius Mela. His words are, 'Si Americam, a Vespuccio repertam, et eum Eoæ Terræ partem, quæ terræ Ptolomaeo cognitæ adjecta est, ad longitudinis habitatæ rationem referrimus, longe ultra hemisphærium habitari terram constat.'"[2]

1 Navarréte, tom. iii. p. 184.

2 "Joachim. Vadian. Epist. ad Rudol. Agricolam, ad calcem Pomponii Melæ de situ orbis, ed. fol. 1530. Latet Parisiorum, in the Boston Atheneum."

The name does not seem to have come into general use until after the middle of the sixteenth century; but it is occasionally met with before that time; and Canovai cites a treatise on the elements of Geography, printed at Venice in 1535, in which it is doubted whether the word *America* should be employed, or not rather *Amerige*.[1] But what deserves to be particularly noticed is the remarkable fact, that the name was not originally applied to the whole continent, but only to that part of it which is now denominated Brazil. This can be made to appear by the most ample testimony. We pass over the authority of Spaniards who once proposed to call this country Fer-Isabellica, from the sovereigns under whose auspices it was discovered, and who, to this day, entertain a sort of horror of the word America, almost invariably speaking of the New World or the Indies.[2] Looking therefore into Cademosto, P. Martyr, Benzoni, and Grinæus, we find that each of them uses the term Novus Orbis, where we should use America. In most of the maps published between 1510 and 1570 America is applied in the limited sense we have stated. Thus Munster, whose Cosmographia, printed in 1550, was long a text-book in Geography, has a map of the world, in which, towards the west of Europe, appear Terra Florida, then, a little below,

1 Canovai, Diss. Gius. No. 51.

2 "Pizarro, Varones Illustres del Nuevo Mundo, p. 51. Others have proposed to call it Orbis Carolinus, as a compliment to the Emperor Charles V."—See *Solorzano*, *Politica Indiana*, L. i. C. ii. S. 18.

CHAPTER XVI.

Cuba, then Hispaniola, and a little south of the line, Americæ vel Brasillii Insula. In another map of Munster's, which is entitled Novus Orbis, are found grouped together Terra Florida, Cuba, Hispaniola, Jamaica, Parias, and lastly, Insula Atlantica, quem vocant Brasilii et Americam.[1]

In a map of the world, prefixed to the Grinæus of 1555, the western part is occupied with a number of islands, which, beginning with that farthest north, are named Terra Cortesia, Terra de Cuba, Isabella, Spagnolla, Insulæ Antigliæ, Zipangru, and then America, an island considerably larger than either of the others, on the northern extremity of which is printed Parias, on the western, Cannibali, and on the southern, Prisilia. If the last word, Prisilia, refers to Brazil, it would seem that some geographers had begun to distinguish it as a part of America. The same edition of Grinæus contains a brief introduction to geography, in which occurs the following sentence: Insulas occidentales, nempe Hispanam, Joannam, Spagnollam, Cubam, Isabellam, Antiglias, Cannibalorum Terram, Americam, et reliquas incognitas terras primi mortalium adinvenerunt Christophorus Columbus et Albericus Vesputius.[2]

Similar quotations can easily be multiplied. Thus Comes Natalis, who flourished about 1680,

[1] Canovai, Diss. Gius. n. 76.

[2] Novus orbis Regionum ac Insularum veterribus incognitarum, fol. The first edition of this work, printed in 1532, is very rare. The one made use of is the edition of 1555, printed at Basle by Hervagius. A copy is to be found in the Library of the New York Historical Society.

CHAPTER XVI.

speaking of the famous expedition of the Huguenots under Villegagnon, says, that the French called Brazil America, because it was discovered by Amerigo Vespucci.[1] Jean de Lery, a Huguenot minister, who visited Villegagnon's settlement in 1550, and twenty years afterwards published a very amusing account of his voyage, entitles it a history of a voyage to Brazil, which is also called America.[2]

Period when the name of America was first used in its present signification.

The present use of the term seems to have been established soon after this time: for Ortelius, in his Theartum Orbis Terrarum, applies the words America and Bresilia as we do now, and delineates the geography of this continent with tolerable accuracy.[3] But the original signification was not immediately forgotten, as we perceive in Gaspar Ensl's History of the West Indies, where he says that the name of America was originally given to the countries explored by Vespucius, although afterwards, on account of the dye-wood found there, common usage superadded the name of Brazil.[4] We will only add to these citations the authority of Rocha Pitta and Barbosa, who, in noticing Pedro Alvarez Cabral, remark that the name of Santa Cruz,

[1] "Comes Natalis. Hist. S. Temp. p. 139, as quoted by Canovai, Diss. Gius. n. 75. See also Southey's Brazil, vol. i. p. 272, note."

[2] "Historia navigationis in Braziliam, quæ et America dicitur de a Joanne Lerio, Burgundo, Gallice Scripta, nunc vero primum Latinitate donata," &c. 1558, 12mo.

[3] "Theatrum orbis terrarum, fol. Antuerpiæ 1584. Apud Christophor. Plautinum."

[4] "Gaspar Ensl, Indiæ Occidentalis Historia, Coloniæ 1612, 12mo. p. 130."

CHAPTER XVI.

which Cabral gave the country he accidentally discovered, was afterwards changed into America, on account of the charts of it delineated by Vespucci, and finally into Brazil, from its producing the Brazil wood."[1]

The opinion of Canovai incorrect.

Canovai is of opinion, that the name originated from the royal letters-patent which were issued by the king when Americus was appointed to the office of chief pilot, through which it came into general use in Europe, as it were under the sanction of royal authority. That the appointment of Americus to this office aided in fixing the name permanently upon Brazil, may have been the case; but it is apparent, from the statements above, that the Italian biographer is partially in error in his idea, that it was the intention of the Spanish king to confer the name as a mark of honour, and that the world acquiesced in the decision, considering it a just reward of the services of the discoverer.[2] In his desire to defend his countryman from the attacks of those who accuse him of artifice and fraud, in endeavouring to secure an eternal remembrance of his name, by

[1] "'Para eterno monumento da sua piedade, intitulou Pedro Alvarez a nova terra com a religiosa antonomasia de S. Cruz. que depois se mudou em America, por ter demarcado as terras e costas maritimas della Amerigo Vespucci, insigne cosmographo, e ultimamente Brazil, pela producaõ da Madeira, que tem cor de brazas. —*Barbosa, Bibliotheca Lusitana*, tom. iii. p. 554. Rocha Pitta is no less explicit: 'Este foy,' says he, 'a primiero descobrimento, este o primiero nome desta regiõ, que depois esquecida de titulo taõ superior, se chamou America, por Americo Vespucio, e ultimamente Brazil, pelo pao vermelho, ou côr de brazas, que produz.—*Hist.' da America Portugueza*, p. 6."

[2] Diss. Gius. No. 78.

making it the distinctive appellation of the New World. Canovai here goes to the opposite extreme. "If Vespucci's priority, in discovering the southern continent," says the article above quoted, "was a valid reason for naming it America, there is equal reason, as Purchas observes, for denominating the northern Sebastiana, or Cabotia; since it is notorious that the Cabots explored the coast from Labrador to the Gulf of Mexico, a full year before any portion of the continent was ever seen by Columbus. But the hand of chance has an influence so predominant in the assignment of honours by the world, that we can hardly feel surprised at the neglect of Columbus and the Cabots, to the exclusive distinction of Vespucci. The fortune of the name of America itself is not a little singular, as an instance of the mutations of human affairs; which, having been first given to a single province, next spread over the whole southern continent, then passed on to the northern, and now, from being the appellation of the whole New World, it seems about to be confined by foreign nations at least to our own youthful and aspiring republic."[1]

[1] N. A. Review, April, 1821, p. 339, 340.

CHAPTER XVII.

Difficulties of the New Expedition.—Perplexity of the Officials of the Board of Trade.—Accession of Philip and Joanna.—Disagreements between Philip and Ferdinand.—The Board of Trade send Americus to Court.—Their Instructions to him.—Death of King Philip.—Complaints of the Portuguese Court.—The Voyage given up.—Ultimate Fate of the Vessels composing this Fleet.—Great Expense occasioned by it.—Absence of King Ferdinand, and his Return.—Americus ordered to Court.—His Occupation there.—Appointed Chief Pilot.—His Death, February 22d, 1512.

CHAPTER XVII.

The new Expedition.

THE new expedition which was in preparation for Americus and Pinzon was the occasion of much perplexity to the officers of the Board of Trade, and for this reason: by the last testament of Queen Isabella, her consort, King Ferdinand, was appointed Regent of Castile during the minority of her grandson Charles, in case of the absence or incapacity of her daughter Joanna, who had given occasional evidence of insanity, during the lifetime of her mother. This princess was, at the time of the death of the queen, with her husband, the Archduke Philip, in Flanders. King Ferdinand at once proclaimed his daughter queen, and assumed the regency, but from the outset was unpopular with the nobles and people, and at length, on the arrival of Philip and Joanna in Spain, was compelled to

ONE OF THE CREW KILLED AND EATEN.

We saw a woman coming from the mountain, carrying a large club in her hand: when she arrived, she came up behind him, and raising the bludgeon, gave him such a blow with it, that she laid him dead on the spot. (SEE P. 227.)

resign his power in Castile and retire to his own kingdom of Arragon.

CHAPTER XVII.

Accession of Philip and Joanna to the Spanish throne.

From the moment of the accession of Philip to the throne, as the consort of Joanna, an entire change took place in all the departments of government. Almost all the old officers of state were dismissed, and new men appointed in their places. The disagreement between the two kings placed those of the old administration, who still retained their posts, among whom were the offices of the Board of Trade, in a very disagreeable position. They did not know how to conduct themselves, and, fearful of offending either monarch, hesitated whether to proceed with the preparations for the armament, or to give it up altogether.[1]

Instructions of the Board of Trade to Americus.

In this dilemma they wrote, on the 15th of September, 1506, about six weeks after the accession of King Philip, to his secretary, Gaspar de Gricio, that they had despatched Americus to give every information to the king respecting the state of the expedition which King Ferdinand had ordered to be prepared. They also informed the secretary, that it would not be ready to sail before the month of February, in the ensuing year. Americus accordingly left Seville for the court, which was then held at Burgos. He was charged with three letters by the Board of Trade: one for the king himself, another for M. de Vila, his grand chamberlain, to whom he had entrusted the despatch of all business connected with the Indies, and a third to the Secre-

[1] Prescott's Ferdinand and Isabella, vol. iii.

CHAPTER XVII.

tary Gricio, to whom they had previously written. Besides these letters, other documents were placed in his hands. These were five memorials, treating of affairs of the New World, prepared in order that he might not want material at hand, to bring about a prompt and favourable course of action in the matter. The Board of Trade also furnished Americus with written instructions as to his mode of procedure, which show the unenviable state of perplexity in which they found themselves. "You will take," say they, "three letters for the king, M. de Vila, and the Secretary Gricio, and five memorials, one upon the despatch of the armament, two others received from Hispaniola concerning the tower which King Ferdinand commanded to be built on the Pearl Coast, and the remaining two upon the caravels which are on service in Hispaniola, and concerning what things are necessary for the fortress which is building there. If Gricio is at court, and attends to the affairs of the Indies, give him the letter, show him the memorials, and he will guide you to the ear of the king, and obtain for you good despatch. We are informed that the king has entrusted the business of the Indies to M. de Vila, his grand chamberlain. If that is the case, go directly to him. What we principally desire, is a full understanding of the agreement which has been entered into between the king, our lord, (King Philip), and the King Ferdinand, in order that we may be able to give to each prince that which is his."[1]

[1] Navarréte, tom. ii.

CHAPTER XVII.

Death of Philip and difficulties with Portugal.

The perplexities of the officials were not, however, destined to end as soon as they hoped. Just ten days after the date of their letter, King Philip suddenly died at Burgos, having enjoyed his power only for two short months. King Ferdinand was absent, on a visit to his Neapolitan dominions, and the Queen Joanna remained in a state of partial insanity, which rendered her incapable of attending to public affairs. The kingdom was thus trembling on the verge of anarchy, and for a time, most public undertakings were suspended. In addition to this unexpected death of the king, the distrust and complaints of the King of Portugal, respecting the object and destination of the expedition, greatly retarded the preparations for it, and finally were the means of breaking it up altogether. Unwilling, probably, to embroil the country in a quarrel with a foreign court, while in such a distracted condition at home, the provisional regency ordered the preparations to be suspended, and that every thing which had been bought for the expedition should be sold.

Fate of the fleet, when the expedition was given up.

The ultimate fate of the ships which were intended for this fleet is recorded by Navarrēte. It was composed of three ships, which had been brought from Biscay for the purpose. The largest was called La Magdelena, and was to have been under the command of Pinzon; the second was a vessel of somewhat less dimensions, of which Americus was to have had the control; and the third, a caravel, was to have served as a tender to

CHAPTER XVII.

the other two, being of much smaller size. The two first of these vessels were despatched with cargoes to Hispaniola. The Magdelena went under the command of Diego Rodrigues de Grogeda, who purchased her on his return. The one which was to have been under the command of Americus carried Juan de Subano as captain. Americus, notwithstanding, appears to have had the management of the concerns of this vessel, as he had previously attended to its fitting out. The caravel went to the Canary Islands, and, returning to Seville in April, 1507, was employed in the voyage of discovery which Pinzon and Diaz de Solis subsequently undertook.

Large expenses of this expedition.

The preparations for the expedition, which was thus broken up, occasioned a very considerable outlay of capital. Besides the large amount of upwards of five millions of maravedis, which the settlement of the accounts, towards the close of the year 1507, showed, as the sum of the expenses, Americus, with his title of captain, received a salary of thirty thousand maravedis per annum. It appears, from the documents which Navarrēte has extracted from the archives of Seville, that his time was principally passed, until the close of that year, in making all the purchases of provisions and equipment necessary for so extensive a voyage as that in contemplation, and his disappointment must have been great indeed, when the order arrived at Seville countermanding the expedition.[1]

[1] Navarrēte, tom. iii. p. 322.

CHAPTER XVII.

Absence of King Ferdinand.

During the absence of King Ferdinand, on his visit to his Neapolitan dominions, there was a manifest slackening of the spirit of discovery. The stirring nature of the events which were taking place at home, and the prospect of change, if not of anarchy and civil war, gave occupation to, or attracted the attention of, most of the adventurers and restless spirits of the day. But as soon as the king found himself again firmly fixed in power in Castile, and ruling there in the name of his daughter, with an authority much more extensive than he had ever enjoyed during the lifetime of Isabella, he recommenced his projects of discovery and acquisition in the New World. He enjoyed, in virtue of the testament of Isabella, a moiety of the revenues arising from the countries already occupied in the West Indies, and was fully aroused to their importance. But that he was not actuated solely by his pecuniary interest in them, is evident from the measures he took to promote further discoveries, and the colonization of territories already acquired.[1]

Americus ordered to repair to court.

On the 26th of November, 1507, about three months after the return of Ferdinand to Castile, he issued an order, commanding Americus and Juan de la Cosa to proceed immediately to court. Thither, accordingly, both repaired, and were soon engaged in active consultation with the king and his ministers, respecting the nautical affairs of the kingdom. In the beginning of February of the

[1] Prescott's Ferdinand and Isabella, vol. iii.

CHAPTER XVII.

next year, Americus, in connexion with Vicente Yañez Pinzon and Juan Diaz de Solis, was charged with the safe conduct to the treasury of the king of six thousand ducats of gold, which had just then arrived from the Indies, and on the 14th of March, 1508, he received by royal order a payment of six thousand maravedis, in consideration of this service.[1]

The distrust which the Spanish court felt at that time towards the rival court of Portugal, induced them to make ready two caravels, which were placed under the command of Juan de la Cosa, to guard and give convoy to the ships which were coming and going, from time to time, between Spain and their new dominions. Americus was charged with the provisioning and support of these vessels, while his friend Pinzon provided their armament and warlike stores. Americus attended to this business at about the time mentioned above.

Americus appointed chief pilot by the King.

Shortly after this date, on the 22d of March, 1508, Ferdinand appointed Americus to the office of chief pilot, with an annual salary of seventy-five thousand maravedis. It would seem, from the decree which was issued on the 6th of August of the same year, that this place was by no means a sinecure. That document was intended to define the duties of the new office, and it clearly appears, that if they were performed by Americus with the fidelity which characterized all the other trans-

[1] Navarréte, tom. iii. p. 323.

actions of his life, but little leisure could have been left to him. This high and responsible post was held by Americus during the remainder of his life, and his appointment to it by Ferdinand was the highest proof of the estimation in which he was held by that monarch that could have been bestowed upon him.

Great excitement in Spain, and extensive emigration.

In order fully to appreciate the weighty responsibility which rested upon him, the great excitement which existed in relation to the newly-discovered continent must be duly estimated. Never before in Spain had the furor for navigation and nautical enterprise been so extended. Day after day fortunate adventurers returned from the Indies with immense wealth suddenly acquired by the discovery of hidden hoards of some of the unresisting natives, and roused the cupidity of their friends and neighbours, by glowing accounts of riches which their own success seemed to prove substantial. The fever of emigration was hourly increasing, and rose at last to such an extent, that in Seville, where Americus established his permanent residence, it was said that few persons were to be seen, save women and young children. On the countermanding of an expedition, which the king had proposed to send to Italy in the year 1512, about three thousand of the cavaliers, who were to have accompanied it, proceeded to Seville and made eager application for service in a fleet then preparing for America, although the ful complement of men to

CHAPTER XVII.

be employed in it was only about half the number of the applicants.[1]

Death of Americus, February 22d, 1512.

Nothing now remains but to record the death of him whose life and writings have occupied the foregoing pages. This event took place at Seville on the 22d day of February, in the year 1512.[2] No account of his last sickness has been preserved. The date and the place of his decease have, until recently, been subjects of discussion, and these have been determined only from the musty files of receipts in the Spanish archives, and from the warrant of the crown appointing his successor. The place of his burial is not certainly known. Vague accounts are current in his native country, that his remains were transported to Italy, and now rest in the tomb of his ancestors, in the church of Ogni Santi in Florence, but they do not carry with them the stamp of authenticity.

After his appointment to the office of chief pilot he made a short visit to Florence, and the portrait of him by Bronzino, taken unquestionably towards the end of his life, is said to have been painted in that city. It has always been preserved as a sacred relic by the Vespucci family, and its authenticity seems never to have been called in question.

[1] Prescott, vol. iii. chap. xxiv.

[2] Navarréte, tom. iii. p 324.

CHAPTER XVIII.

CHARACTER AND WRITINGS OF AMERICUS.

His simplicity.

In perusing the writings and following the history of Americus, one cannot fail to be struck with the modest simplicity and truthfulness of his character. It is difficult to conceive how any one can read his letters, and rise from the reading with any other conviction, than that the writer was actuated by a sincere desire to instruct his correspondents, and furnish them with accurate information. Rarely alluding to his own position of danger and suffering, or of honourable renown, the reader has cause for regret in the very modesty which restrains his pen. He seldom separates himself from his companions, and when enterprise and courageous bearing is his theme, freely admits all to a share of the credit. When occasion offers he particularizes, and brings out in bold relief the virtues and bravery of others, but never his own. If an idea occurs to his mind which emanated from the brain of another, he never fails to give due reference. It has been seen that no petty feelings of jealousy restrained him from acknowledging what is owing to Columbus, for he speaks of his previous discoveries without reserve. He excuses his own deficiency, and

His justice to others.

CHAPTER XVIII.

deprecates a harsh judgment of his writings, recommending that they be read in "more leisure hours," and as a pastime, rather than for improvement.

Repose of character.

In Americus, the historian does not find any of those brilliant combinations of good and bad qualities, which so often dazzle the mind, and produce a false estimate of character. He was not an enthusiast, and never allowed himself to be carried beyond the bounds which reason indicated. He was rather inclined to a philosophical scepticism, ever seeking to detect fallacies with the view of firmly establishing truth.

Patience and forbearance.

The patience and forbearance of his character are no less observable than his simplicity and modesty. "But one word," says Canovai, "did he allow to enter his letters, wherein, though without any indication of resentment or bitterness, he complains of discourteous behaviour towards him."[1] No hasty ebullitions of temper marked the occurrence of disappointment or reverse. He was always calm and persevering.

A proper ambition.

He was ambitious, but with a proper ambition. To acquire an honourable name, which should be the comfort and solace of his old age, was his great aim. It has already been shown, that he could not have endeavoured to perpetuate his fame by the fraudulent method of giving his name to the New World, nor did he seek to do so by undervaluing his associates. His was an ambition which did not lead

[1] Canovai, vol. ii. p. 110.

men to fear or oppose him, and his quiet and unobtrusive manners made him friends even among his rivals.

His lofty enterprise.

He was enterprising, but that was a quality of the age in which he lived. There is this difference, however, in the enterprise of Americus and that of most of those by whom he was surrounded. These laboured for their own good, to recruit their own broken fortunes, or to increase wealth already acquired; he, for advancement of knowledge and science, for the good of the whole human race. He was conscientious. The rights of all were respected by him, according to the notions of the age in which he lived. His scrupulous regard of the property of the helpless and unprotected Indians is manifest in his writings. It is true that the vessels of his expeditions brought home slave-prisoners, but they were taken in fight, and after some atrocious treachery; and conformably to the doctrines then in vogue, the right to do this was undoubted, for all who did not believe in the Christian religion were held to be destitute of natural rights, and the enslaving of the Indians was openly countenanced by the government.

He was a warm admirer of nature. The beauty of the foliage in the new lands which he visited, and the melody of the numerous birds which sang among the branches, never failed to attract his attention and elicit expressions of admiration.

He was full of affectionate feelings for his family, as his care and attention to the education and ad-

CHAPTER XVIII.

vancement of his nephew, and his memory of his relatives in Florence, from whom he had been so long absent, amply testify.

His religious sentiments and character.

Lastly, he was deeply imbued with religious sentiment of the truest and most lasting character. Never did he permit himself to forget the Supreme Being who guarded him in his wanderings, or fail to give thanks for the great mercies received at his hands. Possessed of too philosophical a mind to adopt as truth all that the visionary fanaticism of the age incorporated in the belief of the Christian, yet he never ceased to acknowledge the immediate supervision of Almighty Power; and though passing over, in his accounts, with comparative neglect, the useless vows of pilgrimages and other ceremonies which the superstitious sailors of his fleet were accustomed to make and perform, on the occurrence of a tempest, he enlarges upon his gratitude to the true source of deliverance from danger.

It is a comparatively easy task to place the portraiture of the character of a celebrated man in such a light, that only the brightest portion may be visible, while all the darker points are concealed. The effect of this would be to show a fair but deceptive picture, and such may seem to be the present effort. For although disposed to admit that many faults might have existed in the character of Americus (what mortal is without them?), yet the records of history mention them not, and to the present age they are or should be as if they were not.

His works.

It would be almost as unfair to subject the writings of Americus to the critical tests of the present day as to judge of his character by the partial and disingenuous accounts of prejudiced historians. Few, besides his own countrymen, have read his letters with unbiased minds, and some of those who condemn him most loudly, have probably never read them at all. He who peruses them in the expectation of finding passages of elegant diction, or a blood-stirring narrative of danger and adventure, will meet with total disappointment. They are quiet and unassuming descriptions of what appeared new and strange to him, in simple language, though at times quaint and forcible. Plain and unvarnished statements throughout, they were evidently written by one who, knowing his own integrity, felt confident of due credence from others.

Like all men who live in times of general agitation, when society is passing through radical changes, the great navigator experienced his share of disappointments and reverses. Those men who are chosen by Providence to bring about important events, and lead nations on to brilliant achievements, generally become familiar with trouble—for those names that must live always in the regards and recollections of mankind, are not easily won. But Americus may justly be considered a fortunate man, whatever may have been his reverses. No conqueror, however celebrated, no philosopher, however wise, has yet received, or ever will receive, so bright a reward. No shade obscures his character, no accident can effect his fame—his name is borne by a great continent, and will be transmitted to the last moment of time.

END OF PART I.

PART II.

ILLUSTRATIONS.

EULOGIUM

OF

AMERICUS VESPUCIUS,

WHICH OBTAINED THE PREMIUM

FROM THE NOBLE ETRUSCAN ACADEMY OF CORTONA,

ON THE 15th OF OCTOBER, IN THE YEAR 1788.

LETTER

Of the Etruscan Academy of Cortona, to Count John Louis of Durfort, then Minister Plenipotentiary of France to the Royal Court of Tuscany, accompanying the Premium Eulogy.

LETTER

AFTER the respected judgment of six censors, no less impartial than enlightened, here at last is that eulogy of Americus Vespucius, which your Excellency perhaps contemplated, when, with an incomparable proof of intelligence and generosity, you condescended to remit to the Academy your interesting proposal for it, and the noble premium. The author, who appears to have chosen for his model the celebrated Isocrates, knew so well how to convert to his advantage, and combine intimately in his theme, the various questions proposed to the candidates, that the Grecian orator would perhaps be astonished to see himself imitated, even in the skilful digression where he passes with so much grace from the praises of Evagoras to the deeds of the Athenian Conon. The proposition of your Excellency will be, therefore, a memorable circumstance in the exhibitions of the Etruscan Academy, and might also become a glorious epoch in Tuscany, if the example, so new and so enlightened, should become known in all quarters, and make us feel that the true love of letters is a magnanimous, ardent, and efficacious love, and that admiration of great men is one of the few means of eventually acquiring greatness. France alone, that genial realm, fruitful alike in characters worthy of eulogium, and in literary men capable of appreciating them, has renewed in her academies, in our day, the ancient custom of eulogizing her heroes, with a sublimity equal to their merits. Though the renowned Linguet, perhaps too great a friend of paradoxes, imagined that there was something intrinsically and essentially vitiated in this kind of eloquence, his wise compatriots have well decided that it is better to suffer some abuse of it, than to lose its manifest advantages by a heedless proscription. While therefore Tuscan writers are indebted to your Excellency for this happy opportunity of exercising their powers in a department of oratory so dear to the ancients, and which ought not to be lost to our literature, we shall be eternally grateful to you, that we were selected by your judgment for the fortunate duty of searching out merit, and nobly rewarding it.

EULOGIUM.

——— agit grates, peregrinæque oscula Terræ
Figit, et ignotos montes agrosque salutat.
Ovid, Met. iii. v. 14.

It has been said in olden times, that no eulogium could compare with an illustrious name, and that no words could add to the fame and glory of any one whose name alone was insufficient. But (it must be confessed) that these pompous dicta, which eloquence lavishes so freely, are of no substantial worth, and while thus attempting to express with emphasis an appreciation of merit, and the impossibility of praising it sufficiently, would establish the nothingness and inutility of all praise.[1]

EULOGIUM.

[1] Here we have in view the inscriptions on the monuments of two celebrated secretaries of the Florentine Republic. One reads thus, under the bust of Marcellus Virgilius: "Suprema nomen hoc loco tantum voluntas jusserat Poni sed hanc statuam pius erexit heres nescius famæ futurum et gloriæ. Aut nomen aut nihil satis." The other was placed on the tomb of Niccolo Machiavelli. "Tanto nomini nullum par eulogium." If there could be no eulogium proportionate to the merits of a great man, it is useless to make any whatever, and all praise will be reserved for mediocrity. What an absurdity! This is the true eulogy inscribed to Machiavelli.

The scribe of Florence,
Whose subtle wit discharged a dubious shaft,
Called both the friend and foe of kingly craft.
Tho', in his maze of politics perplext,
Great names have differed on that doubtful text:
Here, crowned with praise, as true to virtue's side,
There, viewed with horror, as the assassin's guide:
High in a purer sphere, he shines afar,
And hist'ry hails him as her morning star.
Hayley, Essay on History, Epist. ii. v. 186.

EULOGIUM.

Praise, the aliment of genius.

Fortunately, it is well known that orators are accustomed to use such apothegms, which rarely influence those who are seeking after truth. What would become of the fine arts, literature, and science, if, acting on this false principle, posterity should neglect to bestow encomiums upon their distinguished cultivators? Praise is the natural aliment of genius, and though unheeded by the mouldering ashes of heroes, at least encourages the imitator of their glorious deeds. Let it be remembered that the great man does not descend wholly into the tomb; he soars immortal upon the untiring wings of fame. He erects for himself a trophy in his great exploits, which neither the ravages of time can deface, nor the mist of oblivion obscure. Let us figure to ourselves in the distance, a hundred nations yet unborn, repeating his name with admiration, celebrating his discoveries with applause, possessing themselves of what is good and true by the infallible guide of his instructions. Such delightful hopes not only wiped the tears and the sweat of labour from the countenances of the valiant Athletæ, but forcibly counteracted the spells of all the malignant spirits which enhanced the difficulties of their enterprises.[1] The germs of greatness are enveloped in the minds of those who are warmed with the love of glory.

There is a manifest connection between pub-

[1] Ceteros ad sapientiæ studium laudibus aliorum propositis exhortamur, ut earum laudum accumulatione incitati, earundem etiam virtutum desiderio inflammentur —*Isocr. Evag.*

lic praise and public happiness.[1] Egypt knew this; Greece was not unmindful of it; all those nations which best understood the economy of the human heart, ever had fortunate experience of it. Ah! whence comes it, that the noble example wants emulators among us, that the shades of our most noble citizens wander about without panegyrists and without eulogium?[2] Ought it to have been expected that a generous foreigner, realizing the sublime idea of perfect patriotism,[3] would come from the banks of the Seine, to awaken our indolent eloquence, and compassionately arouse it to revive the languishing memory of Americus? Senseless Syracusans! thus, perchance, came the great Tully from the Tiber to show you the tomb of the forgotten Archimides.[4]

EULOGIUM.

We accept an invitation which at the same time honours and condemns us. We praise the intrepid navigator, the unwearied discoverer of extensive territories, the noble Tuscan who wandered through

[1] Hoc genus (orationis) tam Græcis quam Romanis usitatum fuit, sumpta, ut opinor, consuetudine ab Ægyptis. Harum finis fuit ut et bene meritis de republica viris honore laudationum aliqua gratia referretur, et adolescentes cupiditate laudis incitati ad virtutem accenderentur.—*Wolf. in Isocr. Evag.*

[2] We have, under the name of eulogy, the lives of many illustrious Tuscans, but the eulogies here referred to are very different om these lives.

[3] Le Patriotisme le plus parfait est celui qu'on possède quand'on est si bien rempli des droits du Genre humain, qu'on les respecte vis-à-vis de tous les peuples du monde.—*Encycl. art. Patriotisme.*

[4] Cicero himself narrates his famous antiquarian discovery, and concludes thus: "Ita nobilissima Græciæ civitas, quondam vero etiam doctissime, sui civis unius monumentum ignorasset, nisi ab homine Arpinate didicisset."—*Tusc. Quæst.* l. 5. c. 23.

EULOGIUM.

the boundless extent of the other hemisphere, and left his name impressed upon it forever. If a vile jealousy has attempted to snatch from his brow the well-merited crown; if a partial history has robbed him of the credit due to his signal enterprise by its malicious silence; if a misguided criticism has unfortunately depreciated his merits and defamed his candour, future ages will see his character in clearer light, and bestowing their just homage of admiration and encomium, will free him from the combined aspersions of his enemies, and cover his cruel adversaries with detestation.

The youth of Americus.

To deny an infancy to an extraordinary man, and gravely pronounce that he was a wonder from the very cradle, would be to fabricate, in imitation of the poets, a fabulous Hercules.[1] To investigate the little anecdotes of this infancy, and dwell at length upon its gradual development, would be but to gratify a puerile curiosity. No, you do not think that Americus was born a prodigy, and came thus into my hands, or that I would wish to follow

[1] Hercules, while yet in swaddling clothes, strangled, according to the poets, two large serpents which Juno had sent to destroy him. But it is so uncommon or unnecessary for great men to begin by being great in boyhood, that the infancy of the greater number of them has remained altogether in obscurity. I only remember, at present, having read something of the kind respecting Pascal, and the following is what is said of him.

"At the age of twelve years he had," they say, "by the force of his genius alone, and without books, mastered the thirty-second proposition of the first book of Euclid. The reader may think what he pleases of it—for my part, I incline to the opinion of Baillet, who was reprimanded by some partisans of Pascal for having doubted this feature of his life. I shall not dissemble, that I suspect it very much of being exaggerated."—*Hist. de Mathém.* t. ii. p. 53.

the feeble footsteps of his early boyhood. When the energy of his mind called from chaos an entire half of the globe, and, almost as if by magic enchantment, spread existence over the vast ocean, it is of slight importance to enquire what went before, or whence he derived his power. Conjecture, therefore, if you please; proportion the means to the result; unite to the most fervid imagination the most scrupulously strict reasoning, the possession of subtle theories to the free use of complicated instruments, uninterrupted study of the planets and stars to accurate knowledge of continents and seas, the valour of the soldier to the prudence of the mariner, the bustling life of the voyager to the solitude of the philosopher, the skill of the merchant to the honour of the citizen, sense to genius, modesty to elevation, vigour to sensibility, boldness to religion, and then, perchance, you will then have a sketch of the sublime qualities and enviable character of Americus.

With such vast endowments as these a man becomes as it were omnipotent. He projects, and nothing is impossible; he wills, and all is done. A thousand secret combinations stand ever at his side, and with emulous rivalry offer him their aid. He manages them with such authority, and applies them to the work with so much rapidity, that the effect of penetration and inconceivable art often appears like the necessary result of natural causes. The soul from its unknown seat, the sun from the centre of its system, produce in no other manner

EULOGIUM. the wonderful motions of the human machine, and the astonishing order of the universe.

The position of Americus.

But where shall we find a place for Vespucius, and what position shall we assign to him, if Spain, his new residence, intoxicated with joy by rising hopes of immense riches and power, recognises no other genius, and commemorates no other name, than the incomparable genius and illustrious name of Columbus? We leave to prostituted pens the vile employment of insulting the great with false reproaches or false praises. I shall not make one of these two the victim of the other. I should know how to weave a eulogium for Newton,[1] without injury to Leibnitz, and I shall speak of Vespucius without detracting from the fame of the Italian Admiral. He has already burst the confines of the Old World; he has already pushed with a noble daring among the virgin waves of a yet nameless sea,[2] and St. Lucia, Antilla, Cuba, Jamaica, and Hispaniola[3] have become the rewards of his

1 It is known that a serious debate arose between Newton and Leibnitz, about the first inventor of the differential and integral calculus, on which Montucla thus pronounces: "Newton had found the principle of fluxions before Leibnitz, but too obscurely to deprive the latter of the merit of the discovery."—*Hist. des Math.* t. H. p. 334. Americus discovered the continent before Columbus, and did not find it at all obscurely.

2 Columbus himself called this sea the North Sea, though not very appropriately.—*Hist. de l'Acad. des Scien., an* 1753, p. 119.

3 Cuba, Jamaica, and Hispaniola are confounded by some geographers with the Antilles, which are more than six hundred miles distant from them.—*Ramus.* t. iii. p. 71. c. This confusion, however, was received by the modern author of the art. 'America," in the Encyclopedia, a century after Columbus and Vespucius.—See *Dissertazione Giustificativa.*

wonderful expedition—vast and fruitful islands, where the greedy European trampled for the first time upon gems and gold, forgetting the famous countries of the Ganges and Cathay. The shout of important conquests ascends from the Mexican Archipelago; nations and kingdoms of long standing are shaken; commerce joyously contemplates her reviving youth;[1] all eyes are fixed upon the leader of the exalted enterprise: he enters Barcelona with more pomp than the Roman Capitol witnessed in other ages at the return of an Emperor in triumph. At this, Vespucius becomes thoughtful, and absorbed in burning meditation. The trophies of Miltiades[2] disturb the dreams of Themistocles, and the repeated announcement of his father's victories dissolves in sighs the magnanimous heart of

EULOGIUM.

[1] A few days before the third edition of this eulogium was issued, I read the work of Genty, entitled "The Influence of the Discovery of America on the Happiness of the Human Race." He repeats many times the truth which is here hinted at; but two quotations must suffice. "The rich productions of the mines of Peru must multiply our relations with the East, and of necessity furnish more abundant aliment for the foreign commerce of Europe (p. 209). The conquest of the New World started commerce from infancy, and gave it wings to soar over the whole universe" (p. 290). I agree, therefore, with the illustrious Genty, not only in his opinion, but also in the figures with which he illustrates it. I shall not fail to quote parallel passages as they occur, which will show the unexpected correspondence of my sentiments with those of so celebrated an author.

[2] It is said that Themistocles was so carried away with a love for glory, that, at the time the barbarians were conquered at Marathon, and when the glory of Miltiades was every where celebrated, although yet a youth, he withdrew by himself, and indulged in nocturnal vigils; and, on being asked the reason, by those who wondered at his conduct, replied that the trophies of Miltiades deprived him of sleep.—*Plutarch. Themistocles.*

EULOGIUM.

Alexander. Ah! there are no more countries for me![1] this terrible despot of the ocean sees and ravishes all. Though I might excel him in daring, yet how can I equal him in fortune and glory?

The spirit of emulation and its effects.

Behold the transports of that lively emulation which springs from the indisputable consciousness of talents, and is nourished by the pure and delicate essence of virtue, which shines uncontaminated in every footstep of the hero! It seems enmity, but is laudable strife; it seems envy, but is a generous ambition. If Columbus had found enemies and rivals resembling Americus, I should not see, as now, the magnificent scene of his triumph so suddenly changed into mourning and horror, the gloomy night of ignominy and mockery succeed the brief light of ephemeral happiness, and that invincible leader who redoubled the power and dominions of ungrateful Castile, groaning under the weight of infamous chains, while he asks for nothing but liberty to carry her arms to the most distant shores of the West. Go now, and turning away your eyes from the atrocious metamorphosis, exclaim, it is chance,—it is fate,—arbitrary sounds and sterile syllables, with which no distinct idea can ever be associated. Alas! are not there imperceptible threads by which a regulating hand guides us through a crooked labyrinth from causes to effects, and prepares in silence

1 Often, when the capture of a noble city or a victory in a memorable battle, by Philip, was announced, Alexander did not seem much rejoiced, but said to his playfellows, "My father is conquering every thing, so that there will remain no great and brilliant exploits for me to accomplish."—*Plutarch. Alexander.*

the events of the universe? Prostrated by implacable vengeance, and despoiled of the exclusive right to discoveries and honours,[1] Columbus pines in inaction, but no new columns of Hercules,[2] beyond which the pilot dares not pass, stand erect before the shores of Mexico. Americus reunites the web of fortunate events. Americus succeeds Columbus.

The eulogist imagines an address to Americus.

At that period might some one have said to him, 'Pause, illustrious Vespucius, and before two worlds, astonished at each other, are united by your means, penetrate with me, for a few moments, the shadows of the future, and observe the memorable results of the union. What merchandise, what treasures to Europe! What rare industry in the arts, what new sublimity in the sciences! The uncertainty of the heavens, the strange laws of the sea, the unknown form of the terrestrial globe, the peculiar formation of mountains and rivers, the hidden virtues of minerals, of vegetables, of animals, all are determined, all are turned to usefulness or pleasure in life. There is not a single corner where the fortunate influence of your discoveries is not felt.[3]

[1] This exclusive right, which is asserted by various historians (*Rob.* v. i. p. 95), does not appear in the contract between Columbus and the Spanish monarchs. It is, however, reported so in the *Hist. Gen. des Voyag.*, t. xlv. p. 17, and by Robertson himself. *Ib.* p. 155.

[2] The twelfth labour of Hercules was, according to Mythologists, to go to the two mountains, Abila and Calpe, and separate them, so as to introduce the ocean into the Mediterranean. Therefore, the two heights which overlook the Strait of Gibraltar are called the Pillars of Hercules. It was said that he dared not pass them, and that they were to serve forever as limits to all navigators. It is known, however, that the Tyrians, Hanno, the Carthagenian, and afterwards many others, passed these limits.

[3] Genty agrees with me. "The

EULOGIUM. What did I say? the Mediterranean and the North Sea are too contracted in space for the new tribute which pours into them. The immense plenitude inundates Africa and Asia. Political society is raised to the highest point of elevation, and the country discovered by you, furnishes an equilibrium to the boasted power of the other hemisphere. But, alas! if this splendid picture is so seductive with its bright prospects of benefit, and so dazzling to your vision, in what colours shall I paint to you the funereal spectacle of innumerable wrongs? You will find there unknown regions of gold; the rocks are rich with it; the sands glitter with it; nature xhibits her richest stores. Inauspicious stores of lamentation and desolation! A vast multitude of hungry adventurers hasten from all quarters. Attracted by the glitter of the dangerous metal, they abandon their ancient seats. Europe sends masters there; Africa, slaves. They are disputed at every step, they are combated on every shore. Some are the prey of the waves, others of fire and sword; many, of a foreign climate ruinous to health; many of an unknown pestilence which devours them, and without peopling the continent which they seek, that which they leave remains desolate and desert-

conquest of the New World extended the domain of the arts and sciences, furnishing them with materials and instruments, and opening to genius a career more vast and more brilliant. It contributed, above all, to perfect natural history, botany, geography, navigation, and astronomy. It brought us the Quinquina; it called us to share in all the productions of nature, and procured us more numerous and more varied enjoyments" (p. 289, 290).

EULOGIUM.

ed.[1] This may be the punishment of their covetousness and debauchery. This may be the punishment of those who hoped to find a peculiar sky, where Nature spoke not with her accustomed language, and where the brutality of their desires might be gratified to its fullest extent. In what have those unfortunate beings sinned, those freemen whom they bind with fetters in their tranquil huts?[2] Can you convince yourself that you have

1 Such is exactly the view of Genty. "It (the conquest of the New World) should have softened the manners of the Europeans, and inclined them to beneficence; but it rendered them more cruel and pitiless.

It should have exalted the dignity of man, and taught him the nobility of his origin; it only swelled the hearts of some despots, and furnished them with new means to oppress and degrade the human species. It ought to have enriched Europe, and it covered it with mourning, and rendered it, so to speak, deserted and miserable (p. 289). The Spaniards made deserts in America, and rendered their own country more than a desert.—*Montesq. Lett.—Persan. Lett.* 121. Since the devastation of America, the Spaniards, who have taken the place of the ancient inhabitants, have not been able to re-people it; on the contrary, the destroyers are destroying themselves, and are being consumed every day."—*Id.*

2 There are ten titles, according to Solorzano (*de Indiarum Jure*, t. i.), which give to Spain the right over America. The gift of God, confirmed by prophecies and prodigies; impulse and Divine inspiration; discovery and occupation; the barbarous customs of the Indians; their infidelity; their sins; the preaching and propagation of Christianity; the obligation of listening to the faith; the power of the Roman Emperor to overcome the infidels; and the donation of the pope. Let every one judge of the solidity of such titles at his pleasure. To me, they seem more evtravagant than all the rights seriously proclaimed by Gonzalo d'Oviedo. "Now, as Spain and Italy took their names from Hesperio XII., King of Spain, so, also, should these islands take it, which we call Hesperides. Hence, without doubt, it may be considered, that in that time these islands were under the dominion of Spain, and under the same king, which was (as Beroso says) 1658 years before our Saviour was born, and because, at present, we are in the year of grace, 1535, it follows that it is now 3093 years since Spain and

EULOGIUM. imaginary rights in Atalanta and the Hesperides, and with the same thought fancy that a man without clothing and without a yoke, merits not the name of man?[1] Oh God! the basest sycophancy has fabricated those monstrous pretensions, in behalf of powerful injustice.[2] Reason blushes at them; humanity shudders at them.[3] The thirst for gold awakens the thirst for blood. Like those cruel persons, who kill the innocent bee in order to become masters of its sweet treasure, we signalize our violation with murder, and bearing fire and the sword in our hands, more cruel than wolves, more barbarous than tigers, mangle a terrified and unarmed herd, that we may reign over a huge mass

its Hesperus exercised dominion over these Indies or islands of Hesperides. On account of this ancient jurisdiction, and judging by the manner in which it has been given, which will be stated hereafter, God has returned this dominion to Spain again, after so many centuries; and it appears that Divine justice wished to return it to her, that she might possess it perpetually, through the good fortune of her two happy and Catholic monarchs.—*Ramusio*, t. iii. p. 65.

[1] Americus relates, that the men seen by him all were naked, and that they have neither king nor lord; that they obeyed no one, and could neither be called Moors nor Jews.

[2] Listen to Genty, who thus begins his second question: "Must this too celebrated revolution be described, which will make all future generations blush with shame and indignation? Must these revolting scenes be painted, these numerous massacres, where all that was most atrocious in barbarity, all that was most hideous in avarice and cowardice, was put in operation against timid and defenceless nations? Must the long chain of crimes, perfidy, and oppression be retraced, which blotted out whole nations from the face of the earth?" p. 33.

[3] The reply of Cortez to the ministers of Montezuma, who boasted of the treasures and the power of their country, is reported by Raynal, t. vi. p. 64. "Behold exactly what we are seeking after—great dangers and great riches." Perhaps the Spanish general had learned this language from the pirates of Tunis or Algiers.

EULOGIUM.

of dead bodies and gold. The lacerated remnants of the horrid carnage howl with mournful clamour, fly among the mountain precipices, conceal themselves in inaccessible forests, and their country, covered with blood and tears, offers nothing to its unhappy children, but a sacrilegious altar with thirty millions of men wickedly immolated to the idol of avarice.[1]

The doubts and decision of Americus.

Whoever, at that juncture, had pourtrayed to Vespucius this double series of events, would, perchance, have induced him to change his determination. His heart, so prone to emotion, his spirit so penetrating and so just, his noble disinterestedness, his scrupulous delicacy, would have united to dissuade him from a voyage, the manifest ambiguity of the event of which might destroy so large a portion of its glory. But very different thoughts were revolving in his mind. Anxious to make known to the world the superiority of the science and nautical skill which had been his for a long time, he listens only to the voice of honour, which calls him, and directing his course to the West, leaves to the enlightened philosopher the task of determining the character of his labours. Difficult judgment! which seems tacitly to constrain to the intricate examination of primitive causes, and to odious com-

1 Thomas, Eloge de Dugay-Trouin. "Taking the calculation of the furious Carvajal, 1500 Spaniards were sufficient to slaughter thirty millions of men. This monster boasted, at his death, of having killed twenty thousand Americans, besides fourteen hundred of his own nation, with his own hand."—*Raynal*, tom. vii. p. 58, with whom Gomara does not disagree, except in the words "with his own hand."—*Cap*. 186, p. 259.

EULOGIUM. parison between the private prosperity of a state, and the public interest of the human race. Tell me, indeed, whether navigation is an absolute advantage, or fix, at least, the relation between its advantages and disadvantages. Tell me if it is possible to find any universal measure of good, or any rules by which to estimate in exact proportion, and by a common criterion, physical, political, and moral benefits. Tell me whether all men belong to the same family, or define to which of the many families of men a preference is due, and I will soon designate to you the proper estimate of the maritime deeds of Americus. If, in the absence of proper data, I declare these general problems insoluble, do not be astonished that a question which is connected with them by such bonds, and is of such manifest affinity, should remain undecided.[1]

The advantages and disadvantages of the discovery of Americus.

It happens sometimes, however, that an aggregate of facts and peculiar analogies authorizes a general conclusion, or it may be that compassion, tender and beautiful virtue, inborn with man, inclines the spirit to favour the oppressed, and the important judgment may seem to you already pronounced. At the horrid sight of the carnage, the pretended advantages sink into insignificance. The warm invectives of the philosopher are united with

1 The work of Genty considers the present question exactly, and has an exposition of it much better than any thing that can be given in a eulogium. It ought to be spoken of here, but however advantageous for me the accordance of my opinions with those of Genty may be, it will be easily seen, that a longer discussion of the point would have been quite foreign to my subject.

BURNING A HUT AND EIGHT WARRIORS.

Eight of the bravest Indian warriors threw themselves into a hut, whence they discharged such showers of arrows that for a time the hardiest of the assailants were kept at bay. At last, fire was applied to the hut, which in an instant was in a blaze, and the eight warriors perished in the flames. (SEE P. 381.)

EULOGIUM.

the eloquent tears of the ignorant, and that fatal art is deplored, which, in spite of a visible prohibition of Providence, showed the way to the unlucky shores of the New World. I would not mask the truth, in order to secure fame to Vespucius. Sincerity of intention, and the impossibility of foretelling the future, justify him sufficiently. But if all the great elements of the question are considered, how shall the decision be given with judgment and equity? Has the culture of those wild and savage nations ever been estimated? Has the price of religion ever been calculated? Yet these benefits hold a rank so elevated, and offer rewards so certain to the feeble nature of man, that the dubious light of every other good is obscured in comparison; they are competent even to soften anguish, calm terror, enlarge the mind, and spread oblivion over the barbarity of conquerors, and the wickedness of tyrants. It is a crime, I do not deny it, it is the blackest of all crimes, to change the institutions of religion into sanguinary instruments of death, and reduce a desperate people to execrate those revelations and that God, to whom they ought to give themselves up with gratitude and transport. But these revelations are adopted, and that God is worshipped now in America.[1] Forget

[1] It has been said that this intelligence is producing its effects. But it will be seen in the course of this eulogium, that it could not be throughout America, and neither so soon nor so easily developed. These ideas are presented by Genty: "Nature," he says, "and philosophy will unite their voices to applaud these happy changes, to prepare them, and understand their effects. Religion

EULOGIUM. all evils in the presence of one good so incomparable;[1] and since these were the pure designs of the eager Voyager,[2] in whom neither covetousness nor fanaticism ever fostered the cruelty of a Cortez,[3] a Pizarro, or an Almagro, let him disembark tranquilly upon the shores of that strange land, and greet in peace their unknown mountains and untrodden fields.[4]

will continue to invite the savages to a participation in its mysteries. It will conquer them by its tender exhortations, it will soften their hearts by its promises and its consoling dogmas—it will make men of them."—P. 321.

1 Thus is the first question decided—The advantages and disadvantages of the discovery of America, as proposed in the programme of the Etruscan Academy. It was raised, not with regard to Europe only, but without any limitation, and it was necessary, therefore, to reply to it in full.

2 Not only was Americus eager to inculcate in the minds of the savages religion and morality, but he was also so happy as to succeed in it. "In this country (in Paria, that is), we established baptismal fonts, and a great number of people were baptized. They called us in their language, Carabi, which means men of great wisdom. We endeavoured many times to draw them into our opinions, and admonished them often, that they might finally be willing to abandon such an infamous custom as an abomination, and they promised us many times to abstain from such cruelty."

3 The moderation which Americus observed towards the savages was quite remarkable. "We took from them (from the traitors who had assaulted him) many things of little value, and we would not burn their houses, as it was a matter of conscience with us." "We resolved not to touch or take away any of their things, in order the better to assure them, and we left many of our things for them in the houses." "It was determined that since this people wished to be at enmity with us, we would have a conference with them, and do every thing to make them friends." "We discharged two guns at them (at those who had followed him shooting arrows), more to frighten than to do them injury." Americus was not, therefore, inferior to Cook, in an age which was not like the age of Cook; and though he was obliged to fight many times, it was to defend those savages who were his friends, or in his own defence.

4 " " Agit grates, peregrinæ que oscula Terræ
Figit, et ignotos montes agrosque salutat. " "

Thus speaks Ovid of Cadmus, who brought letters into Europe,

EULOGIUM.

Comparison of the tracks of Columbus and Americus.

The daring Columbus should first have landed here, had he intended to deprive others of the hope of surpassing him. Every effort is now vain, and whoever regards the discovery of the continent as a poor appendage to the discovery of the islands, militates with the truth, though he cannot wound the invulnerable glory of Americus; because the acute Archimides, because Wallis and Brouncker and Fermat approached closely the new analyses, it does not follow that the divine geometrician who courageously opened the formidable gates of infinity, and trod those perilous regions with a sure foot, has not eclipsed them. Newton found assistance in the labours of many great men. But there was nothing in common between the two navigators. Neither the line of the voyage, the conduct, nor the termination were similar. What an uncertain and tortuous circuit was that of Columbus, who from the Canaries returned to the south so far that he saw in the tropics the neighbouring heights of Cape Verd, and turning thence to the west and to the north, arrived at Guanahani! He roved nearly three years from island to island, and from coast to

and perhaps religion also, as Americus introduced religion and the first seeds of moral culture into America. The custom of rendering thanks to God at the sight of land was then general among navigators. "They set their feet on terra firma," writes Boccacio, "and saluted the neighbouring mountains," &c. Robertson also intimates it. "The crew of the Pinta sang the Te Deum, and those in the other vessels responded to it". . . ." The Spaniards who followed Columbus, fell on their knees and kissed the earth which they had so long desired to see." —*Hist. de l'Am.* t. i. p. 176, 177. Hear Americus himself: "Having seen the land, we gave thanks to God."

EULOGIUM. coast, and attracted by an invisible magnetism within the narrow circumference of past discoveries, never saw the boundless country which was laid temptingly before his face, and seemed to open its bosom, and invite him to repose upon it.[1] Americus, on the contrary, avoids the seas already known, shuns the islands already discovered,[2] does not propose to return to Europe by the way of Japan and China, and impelled by intelligence and genius, runs in thirty-seven days from the Fortunate Islands to the Oronoko. The spacious plains of Terra Firma, the curious little island of Venezuela, the pleasant forests of Paria,[3] present an inexhausti-

[1] Jamaica, Cuba, Hispaniola, and the other islands adjacent to the Gulf of Mexico, having been discovered, it might have been said that the gates of the New World were thrown wide open, and that nothing further remained to be done by the voyagers who followed Columbus, but to enter them. But I would ask, why did not Columbus enter Mexico through those gates which he himself had thrown wide open?

[2] It was only in his second voyage that Americus went to the islands of Antilla and Hispaniola, already discovered by Columbus.

[3] The land discovered by Vespucius in his second voyage was, according to his own account, continuous or contiguous to the land discovered in his first; therefore, if that of the second lies a little beyond the equator, in the southern hemisphere, it is reasonable to conclude that of the first to be near the line in the northern hemisphere: hence his "Lariab" is certainly "Paria," as in the Geography and Cosmography, Munster accurately translates it.—(*Geog. Tab. Nov. Ins. Cosmog.* p. 1109.) But it is not easy to understand how Lariab or Paria is located by Americus under the Tropic of Cancer, where New Galicia and Panuco are situated. From observing that Martiniere (V. Paria) does not recognize any province of this name further East in America, and that De l'Isle took it entirely from his charts, I suspected that in the first period of the discovery, this might have been the general denomination of America as then known; neither do I think I have been deceived, since Geraldini, Bishop of St. Domingo, wrote to Leo X., concerning that island which the unlearned call the continent of Asia, and others denominate America or Paria.—(*Can-*

ble harvest for his meditations, and give repose to the cosmographer to employ the philosopher. Neither is he satisfied with a passing and fugitive glance, but having measured once more the fourth part of the terrestrial perimeter,[1] sees again the shores with which he is enamoured, again explores vast and almost boundless tracts of territory, visits the northern shores,[2] where men of gigantic stature are found,[3] certain of bearing, as a tribute to covetous

cell. Diss. Sopra Crist. Colomb. p. 224.) It is certain that one map, as late as 1535, printed in Basle, places Paria in 24 or 25 degrees of south latitude (*Margar. Philos.* p. 1434); in the maps of Apianus, Grinæus and Munster, Paria is located in the environs of the equator; and in that of Villanovano, published in 1541, Paria is placed at 45 degrees of north latitude. Seventy degrees of latitude being thus included by different geographers, it is fair to conclude that all America was Paria; and perhaps for this reason Martyr says, "in the immense tracts of Paria" (*Dec.* ii., L. ix. p. 39.), and called the "Sea of Paria" the ocean which bathed the New World (*Majol. Dies. Canic.* p. 509). In fact, Vespucius himself testifies, that after having moved ten degrees from the equinoctial line, he continued to sail towards the north, and passed into a gulf which is called the Gulf of Paria. This is certain proof that Paria extended much beyond eight or nine degrees north latitude, to which, with evident error, others have been disposed to limit it, not knowing that New Castile and New Andalusia were two provinces of Paria, and that the six hundred leagues of coast, traversed by Pinçon, amounted to more than 36 degrees (*Ram.* t. iii. p. 13. B. p. 23. B).

[1] Americus was more than 52 degrees distant from Cadiz; hence he had passed over nearly the fourth part of the terrestrial circuit.

[2] "We resolved to turn our course to the northwest," says Americus. "We determined to sail to the northern parts; we changed our navigation towards the north." In fact, Venezuela, which Americus arrived at, is changed to Tramontana, and from the particular position of the ocean in that place, Columbus took the occasion to call it the North Sea, as I have said in another place.

[3] Various writers think these giants were Patagonians, which would carry Americus towards the land of Magellan, at the south, while in fact he went to the north. It appears that similar gigantic persons inhabited Yucatan, as Solorzano observed, on the au-

EULOGIUM.

Spain, three thousand miles of continent. His companions were astonished, and with ravenous eyes viewed the rich ear-rings and jewelled necklaces of the naked Indians.[1] He admired their proportions, studied their language, considered their customs, and softened by the complaints and grievances of these friendly hosts, turned his sword against the deadly cannibals, who tore them in pieces to satiate their hunger.

Cosmographical calculations of Americus.

Meanwhile, abandoned cosmography recalls him, and at her imperious nod, Americus retraces his footsteps, and reasons with himself. Where am I? in what part of the globe? at what distance from Calpe? Physical wonders are redoubled every moment. The pole that was elevated so lucidly above the horizon, is now sunk in the abyss of the ocean. That zone which inexperienced philosophers declared fatal to respiration and to life, contains within its beautiful boundaries an innumerable multitude of inhabitants. Perhaps I am now at the antipode of the Tartar or the Chinese. Will my story be credited in Europe, if the new Eden through which I wander[2] should be lost, like

thority of Herrera.—*De Ind. Jur.* l. i. c. 10, n. 54. These and many similar accounts of the early navigators have proved to be exaggerations.—*Trans.*

[1] The Spaniards, greedy for riches, were never sensible of the beauties and charms of the lovely climates of America. Like the Mammon of Milton, who, forgetting every delight in Heaven, always kept his eyes fixed on the golden pavement.—*Raynal*, t. vi. p. 70. Americus very cautiously observes, "The navigation has been very profitable, which is now a matter of high consideration, and particularly in this kingdom, where inordinate covetousness prevails."

[2] The idea of having found in America a terrestrial paradise,

EULOGIUM.

the old, in the immensity of space? Many times the setting sun left him pondering upon these grave considerations, and many times surprised him deeply absorbed in them when it rose. To discover in the Antarctic heavens a motionless star, to guide the pilot through the regions of the South, and from the various intersections of the meridians with the equator,[1] to determine both the position of the country, and the extent of the voyage—this was the double knot, to unravel which, Americus devoted the silent night. It was more a matter pertaining to his glory, than a thing absolutely essential to designate in the firmament the opposite pole; but to secure the honour of having trodden unknown countries for the first time, it was indispensable to be able to show the way to them again. Meanwhile, an exact determination of the geographical longitudes, may contend in point of difficulty with the discovery of a continent. What did not the old philosophers do, what had not more recent ones attempted, to solve the contumacious problem? Despairing of solving it by the too

was common to Columbus and Americus; but while Columbus spoke of it with gross fanaticism, (*Hist. Gen. des Voyag.*, t. xlv. p. 219), Americus treated the idea with a sobriety and a delicacy which do honour to his good sense. "The trees are so beautiful and so odoriferous, that we seem to be in a terrestrial paradise." "If there be a terrestrial paradise on earth, doubtless it cannot be far from these regions."

[1] Imagining every point of the globe cut by a meridian, and taking for the first any point whatever, as that of Paris, the distance of this from others, counted upon the equator, is called longitude. Thus the meridian of Florence cuts the equator at 8 degrees, 56 minutes, 59 seconds east; that of London, at 2 degrees, 5 minutes, 9 seconds west; and this difference of the two meridians, in crossing the

EULOGIUM.

feeble aid of latitude and the rhombi,[1] they brought to bear upon it the boldest computations, they invested it with the most formidable analyses, and reduced it almost to a surrender by their experiments with a hundred orreries.[2] What then? Their fruitless exertions left them finally to learn from Vespucius the art of subduing the rebel. His inventive genius pursues the question through the two tropics;[3] he watches; he meditates; he reasons. It may be said, that abstruse formulas and imperfect instruments were impediments to his career. He notes the moment of an astronomical conjunction, proceeds at once to the determination of the longitude, and either the tables to which he recurs, or the instruments he employs, lie. But he is the possessor of the secret; his method is certain; no one knew it before Americus, no one has abandoned it since.[4] Well may all the discourteous forgetfulness of men vanish, because this original method which the ingenious European brought forth for the first time under a savage sky, and employed for the first time in fixing its geographical character, does not appear in the first place in the American memorials of Astronomy—the inestimable anticipated fruit of the civilized hemisphere.

Rejoicings at Florence in consequence of the discoveries of Americus.

Fortunate Florence rejoiced at the proclamation

equator, determines the longitude of Florence and London.

[1] Encycl., art. Longitude.

[2] Bailly, Hist. de l'Astr. Mod. p. 111, &c.

[3] All the instruments of Americus, in this very difficult research, were a quadrant and an astrolabe; all his books, the almanack of Monteregio and the tables of Alphonso. Genius is like nature—it is contented with little.

[4] Diss. Gius., No. 79.

EULOGIUM.

of these discoveries. The noble emporium of literature and commerce, foreseeing their remote consequences, with joyful illuminations, hastened to render to her son a portion of the honour by which he has made her so illustrious and so renowned.[1] With joyful illuminations! Ah! deplore the wretched reward, if the follies of a devastating luxury, and magnifieent spectacles giving evidence of corruption and slavery, have abolished in you the august traces of republican simplicity.[2] If you still nourish any feeble sparks of ancient virtue, confess that Athens and Rome, while erecting statues to Miltiades, or crowning the brow of Postumius with a wreath of myrtle, exhibit a far superior greatness, than while decreeing three hundred statues to Valerian, or while erecting arches and temples to Antony.[3] Americus received at the

[1] Band. Vit. d'Am. Vesp. p. xlv. Though such festivities are narrated by Bandini to have taken place before the voyages of Vespucius, in the service of Portugal, it would seem that they followed the voyage of 1501 to Brazil. The reason is, because the relation to Soderini did not arrive in Florence till after the year 1504, and that alone, as a public document, might have given rise to the festivities.

[2] The most enlightened sovereigns, fathers of their subjects, have always abhorred useless pomp. For example, Adrian, Marcus Aurelius, and Alexander Severus. The truly philosophic character of Leopold, Grand Duke of Tuscany, and his noble refusal when the gratitude of the people offered him an equestrian statue, may be cited as another example.

[3] Cujus victoriæ non alienum videtur quale præmium Miltiadi sit tributum docere. Ut populi nostri honores quondam fuerunt rari et tenues, ob eamque causam gloriosi—sic olim apud Athenienses fuisse reperrimus. Namque huic Miltiadi—talis honos tributus est in Porticu quæ Poecile vocatur—ut in decem Prætorum numero prima ejus imago poneretur—Idem ille populus postea quam corruptus est, trecentas statuas Demetrio Phalerio decrevit.—*Cor. Nepos. Miltiades.*

EULOGIUM hands of his native country the illustrious rewards of a respected citizen, while Spain, forgetful of the foreigner who boasted no titles but those of courage and genius, rewarded him only with the usual stipend of a faithful subject.[1] Great men are certainly great phenomena in nature; rare among a multitude of ordinary productions, and unmoved by the confined powers of vulgar systems, they excite ideas of the admirable, and present to the curious philosopher an immense perspective of new combinations. It is a strange misfortune that such great similarity of endowment is coupled with so different a fate, and that a great phenomenon may be great with impunity, while a great man cannot.

[1] Everything convinces me, that in 1500, a cabal was in operation to ruin Americus with the court of Spain, although, conscious of his rectitude, and the benevolence of the king, he seemed not to have feared it. It is certain, that returning from his second voyage, he was very ill-treated at the Antillas by the companions of Columbus. "I think through envy," he says himself. Who can be persuaded that this envy ended in the Antillas, and did not follow him to Europe? He had scarcely arrived in court, when the king, moved by the greatness of his services, engages him, in the same year, 1500, for a third voyage, with the rank of commander of three vessels. "They are fitting out three ships for me here, and I think they will be ready by the middle of September." But behold the whole face of things suddenly changed. In spite of the esteem of the king, the meditated voyage vanishes, Americus leaves Seville secretly, and, in the month of May of the following year, 1501, we find him upon the ships of Portugal. This change of circumstances, which would be in vain attributed to the caprice or inconstancy of Americus, cannot be explained, without supposing some interference of his enemies. Here is something confirmatory of this view. "The Spaniards having shown very little gratitude to him (to Vespucius) for all his discoveries, their ingratitude mortified him keenly. Emmanuel, King of Portugal, jealous of the success of the Catholic kings, informed of the dissatisfaction of Vespucius, enticed him into his kingdom."—*Nouv. Dict. Hist. Art. Americ. Vespuce.*

Both confront prejudices and prostrate them ; both contend with ignorant pride, and confound it. But that encounter, and that contest, which render a great phenomenon more famous, expose the great man to the fatal action of inexorable circumstances, and although sometimes he is triumphant, he is often left without a single mark of his triumph. Implacable envy resists him ; dark calumny lacerates him ; he who was yesterday the wonder of his age, to-day is deserted ; and at the sound of his ruin, rewards and honours desert him. This is the reason why history, so fertile and diffuse in the catalogue of celebrated personages, seems so limited and barren in her description of their rewards.[1] Every age boasts some transcendent spirits, but not in every age are found generous and feeling hearts. EULOGIUM.

This cruel truth has often led to the very borders of absurdity. Superior talents seemed an unfortunate gift of Heaven, and in order to hide them from the jealousy of tyrants, they have often languished in degradation and stupid inaction.[2] As if

[1] The large dictionary of Moreri is in four large volumes, and might be augmented. We grant three quarters of the work to the names and matters which are foreign to our subject; the names of truly great men would occupy but one volume folio. The work of Du-Tillet, "An Essay upon the honours and monuments granted to illustrious scholars," is a little volume in 12mo.

[2] Descartes and Newton, by concealing themselves, as it were, are a proof of it. The former was so disturbed by the imprisonment of Galileo, that he was on the point of burning all his writings—Thomas Elog. de Descar.—the latter suppressed his "Method of Fluxions," discouraged by the silly objections with which his discoveries were assailed.—*Montucla*, t. ii. p. 312.

EULOGIUM. the moon should renounce her usual course to appease the barkings of the capricious mastiff; or the sun cease to dispense his rays, because the senseless Ethiop, from the sultry atmosphere of a fiery zone, throws javelins and reproaches at it.[1] Americus did not follow such counsels. The star which is never darkened, leaves the misty horizon involved in its clouds, and sheds its light elsewhere. See him upon the ships of Portugal, making the winds and the ocean show him the new line of the Vatican.[2]

* * * * * * * *
* * * * * * * *

[The programme of the academy required the introduction of some eulogistic remarks respecting the King of France and the Grand Duke of Tuscany, which the writer ingeniously brought in, at this place. Being foreign to the subject, they are omitted.—*Trans.*]

The voyages of Americus in the service of Portugal.

But was Heaven wearied with favouring his designs? A thick mist suddenly darkens the serenity of the day, with the whispering of the exaspe-

1 Solem orientem occidentemque dira imprecatione contuentur (Æthiopes) ut exitralem ipsis agrisque.—*Plin.* l. 5. c. 8. Perhaps Job alludes to this custom when he speaks of those who curse the day. On the reverse of a medal prepared in honour of the immortal poetess, Corilla Olimpica, the sun is seen pierced with arrows by some Ethiopians, with the legend taken from Job, "Who curse the day."

2 Alexander VI., in the year 1493, issued a bull in which (taking 100 leagues beyond the Azores, an ideal meridian, as a line of demarcation) he conceded to Spain all discoveries to be made towards the West, in the extent of 180 degrees, and to Portugal all those which should be made towards the East in the remaining 180 degrees. The limit was afterwards changed.

EULOGIUM.

rated winds mingles the wild burst of thunder and the lurid glare of the lightning. The Atlantic rolls a thousand whirlpools beneath the trembling fleet. His companions lose all hope, and without knowing through what region they are wandering, or where the mad encounter of the waves may drive them, feel only that they are running helplessly to shipwreck and death. Then appeared the valour of those skilful commanders,[1] to whom, in order to undervalue Americus, the merit of the discoveries is attributed. Abominable ignorance and pride! Contemptible band of greedy traffickers![2] In vain would ye have invoked with your dying exclamations the impotent riches with which ye had equipped your fleet, had not Americus come to your succour. To abandon the command, to grasp the helm, to consult the faithful instruments of his beloved science, and restore calmness and safety to the disheartened mariners, was the work of an in-

1 See Tirab. p. 189; Diss. Giustif. No. 34.

2 Although history seems to justify the idea that Americus sailed at the expense of the sovereigns of Spain and Portugal, it is very probable that after the first voyage of Columbus, another usage was introduced into the two kingdoms. "The forces of Cortez were not supported by the government, which, in the attempts which were made to discover new countries, and in forming new establishments, gave only the aid of its name. All was executed at the expense of individuals, who, if fortune had abandoned them, would certainly have been ruined. But their enterprises always extended the dominions of the mother country. After the first expeditions, she never formed a plan, never opened her treasury, never recruited any troops.—*Raynal*, t. vi. p. 53. Thus navigated Ojeda, Pinzon, &c.—*Robert.* D. i. p. 294. Americus himself does not leave us in doubt about this, when he relates what share he had in the sale of 200 slaves, which, but for that, would have belonged to the crown.

stant. This was little. He returns not to Nigritia, from which he had departed, he turns not to some known country, where he may rest securely, but not fearing the absence of the sun, at the time tending to the summer solstice, and defying the most terrible dangers, he follows for two thousand miles the circle of the equinoxes; and, victor over the storms and the winter, discovers the rich country of Brazil, and presents it in homage at the foot of the throne of Portugal.[1]

Importance of the discovery of Brazil.

It was in Brazil that Americus showed the great talents of a Theophrastus and a Pliny. A passionate admirer of nature, full of lively desire to search into its divine beauties, and endowed with the finest sensibility to feel and describe them, see him wandering with ecstacy through the woods and over the mountains; arrested at the sight of a tree, a bird, or a stone; gathering the beautiful fruits, the pure gums and balsams; contemplating with transport the fertility of the soil, the temperature of the climate, the great quantity of nutritious roots, the power of medicinal juices, the health, the vigour, the long life of the inhabitants, and courageously defying the naturalist of the Old World, to find in Europe or Asia so much to interest the student, as Brazil alone offers at every step to the observation of the stranger. Night does not snatch

[1] Brazil was discovered by Vespucius while he was navigating for Ferdinand (*Diss. Gius.* No. 71), but Spain made no account of it, for various reasons. It was then carefully visited, and almost discovered anew, by him, while in the service of Portugal.

from him the pompous spectacle of the earth, but varies his delight with her changing meteors and her unchanging lights of the firmament. He will tell you the magnitude of them, their places, their order, and their motions;[1] he will enumerate them; he will draw curious figures of them; that the South may not envy the North its advantages and its fame, he will enrich with Southern constellations[2] the interesting catalogue of the fixed stars. Ah! where is that precious volume to which Vespucius consigned such vast treasures of natural science and astronomical erudition! What unworthy plot, or what secret disaster, caused it to perish miserably in the hands of a sovereign, who, for the fortune and glory of Portugal, should have jealously guarded it? Let him who doubts this great loss, who pretends that this important work still lies buried among dusty archives, turn to Brazil, and explain, at least, how this happy land is suddenly transformed into an abominable and cursed land, into an

EULOGIUM

[1] The Southern Cross is perhaps the most celebrated of the figures or constellations observed by Vespucius. They are spoken of as an admirable order of stars, and a notable circumstance, by Andrea Corsali and Gonzalo d'Oviedo.—*Ramus*. t. i. p. 177, D. t. iii. p. 73, F. Merian also, reflecting upon the famous verses of Dante, thus expresses himself: "What a wonderful thing! Those four stars are found in the place indicated—three of the second and one of the third magnitude—they form together the most brilliant of the circumpolar constellations. The foremost has nearly 62 degrees of apparent southern declination, and consequently is 28 degrees distant from the pole. Let us imagine the surprise of Americus Vespucius, when, after having passed the line 6 degrees, he suddenly discovered those stars, and recollected immediately the verses of the poet (or shall I say, of the prophet?)."—*Toscan. Nouv. Mem. de Berlin, an.* 1784, p. 515.

[2] Riccoli Alm. Nov. L. 6, p. 410.

EULOGIUM. opprobrious prison for the wicked, an infamous receptacle for the dregs of a kingdom.[1] Ah! if the Portuguese, no less greedy than the Castilian, had possessed those faithful memorials wherein Americus, after picturing its splendid climate, gives magnificent descriptions of pearls,[2] diamonds, and gold, full well I know that Brazil would not have waited two centuries to become the delight and the treasury of Portugal.[3]

Thoughts respecting the civilization of American aborigines.

The consideration of this speaking example enlightens me. How can we hope to civilize America,[4] if, despising her when she is poor, and running to spoil her as soon as she proclaims her riches, we give ample intimation that we would willingly change a savage into gold, but are little disposed to change him into a citizen or a scholar. There gleams, I know it well, in Northern America, a splendid Aurora of pleasing hopes,[5] and from the union of friendship and peace which binds the shore-provinces together, I have a right to augur for the West more fortunate and more pleasing days. Moral culture and science are not propagated with

[1] Raynal, t. ix. p. 7.

[2] The country does not produce any metal except gold, of which there is a great abundance. They have many pearls and precious stones (*Vesp.*). "What negligence, what unskilfulness in those commissaries who, in the sixteenth century, assured the court of Lisbon that there was neither gold nor silver to be found there!"—*Raynal*, t. ix. p. 7.

[3] Raynal, t. ix. p. 115.

[4] In the programme of the Etruscan Academy, it is also desired that in the Eulogy of Americus, some notice may be taken of the future civilization of America, and it is sketched in this place.

[5] "The independence of the Anglo-Americans is the most propitious event to accelerating the revolution which is to reproduce happiness upon earth."—*Genty*, p. 317.

the celerity of light.[1] How many generations will live and die, how many ages will pass away before the muses find a kingdom in America, with its academies and lyceums equalling the number of the bulwarks which encircle her mines. Perhaps the wandering inhabitants of those rich forests will resist forever the social yoke of which they feel not the necessity;[2] perhaps they will never be able to extirpate from the spirit of a Patagonian and a cannibal those ideas that are insuperably opposed to instruction, and close every avenue to images of the beautiful and the true; perhaps, being contented with merely inspiring their limited understandings with a religious feeling, and then leaving them in their native infancy, will have a less evil tendency than bringing them to that indefinable compound of knowledge and vice, which constitutes, in fact, the superiority of European worship over that of the ignorant native. Who can say whether there will ever be on the earth generous mortals to attempt the laborious enterprise, and who will have the heart and the head to succeed in it?[3] We EULOGIUM.

[1] It must not be expected that every thing will be reduced to order in a few years, and that the present generation will enjoy the enchanting spectacle of general felicity.—*Genty*, p. 316. While I was thinking thus, in the year 1788, the greatest men, Borda, La Grange, La Place, Monge, and Condorcet, were writing similar words in France.—*Hist. de Acad. R. des Sci. an.* 1738, p 10.

[2] The sentiment is from Plato. "For when they asked him (the Cyreneans asked Plato) to write some laws for them, and bring the people into some kind of order, he said it was a difficult thing to introduce laws for the happy Cyreneans, for that nothing must be taken away from men without their consent."—*Plutarch. Lucullus.* Raynal makes the same reflection, t. vii. p. 65.

[3] He (Tupia, a native of Tahiti)

EULOGIUM. find but two examples through the long course of three centuries, Americus and Las Casas, who may be cited as the possessors of such qualities. But Las Casas, with superhuman talent, and with the celestial fervour which animated him, wanted power and assistance; and Americus, now bent with the weight of laurels and years, could only point the Europeans to the blameless path which he had marked out for their guidance.

The name of America, his reward.

Permit me to pass over in silence his other passage across the line, and the little he received from repentant Castile. All is little, all is common, after what I have told you. Let it suffice that the universe, astonished at his deeds, regarded him as the confidant of the stars, as the father of cosmography, as the wonder of navigation, and having, by the unanimous suffrages of all nations, abolished that primitive denomination, the New World, willed that the continent should derive its name from Americus alone, and with sublime gratitude and justice, secured that reward to him, and an eternity of fame. But, will you believe it? Italy, though a participator in his glory, and England, though enlightened and sagacious, still nourish hearts so ungrateful and minds so narrow, that they have not

was in fact a more proper person, perhaps, than any European whatever, to bring them to a civil and social state, because some of our people knew how to take the shortest and most efficacious way in instructing them, not seeing exactly, in the progress of their elementary ideas, those intermediate links which unite the weak notions of such people to the extended sphere of our own knowledge.—*Cook*, b. v. p. 263. On the incapacity of the Europeans for converting the Americans, see also *Robertson*, *Hist. of America*.

EULOGIUM.

only dishonoured with satire the incomparable deeds of Vespucius, but, expostulating loudly against the unanimous decree of the nations, have made it criminal in Americus that his name has been thus adopted, and have depicted him in the black colours of an ambitious usurper. O shame! O blindness! Should not Italy remember Mezio; England, Guerk; and both, the renowned Conon? The artist of Holland fabricated that admirable telescope which is called Galilean;[1] the consul of Madgeburgh[2] invented that interesting machine which bears the name of Boyle; the geometrician of Samos described the celebrated curve which was afterwards called Archimedean; and he deserves to give his name to a country who first had the intrepidity to penetrate or conquer it, rather than he who is satisfied to reconnoitre it at a distance.[3]

Death and memory of Americus.

No, it is not true that death silences envy. After fifty lustrums, the memory and the ashes of Americus are insulted. Oh! if his native country, whose name he always bore engraved on his affectionate heart, if the gentle friends among whom he longed to pass his last days, could have foreseen his un-

1 Montucla, Hist. des Mathém., tom. ii. p. 166.

2 Newton. Opt. L. 2, part 3, prop. 8.

3 Montucla, Hist. des Mathém., t. i. p. 237, where he concludes with these words, which are literally adapted to Americus: "He who penetrates farthest into a country, has a better title to give it his name, than he who only reconnoitres it." Americus first made the conquest of this country, not by sacking and depopulating it, but by discovering it, by penetrating it, by observing its immense riches, and by giving a minute account of it.—*Lettera al. Sig. P. Allegrini*, p. 11.

EULOGIUM. worthy fate, with what proofs, with what authentic testimonies, would they not have disarmed the rancour of an incredulous posterity! But, placing too much confidence in the rich light that encircled the citizen and the friend, they wept his loss with bitterness, though they neglected to establish his glory. He died.[1] Seek for his sepulchre in Terceira, in the bosom of the ocean, between the two continents which are indebted to him for power and name.[2] How much better could we show the stranger his monument in his own land! in the midst of us! Look at the urn of Galileo: does it not seem to want at its side the tomb and image of Vespucius? The memory of the two divine geniuses who discovered so large a part of the earth and of the heavens, would arrest the steps of the traveller, and while redoubling his encomiums on the famous Florentine, he would confess with transport, that the Athens of Italy was not contented with producing great men, but knew also how to value the honour of having produced them.[3]

1 "Americus Vespucius died in Terceira, one of the Azore Islands, and it is the common opinion that his death happened in 1508. Others think, on the authority of the archives, that he died in Seville in 1512, but the archives are entitled to credit only when they can be found by all." Canovai was undoubtedly in error as to the place of the death of Americus.—*Trans.*

2 Between America and Spain lie the Azores, nine islands which are called Flandricæ, from the discoverer Flandro.—*Chev. Intr. in Un. Geogr.* p. 666. The Indians alone can be ignorant that the discovery of America has produced the power of Europe. Thus she has known how to profit by it!—*Genty*, p. 211, &c.

3 Averani was accustomed to say, that "Galileo and Vespucius had so ordered it, that we could not raise our eyes to heaven, nor cast them down to the earth, without remembering the glory of the Florentines."—*Algarot.* t. iv. p. 137.

TRANSLATOR'S REMARKS.

THE foregoing Eulogium produced a great sensation in Italy. It was one of the first fruits of the influence, then just beginning to be felt, of the vast intellectual activity which pervaded France at the period of its delivery. The strongest French writers of the Republican Era, whose works and speeches upon the inalienable rights of man were then electrifying the world, found nowhere a readier response than that which came from the ardent hearts of the Patriots of the Italian States. The reader cannot have failed to remark the warm and enthusiastic love of country which dictated many of the sentences of the Eulogist. Immediately following its delivery and publication societies and clubs sprang into existence in every part of the Peninsula, whose object was to furnish premiums for similar orations, devoted to the illustration of the lives and characters of the many scientific and patriotic men who had, in previous ages, shed lustre on the annals of the old Republics. Too deeply fired with national feeling to suit the ruling powers, many of these productions never saw the light; but, passing from hand to hand in manuscript, they made many a youthful heart glow with brighter hopes for his country, and prepared in advance a warm welcome for the French armies when they came victoriously over the Alps.

EULOGIUM.

In order fully to appreciate the merit of the Eulogist, his work should be read in the language in which it was written. Every species of composition loses something by a translation, and none suffer more than works of this nature. There is a certain wealth and fulness of expression in the Italian tongue, which, though mellifluous beyond expression to an Italian ear, adds much to the difficulty of a translation. This, perhaps, is the reason why so few of the works of the authors of Italy, compared with those of other countries, have been rendered into English. There are mines of wealth yet unattempted in her literature, and open only to those who are familiar with her language.

There are some exaggerations and historical inaccuracies in the Eulogium. They are, however, of trifling importance, and, for the sake of a faithful translation, have been allowed to stand unaltered. The reader has either perceived and corrected them in his own mind, or they have been of no material disadvantage to him.

Motives of Canovai in writing the Eulogium.

At the commencement of his Justificatory Dissertation, Canovai gives the motives which led him to undertake the composition of the Eulogium, as well as the dissertation itself.

"Just relieved," he says, "from the extraordinary occupations in connexion with astronomy, which my colleague engaged me to undertake, in the month of May, in the year 1788, I turned my attention to Americus Vespucius, and more to relieve my mind from too severe application than from any other motive, I determined to write a eulogium of him. I confess I was surprised at the names and number of the enemies of this immortal man; but the History of Italian Literature by Tiraboschi alarmed me more than any other book which I consulted. I there found collected into one mass all the alleged crimes of the Florentine navigator. The high estimation which this writer enjoyed in Italy made me almost despair of Vespucius, for Tiraboschi, satisfied with merely desiring his defence, had refrained from undertaking it. EULOGIUM.

I would have given up the idea of praising a man so little worthy of praise, if the programme of the learned Etruscan Academy had not revived my courage. Was it possible that so famous a body of literary men could decree a eulogy to one who merited a satire, if it were possible to sustain so many accusations? Having, therefore, in the extremely limited space of time allowed me, combined in the best manner I could, a defence of the truth, of which I felt persuaded, I wrote the Eulogy, appended some notes to it, to serve as a foundation, and at the time appointed, sent it, as other writers did, to its destination. From that moment a lively desire to purify completely the character of Americus has constantly haunted me. Meaning to compose, at one time or another, an argumentative dissertation on this subject, to present to the Academy, I gladly consecrated to the accumulation of materials all the few leisure hours which my profession allowed me for three months. I never imagined that

EULOGIUM. an occasion, or rather a necessity for putting my design into execution, would offer so soon. The dissertation sprang up under my pen in a few days, and I only gave it to the Academy and the public as an essay, showing what might be said in favour of the accused Vespucius, since the weakness of his defenders has greatly augmented the audacity of his enemies.

The history of Tiraboschi. The convenience I derived from finding myself furnished by Tiraboschi alone with all that has been invented against Americus, made me prefer the "History of Italian Literature" to all other works. I have quoted it, and I have attacked it more freely than usual, as a new collection of observations, of authorities, of information, which that historian either suppressed or did not value, and particularly as the frequent complaint of various writers, have obliged me to consider its criticism and its apathy with more serious attention."

II.

A NARRATIVE

ADDRESSED TO

LORENZO DI PIER-FRANCESCO DE' MEDICI;

Giving an Account of the Voyage and Discoveries of Vasco de Gama beyond the Cape of Good Hope, the Authorship of which, has been attributed to Americus Vespucius.

VOYAGE OF DE GAMA

THE following letter is given by Bandini, in one edition of his "Vita e Lettere," as a veritable production of Americus. Canovai rejects it, and does not publish it in his work. In his preface, he writes respecting it as follows: "To him who asks me why I do not publish in this work 'The Relation of the Voyage of Gama,' freely attributed to Americus by Bandini, and printed with the direction to De' Medici, among his other letters, I would reply without hesitation, that I cannot believe it to be a work of Vespucius. It is demonstrated not to be by the assertion of Ramusio, that 'the Relation was written by a Florentine gentleman, who happened to be in Lisbon at the return of said fleet.' Gama returned to Lisbon while Americus was in the West Indies, and as far as we know, he was not again in Portugal before 1501.

Reasons of Canovai for discrediting the narrative.

Leaving as a matter of controversy this statement of Ramusio, Bandini adds that in the Riccar-

VOYAGE OF DA GAMA.

diano records "the diction and the character are those of Vespucius." This is a most erroneous assertion with regard to the diction, for it is certain that the slightest comparison of the letter to De' Medici with the "Relation of the Voyage of Gama" (consecutive pieces in those records) is sufficient to convince one at a glance that the two writings, though perhaps in the same character, cannot be the production of the same author. The letter speaks of latitudes, longitudes, astronomical methods, American languages, &c., and speaks of them in a certain peculiar style, and with words and phrases so purely Spanish, that it displays distinctly the genius of him who wrote it, and particularly the mingled idiom which he used in writing. Now there is none of this in the Narrative. We find there, in the most simple Tuscan language, a description of the popular customs of Calicut, the merchandise, the prices of the most valuable commodities, the money current in trade, the traffic which might be carried on there with European productions, the time necessary to transport them from Lisbon; yet with all his various accounts of gems, spices, and dye-wood, the latitude of the country is never mentioned. Is it possible that Americus would have treated the subject so stupidly?

But the most decisive reason against Bandini, is an inscription in the same character as that of the Narrative, which appears on the manuscript, "Copy of a letter from the King of Portugal." The Riccardiano Narrative is then a copy, and not a letter from Americus. In fact, by what we can gather from his few hints at the close of his first letter to De' Medici, he was not then so greatly enamoured with the voyage of Gama as to write a relation of it. That Admiral did nothing but reach a particular destination by a new route."

VOYAGE OF DE GAMA.

The arguments of Canovai considered.

Notwithstanding these arguments of Canovai, it is certainly within the range of possibility that the Narrative was written by Americus. He admits that the character of the handwriting was similar to that of the Letter to De Medici in the Riccardiano records; and the fact that the style was not corrupted by Spanish idioms, would weigh as strongly against at least one of his letters, which is well authenticated, as against the Narrative. That Americus was not in Portugal at the date of the arrival of De Gama, is well known, but neither that fact, nor the circumstance that he made no mention of the latitudes of ports which were visited, is of much importance in the consideration of the authorship. It is very possible that Americus prepared the statement from the words of one of the companions of De Gama, for the information of his patron, either before or after his return from his first voyage to the West, in the service of Portugal, in which case he could not, of course, fix the geographical positions of the places visited, from his own knowledge.

The Narrative, in its general features, bears marks of similarity to the other writings of Amer-

VOYAGE OF DE GAMA.

icus. It is devoted to a subject which would very naturally have employed his pen, and is addressed to one who had long been his correspondent and patron. Although in one of his letters Americus appears rather disposed to undervalue the expedition of De Gama, when considered in the light of a voyage of discovery, yet he speaks of the great profit which he thinks will be derived from another expedition about to sail to the same parts. This was probably the very reason which led to the composition of the Narrative, for it contains much matter of mercantile interest, valuable to a person as extensively engaged in commerce as De Medici was at that time.

Canovai may have been correct in rejecting this narrative as not authentic, for no positive proof can be adduced that it was so. The impression which the document itself produces upon the mind of the reader is, however, of some weight in the solution of the question, and in connection with its intrinsic interest, this consideration has led to its publication in this work. The following translation has been made from a German version of Bandini, published in Hamburg in 1748. A very limited number of copies, of that edition of the Italian biographer, which contained the Narrative, were printed, and the one in possession of the translator having been unfortunately stolen, just as the translation was about to be made, it was found impossible to procure another copy in America.

VOYAGE OF DE GAMA

THE RELATION OF THE VOYAGE OF GAMA.

The vessels which our gracious King of Portugal sent upon this voyage of discovery were three new caravels, namely, two of ninety tons burden each, and one of fifty tons, besides a ship of one hundred and ten tons, which was laden with provisions. These vessels were manned by one hundred and eighteen men, and sailed on the 19th of July, 1497, under the Captain Vasco de Gama, from Lisbon. On the 10th of July, 1499, the caravel of fifty tons returned to the city of Lisbon. The Captain Vasco de Gama remained with one of the caravels of ninety tons at the Cape Verd Islands, in order that he might put his son, Paul de Gama, on shore, for he was sick unto death. They had previously burnt the other caravel, because they had too few people to man her properly, and also the vessel which acted as tender, because she was not sea-worthy. On the return voyage fifty-five of the crew died, of a sickness which commenced in the mouth and spread back into the throat, and also caused those who were attacked with it, great pain in the legs from the knees to the feet.

Discovery of lands beyond the Cape of Good Hope.

They have discovered new lands about one hundred and eighty miles from that already discovered, which bears the name of the Cape of Good Hope, and was visited in the time of King John. Coasting this shore for about six hundred miles, they met

VOYAGE OF DE GAMA.

with a great river, and at the mouth of the same a large village inhabited entirely by negroes, who are subject to the Moors that live in the interior, and have conquered them in war. In this river there is an abundance of gold, as the negroes have showed them; they told our people, that if they would remain there a month, they would provide them an immense quantity of gold. The commander, however, would not tarry, but sailed onward.

When we had progressed about three hundred and fifty miles, he found a large town surrounded by a wall, whose inhabitants were grey like the Indians, with very handsome houses built of stone and chalk, after the Moorish fashion. They landed there. The Moorish King of the country saw them arrive with pleasure, and furnished them with a pilot to conduct them across the Gulf. The name of this place was Melinda, and it lies at the entrance of the Great Gulf, the entire shore of which is inhabited by Moors. The pilot, whom the King of Melinda gave them, spoke the Italian language.

Departure from Melinda.

They sailed from Melinda across the Gulf, a voyage of about seven hundred miles in extent, and then came to a large town, inhabited by Christians, which is much larger than Lisbon, and is called Calicut. The entire coast of this gulf is reported to be inhabited, and covered with Moorish towns and castles in every direction. At the upper end of this gulf is a strait, and on passing through

VOYAGE OF DE GAMA.

this strait the voyager comes to another bay or sea, on the right hand, which is the Red Sea. From this strait to the temple at Mecca, where Mahomet's coffin is suspended, it is not more than three days' journey. Round about this temple of Mecca is a large town inhabited by Moors. According to my opinion this gulf is the same which Pliny speaks of, and which, he says, was reached by Alexander in his campaigns, and which the Romans also arrived at in their wars.

Description of the city of Calicut.

Now to speak more at length of the town of Calicut. It is larger than Lisbon, and is inhabited by a race of Christian Indians, who are of an ash-grey colour, and neither black nor white. They have churches with bells, but neither have they any priests, nor do they make any offerings. They use in their churches a basin with water, as we use the holy water, and another vessel very similar to a censer. Every three years they baptize in the river which flows by the town. In the town their houses are built of stone and chalk, and strait streets are laid out, as regular as those in Italy. The monarch of the country is very splendidly apparelled, and maintains a royal retinue of servitors, squires, and chamberlains, and has, moreover, a very beautiful palace.

When the commander of these vessels arrived there, the King was absent from the city, at a castle five or six miles distant. The moment he heard the news of the arrival of the Christians, he immediately came to the city with a guard of five thou-

VOYAGE OF DE GAMA.

sand men. Before him stood a body-guard, whose lances were tipped with silver. The Christians were received in a room where the King reclined on a low couch. The floor of this room was covered with white cloth, beautifully embroidered with gold thread. Over the couch was suspended a most sumptuous canopy. The King immediately inquired of the commander what he desired. The commander answered that it was customary among Christians, whenever an ambassador laid his embassy before a monarch, that he should do so privately, and not in public. The King at once ordered all those persons who were present to retire, and the commander then said to him, that a long time had elapsed since the King of Portugal had heard of his grandeur and magnificence, and as he was a Christian King, and had a desire to cultivate his friendship, therefore he had sent him as an ambassador to visit him, as was customary among the monarchs of Christendom. The King received this message most graciously, and commanded that the ambassador should be taken to the house of a very rich Moor, and sumptuously entertained there.

The Moorish merchants of Calicut.

In this city live many extremely wealthy merchants, and the whole power of the kingdom is in their hands. They have a magnificent mosque in the market-place. The actions of the King are entirely under the control of a few of the principal men among these Moors, either on account of the presents which they make him, or in consequence of their intrigues. They have the entire government in their hands, for the Christians are stupid people, and but little given to intrigue. VOYAGE OF DE GAMA.

Every kind of spice is found in this city of Calicut; cinnamon, pepper, cloves, ginger, frankincense, besides inestimable quantities of gumlac and sandal wood, of which all the forests are full. These spices, however, do not grow in this neighbourhood, but in certain islands distant about one hundred and sixty miles from the city. These islands are only about a mile distant from the shore, but by land it is twenty days' journey there. They are inhabited both by Moors and Christians, but the Moors are the masters.

The currency of the country.

In the town of Calicut the majority of the coin which is current consists of serafi of fine gold, a coin of the Sultans, weighing two or three grains less than our ducat, and which is here called serafino. They have also a few Genoese and Venetian ducats, as well as a small silver coin, with the Sultan's stamp on it. There are large quantities of silk goods in Calicut, and velvet of all colours, besides a cloth made very much like velvet. Damask, taffeta, and fine plush abound. I think that most of these stuffs are brought from Cairo.

The Portuguese remained three months in this city, namely, from the 19th of May to the 25th of August, during which time they saw an innumerable quantity of Moorish ships. They say that fifteen hundred Moorish ships, laden with spices, sail from this port. Their largest vessels are not over two hundred tons burden. They are of various kinds, some large and some small, but have only one mast, and they never try to sail them excepting before the wind. On this account it often happens that they have to wait from four to six months for a fair wind, and are not unfrequently shipwrecked. They are constructed in a most singular manner, are very weak, and carry no arms or ordnance. The ships which sail to the Spice Islands, to bring spices to Calicut, are flat-bottomed, and draw but very little water. Some of them are made without the least particle of iron, because they are obliged to pass over the magnet, which lies not far from these islands. All these vessels, when they are at the city, lie inside of a pier at the Lagoon, and only furl their sails when the sea is high, because they are here safe from winter and the sea. There is no good haven there, and the sea flows and ebbs every six hours, as it does with us. There are often in port at the same time from five to six hundred ships, which is a great number.

Prices of the different articles of produce.

Cinnamon costs in this city from ten to twelve ducats, for what with us would weigh about five stones, that being about the highest price, that is, ten to twelve serafi. In the islands where it is gathered, it is not worth so much, of course. Pepper and cloves are worth about the same; ginger about one half less. Gumlac is worth almost nothing, for there is so much of it, that they use it to ballast their ships, and the same may be said of sandal wood, of which the forests are full. They will receive nothing in payment but gold and silver. Corals and our usual wares they value but little, with the exception of linen. This would be a good article to send there, because the sailors made some very good bargains, by exchanging their shirts for spices, but the linen must be very fine, and white bleached. They are at present obliged to get it from Cairo. There are the same custom duties there as with us ; all imports pay five per centum.

VOYAGE OF DE GAMA.

The voyagers brought back very few precious stones, and these of no great value, because they had no gold and silver to buy them with, and they say they are very costly. I am inclined to think that pearls would be a good article to buy there, but all which the Portuguese saw, were in the hands of the Moorish merchants, who wished to sell them at a fourfold price, as is their common custom. They have only brought a few sapphires and brilliants, and a peculiar kind of rubies, and a considerable number of garnets. They say that the commander has brought some very costly stones. He took his silver with him, and bartered it all for precious stones.

Precious stones

Spices are brought to this Christian town by ships, which afterwards cross the great gulf, over which the Portuguese came, and pass into the strait before mentioned. Then they sail through the Red Sea. From thence the journey is performed by land to the temple at Mecca, which is thirty-six days' journey. Still further on, they journey on the way to Cairo, crossing Mount Sinai on foot, and

VOYAGE OF DE GAMA.

again still further across the desert, where, as they say, the high winds raise mountains of sand into the air, and bury travellers who journey there. Some of their ships sail to the towns on the gulf, and others to the river before mentioned, where the negroes live, who have been subjected by the Moors of the interior. The Portuguese found in store, in this Christian town, butts of malmsey wine from Candia, which, as well as their wares, must, in my opinion, have been brought from Cairo.

Arrival of strangers at Calicut.

It is about eighty years since there arrived at this town of Calicut some vessels navigated by white Christians, with long hair like the Germans. They wore long mustachios on the upper lip, but with that exception, were shaved after the common fashion, like the courtiers at Constantinople. The men were provided with cuirasses, and wore caps and ruffs. They carried weapons similar to spears. On board of their ships they used short arms like our own. Ever since their first arrival, a fleet of twenty to twenty-five ships has come every two years to Calicut. The Portuguese do not know what nation these people belong to, nor what other merchandise they bring, besides fine linen, iron, and brass. They load their ships with spices, and all the vessels have four masts, like the Spanish ships. If they had been Germans, we should have had some account of it. It is possible that they may be Russians. If they have a port upon the sea, we shall find it out from the pilot whom the Moorish king gave to the Portuguese, and who speaks Italian. He is at present in the commander's caravel —for they have taken him against his will.

VOYAGE OF DE GAMA.

In this town of Calicut there is an abundance of wheat, which the Moors bring there in their ships. Three small measures of bread is sufficient to satisfy one of the inhabitants for a day, but they make no leavened bread, and only bake a kind of cake under the hot ashes, and have it fresh every day. As a substitute they make much use of rice, of which there is a great abundance. They have cows and cattle, but they are all small. They use milk and butter. There is an abundance of oranges, but they are all sweet; lemons, also, large and small citrons, very fine melons, dates, and many other delicious fruits.

The monarch's mode of life.

The king of this town makes use of neither flesh nor fish for food, and touches nothing which has been killed. The same custom is followed by all his court, and generally by the wealthiest and most important persons of the kingdom. Their reason for this is, that Jesus Christ has ordered in his laws, that he who kills shall be killed, and therefore they eat of nothing that dies. The common people eat both flesh and fish, but very sparingly. They never kill an ox, but entertain a high respect for the animal, because they say it is an animal which brings a blessing with it, and whenever they meet one on the street they caress it and pat it with their hands. The king lives upon rice, milk, butter, wheaten bread, and many other vegetable articles, and the courtiers and other persons of quality follow his example. He drinks palm wine out of a silver tankard, but never puts the rim to his lips, for he opens his mouth and pours it down from the spout of the tankard in a stream.

The species of fish which they saw were similar to our own. The Christians use very little, but the Moors considerable quantities. They ride upon elephants, of which great numbers exist in the country, and are very tame. When the king goes to war any where, the largest part of his force follows him on foot, but a part ride upon elephants. When he moves from one place to another, he is carried upon men's shoulders, and this duty is performed by his principal servants. All the people are clothed from the middle of the body to the feet, mostly with cloth made of cotton, which is found there in great abundance, but the upper part of the body is left naked, as well by the nobility as by the common people. The first, however, dress themselves in silk stuffs, and garments of various colours, each according to his particular rank. The same may be said of the females, except that the women of quality wear over their heads white and delicate veils. Many of the lower classes go entirely uncovered. The Moors dress in their own fashion, with undercoats and long robes.

Calculation of distance from Lisbon.

The distance from the port of Lisbon to this city is thirty-eight hundred common miles, so that allowing four and a half Italian miles to one common, it makes seventeen thousand one hundred Italian miles. It is easy to calculate from this how long a voyage there will necessarily be. It cannot be less than fifteen or sixteen months.

VOYAGE OF DE GAMA.

Their navigators all sail with the north wind, and make use of certain wooden quadrants. They always go to the right when they sail across the gulf. The pilot before mentioned says, that there are more than a thousand islands in this gulf, and that the navigation between them leads to almost certain shipwreck, as they are very low. They must be the same islands which the King of Castile has just begun to discover. In this city they have some information concerning Prester John, but not much. In the interior there must be some intelligence to be gained respecting him. They know that Jesus Christ was born of a virgin without sin, that he was crucified and killed by the Jews, and afterwards buried at Jerusalem. They have heard also of the Pope, and know that he lives at Rome, but have no further knowledge of our faith. They have letters and a written language.

They have an abundance of elephants, which are extremely useful to them, and cotton, sugar, and sweetmeats. In my opinion, all the riches of the world are now discovered, and nothing more remains to be found out. It is thought that wine would be a good article to barter for Indian wares, for these Christians drink it very willingly. They have also enquired about oil.

In this town justice is very well administered. Whoever steals, murders, or commits any other

VOYAGE OF DE GAMA.

crime, is impaled after the Turkish fashion, and whoever undertakes to cheat the laws, loses all his goods.

Productions of the country.

There is found also in the town of Calicut, civet, nutmegs, ambergris, storax, and benzoin. The islands where these grow are called Zelotri, and are one hundred and sixty miles distant from the town of Calicut. In one of these islands no other trees grow but cinnamon trees, and a few pepper trees, but not of the best kind. The pepper comes mainly from another island. When the trees which produce pepper and cinnamon are planted in the neighbourhood of Calicut, the fruit is not so good. Cloves are brought there from distant countries. Rhubarb is plenty, and all other common spices. Ginger grows best on Terra Firma. The countries of the Gulf are entirely inhabited by Moors, but I have lately learned more particulars of the truth, and find that it is only on the seashore of one side that they dwell, the whole of the other side being inhabited by Christian Indians who are white as we are. The country is extremely fruitful in wheat and other descriptions of grain. Fresh fruit and all kinds of provisions are shipped to Calicut, for the region where this town lies is sandy and unfit for grain.

Two winds prevail in this region; the west wind in winter, and the east wind in summer. They have very skilful painters there, who paint figures and pictures of every kind. This town of Calicut

VOYAGE OF DE GAMA.

has no walls, and the same may be said of all the other towns. Still there are many very beautiful Moorish houses and regular streets. In the island mentioned before, where the best cinnamon grows, civet and many sapphires are found.

III.

LETTERS OF PAOLO TOSCANELLI TO COLUMBUS.

LETTERS OF TOSCANELLI.

The letters of the Florentine physician to Columbus produced such a strong effect upon his mind, and rendered him so confident in his belief in the practicability of a passage to the Indies by the west, that they merit a place among the illustrations of the discovery of the New World. They are preserved in the History of the Admiral, by his son Fernando, and the translation of them, found in Pinkerton's Collection of Voyages, has been followed, with some trifling alterations. No writings contributed more to occasion the discovery than these two short letters. Some Italian writers even go to the extent of asserting that the idea of a western passage to India originated with Toscanelli, before it struck the mind of Columbus, and by him was communicated to the admiral. It is highly probable that this was the case. At the time of the date of his letters, Toscanelli was already an aged man, while Columbus was in the prime of life, and it is evident that the opinions he expresses were arrived at after many years of examination and study.

LETTERS OF TOSCANELLI.

THE FIRST LETTER.

To Christopher Columbus, Paul, the Physician, wishes health.

I perceive your noble and earnest desire to sail to those parts where the spice is produced; and therefore, in answer to a letter of yours, I send you another letter, which some days since I wrote to a friend of mine, and servant of the King of Portugal, before the wars of Castile, in answer to another that he wrote to me by his Highness's order, upon this same account, and I send you another sea-chart like the one I sent to him, which will satisfy your demands. The copy of the letter is as follows:

To Ferdinand Martinez, Canon of Lisbon, Paul, the Physician, wishes health.

I am very glad to hear of the familiarity you enjoy with your most serene and magnificent king, and though I have very often discoursed concerning the short way there is from hence to the Indies, where the spice is produced, by sea, which I look upon to be shorter than that you take by the coast of Guinea; yet you now tell me that his Highness would have me make out and demonstrate it, so that it may be understood and put in practice. (Letter of Toscanelli to Martinez.)

Therefore, though I could better show it to him,

LETTERS OF TOSCANELLI.

with a globe in my hand, and make him sensible of the figure of the world; yet I have resolved, to make it more easy and intelligible, to show the way on a chart, such as are used in navigation; and therefore I send one to his majesty, made and drawn with my own hand, wherein is set down the utmost bounds of the earth, from Ireland, in the west, to the farthest part of Guinea, with all the islands that lie in the way; opposite to which western coast is described the beginning of the Indies, with the islands and places whither you may go, and how far you may bend from the North Pole towards the equinoctial, and for how long a time; that is, how many leagues you may sail before you come to those places most fruitful in spices, jewels, and precious stones.

Do not wonder if I term that country where the spice grows, West, that product being generally ascribed to the East, because those who sail westward will always find those countries in the west, and those who travel by land eastward, will always find those countries in the east. The straight lines that lie lengthways in the chart, show the distance there is from west to east; the others which cross them, show the distance from north to south. I have also marked down in the chart several places in India, where ships might put in, upon any storm or contrary winds, or other unforeseen accident.

Moreover, to give you full information of all those places which you are very desirous to know about, you must understand that none but traders live and

LETTERS OF TOSCANELLI.

reside in all those islands, and that there is there as great a number of ships and seafaring people with merchandise, as in any other part of the world, particularly in a most noble port called Zaitun, where there are every year an hundred large ships of pepper loaded and unloaded, besides many other ships that take in other spices. This country is mighty populous, and there are many provinces and kingdoms, and innumerable cities under the dominion of a prince called the Great Khan, which name signifies king of kings, who for the most part resides in the province of Cathay. His predecessors were very desirous to have commerce and be in amity with Christians; and two hundred years since, sent ambassadors to the Pope, desiring him to send them many learned men and doctors, to teach them our faith; but by reason of some obstacles the ambassadors met with, they returned back without coming to Rome. Besides, there came an ambassador to Pope Eugenius IV., who told him the great friendship there was between those princes and their people, and the Christians. I discoursed with him a long while upon the several matters of the grandeur of their royal structure, and of the greatness, length, and breadth of their rivers, and he told me many wonderful things of the multitude of towns and cities founded along the banks of the rivers, and that there were two hundred cities upon one only river, with marble bridges over it of a great length and breadth, and adorned with abundance of pillars.

LETTERS OF TOSCANELLI.

This country deserves as well as any other to be discovered; and there may not only be great profit made there, and many things of value found, but also gold, silver, many sorts of precious stones, and spices in abundance, which are not brought into our parts. And it is certain that many wise men, philosophers, astrologers, and other persons skilled in all arts, and very ingenious, govern that mighty province, and command their armies.

Distance from Lisbon.

From Lisbon directly westward, there are in the chart, twenty-six spaces, each of which contains two hundred and fifty miles, to the most noble and vast city of Quinsai, which is one hundred miles in compass, that is, thirty-five leagues. In it there are ten marble bridges; the name signifies a heavenly city, of which wonderful things are reported, as to the ingenuity of the people, the buildings and revenues. This space above mentioned is almost the third part of the globe. The city is in the province of Mangi, bordering on that of Cathay, where the King for the most part resides. From the island of Antilla, which you call the Island of the Seven Cities, and whereof you have some knowledge, to the most noble island of Cipango, are ten spaces, which make two thousand five hundred miles, or two hundred and twenty-five leagues, which island abounds in gold, pearls, and precious stones: and you must understand, they cover their temples and palaces with plates of pure gold; so that, for want of knowing the way, all these things are concealed and hidden, and yet may be gone to with safety.

LETTERS OF TOSCANELLI.

Much more might be said, but having told you what is most material, and you being wise and judicious, I am satisfied there is nothing of it but what you understand, and therefore I will not be more prolix. Thus much may serve to satisfy your curiosity, it being as much as the shortness of time and my business would permit me to say. So I remain most ready to satisfy and serve his highness, to the utmost, in all the commands he shall lay upon me.

Florence, June 25, 1474.

A short time after this letter was despatched, Toscanelli wrote a second letter to Columbus, of which the following is a translation.

To Christopher Columbus, Paul, the Physician, wishes health.

I received your letters with the things you sent me, which I take as a great favour, and commend your noble and ardent desire of sailing from east to west, as it is marked out in the chart I sent you, which would demonstrate itself better in the form of a globe. I am glad it is well understood, and that the voyage laid down is not only possible, but true, certain, honourable, very advantageous, and most glorious among all Christians.

You cannot be perfect in the knowledge of it, but by experience and practice, as I have had in

LETTERS OF TOSCANELLI.

great measure, and by the solid and true information of worthy and wise men, who are come from those parts to this court of Rome, and from merchants who have traded long in those parts, and are persons of good reputation. So that when the said voyage is performed, it will be to powerful kingdoms, and to most noble cities and provinces, rich, and abounding in all things we stand in need of, particularly in all sorts of spice in great quantities, and store of jewels. This will moreover be grateful to those kings and princes who are very desirous to converse and trade with Christians of these our countries, whether it be for some of them to become Christians, or else to have communication with the wise and ingenious men in these parts, as well in point of religion as in all sciences, because of the extraordinary account they have of the kingdoms and government of these parts.

For which reasons, and many more that might be alleged, I do not at all wonder that you who have a great heart, and all the Portuguese nation, which has ever had notable men in all undertakings, be eagerly bent upon performing this voyage.

DISCOVERY OF ALONZO DE OJEDA.

Extended on these roots, with his buckler on and his sword in his hand, but so weakened by hunger and fatigue that he was unable to speak, the Spaniards found Alonzo de Ojeda. (SEE P. 383.)

IV.

MARCO POLO AND HIS TRAVELS.

MARCO POLO.

TOSCANELLI was led to a consideration of the subject of a western passage to India mainly by the accounts of Marco Polo. The influence which this traveller exercised over the minds of the early discoverers, renders some notice of him and his works necessary. The history of his life is singular and interesting, and is abridged from Kerr's Collection of Voyages and Murray's Translation of the Travels of Marco Polo, whence also are taken the extracts which are given from his writings.

Marco Polo was born at Venice about the year 1260. His father, Niccolo Polo, and his uncle Maffei, were of a noble Venetian family, who were extensively engaged in commerce. They left Venice, in the prosecution of their business, just before the birth of Marco, whom his father never saw till his return to Venice in 1269, at which time he was about nine years old. They went first to Constantinople, and from there into Armenia. They remained a year at the camp of Bereke, the khan or ruler of the western portion of the vast empire of the Mongals, and then pursued their journey into

Bochara, where they staid three years. Another year more was occupied by them in travelling to the court of Kublai Khan, the powerful emperor of the Mongals or Tartars. At the court of this potentate they remained about a year, and then consumed three years in their return to Europe.

Soon after their return, they again started for the East, taking with them the young Marco. It was probably in the year 1270 that they departed on their second journey, for upon the election of Gregory IX. to the pontifical chair, he despatched an express after them, which overtook them in Armenia, where they were detained some time, in order that they might receive the final instructions of the Pope.

Election of Visconti to ne Papal chair.

The cause of this delay was, that by the death of Clement IV., the Papal See had been left vacant for two years. Niccolo and Maffei Polo learnt the news of this fact at Acre, while on their return from their first journey. They saw there the papal legate, Tibaldo Visconti, of Placentia, who was greatly interested in their descriptions of their travels, and advised them to wait for the election of a new pontiff before setting out again for the East. Finding, after their return to Venice, that the election did not take place so soon as they anticipated, they became very anxious lest the Great Khan should become impatient at the postponement of the conversion of himself and his nation, and accordingly started before the cardinals had been able to effect the choice of a new successor of St. Peter. Once more passing through Acre, they were kindly entertained by the Legate, who furnished them with letters to the Khan, exculpatory of their conduct in not returning sooner, and with letters from the Pope. He also procured them a sufficient supply of oil from the Holy Sepulchre, which had been expressly desired by the Khan, through belief in its miraculous powers. Hardly, however, had they departed from Acre, in the prosecution of their journey, when letters came to the legate, informing him that he himself had been chosen Pope. He took the name of Gregory, and immediately issued a bull providing, that in future, on the demise of a pontiff, the cardinals should be confined together until they had selected his successor.

Friars sent by the Pope to accompany the Polos.

Before proceeding to Italy to take possession of the papal chair, he despatched those messengers who caused the delay of the travellers. In a short time, new letters were prepared by him to deliver to the Khan, containing complimentary expressions and a long defence or exposition of Christian doctrine. These were brought to the Polos, by two priests, Nicolo of Vicenza and Guelmo of Tripoli, both men of distinguished learning and discretion, who were intended to accompany the travellers in their journey. They were furnished also with splendid presents of great value for the eastern monarch, and were endowed with ample powers and privileges, and authority to ordain priests and bishops, and to grant absolution in all cases, as fully as if the Pope were personally present. These two friars, however, proved themselves to be wanting in the hour of danger. Learning that the Sultan of Cairo had led a large army to invade Armenia, where he was committing the most cruel ravages, they were fearful of their own safety, and delivering the letters and presents of the Pope to the Polos, and preferring to avoid the fatigues of the route and the perils of war, returned to Acre.

The Polos pursue their journey.

The three Venetians, however, pursued their journey boldly, in spite of many difficulties and dangers, and at length, after a journey of three years and a half, arrived at the great city of Clemenisu or Chambalu, which means the city of the Khan, and is the modern Pekin. In this long journey they were often compelled to make great delays, on account of the deep snow and extreme cold, and in consequence of the floods and inundations. When the Khan heard of their approach, he sent messengers forty days' journey to meet them, that they might be conducted with all honour, and be provided with every accommodation during the remainder of their journey. On their arrival at court they were introduced into his presence, and prostrated themselves before him, according to the custom of the country, but they were commanded to rise, and were most graciously received. The Khan demanded an account of their proceedings on the way, and of what they had effected with the Pope. They related all this distinctly, and then delivered the Pope's letters and presents, which the Khan received with great pleasure, and commended them

MARCO POLO.

for their fidelity. The holy oil which they had brought, at the request of the Khan, from the sepulchre of the Saviour at Jerusalem was reverently received, and preserved with scrupulous care.

The Khan very naturally inquired who Marco was; on which Niccolo replied, "He is your Majesty's servant, and my son." Thereupon the Khan received him kindly, and had him taught to write among his honourable courtiers. He was much esteemed by the court, and in a very short time learned to read and write four different languages, and made himself familiar with the customs of the Tartars.

Marco Polo sent on embassies by the Khan.

Some yeas after, in order to try his capacity, the Khan sent Marco upon an embassy to a great city called Carachan or Carazan, at a distance of almost six months' journey. He executed this service with great judgment and discretion, and very much to the satisfaction of his imperial patron, and well knowing that the Khan would be pleased with an account of the manners and customs of the inhabitants of the countries through which he passed, he made a minute of every thing that appeared worthy of note, and repeated it to him on his return. In this way he rose to such high favour, that he was continually sent by the Khan on business of importance to all the different parts of his dominions, which was the means of his acquiring so much information respecting the affairs and places of the East.

After remaining many years at the court of the

MARCO POLO.

Khan, and acquiring immense wealth in jewels of great value, they began to consider the possibility of returning home. This they thought would be impossible if the Khan, who had then become quite aged, should die, and they became, of course, exceedingly anxious to obtain permission to return to Venice. One day, therefore, finding the Khan in an excellent humour, Nicolo Polo asked permission to return to his own country with his family. He was greatly displeased at the request, and could not conceive what inducement they had to undertake so long and dangerous a journey; adding, that if they were in want of riches, he would gratify their utmost wishes, by bestowing upon them twice as much as they already possessed, but from pure affection he refused to part with them.

Their scheme to return to Venice.

Not long after this, it happened that a King of the Indies, named Argon, sent three of his counsellors as ambassadors to Kublai Khan, on the following account. Bolgana, the wife of Argon, had lately died, and on her death-bed had requested her husband to choose a wife from among her relations in Cathay. Kublai yielded to the request of the ambassadors, and chose a fair young maiden, seventeen years of age, named Cogalin, who was of the family of the late queen, and determined to send her to Argon. The ambassadors departed with their fair charge, and journeyed for eight months on their return, by the same road over which they came. Then they found that bloody wars were raging between some of the Tartar princes, and were com-

MARCO POLO.

pelled to come back again, and acquaint the Khan with the impossibility of their proceeding on that road. Meantime, Marco, who had been absent at sea, returned with certain ships belonging to the Khan, and reported the peculiarities of the places he had visited and the facility of intercourse by sea between Cathay and the Indies. This came to the knowledge of the ambassadors, who conversed on the subject with the Venetians. It was agreed between them that the ambassadors and the young Queen should ask permission of the Khan to return by sea, and should request to have the three Europeans who were skilful in nautical affairs, to accompany and conduct them to the dominions of Argon.

Though dissatisfied at this proposal, the Khan at last gave a reluctant consent, and calling the Polos into his presence, after many demonstrations of affection and favour, he made them promise to return to him, when they had spent a little time among their relations in Christendom. He caused a tablet of gold to be given to them, on which his orders were engraved, directing his subjects throughout his dominions to furnish them with every convenience on their passage, to defray all their expenses, and to provide them with guides and escorts whereever necessary. He also authorized them to act as his ambassadors to the Pope, and to the kings of France and Spain, and other Christian princes.

Departure from Cathay.

The Khan ordered fourteen ships to be prepared for the voyage, each having four masts and carry-

MARCO POLO.

ing nine sails. Four or five of these were so large as to have about two hundred and fifty mariners in each, but the rest were smaller. In this fleet the Queen and ambassadors embarked, accompanied by the three Venetian travellers. The Khan, on taking leave of them, presented each with many rubies and precious stones, and money enough to defray all their expenses for two years. Setting sail from Cathay, or China, they arrived in three months at Java, and sailing from there, in eighteen months at the dominions of Argon. Six hundred mariners and one woman died during the voyage, and only one of the ambassadors reached home alive. On their arrival at the dominions of Argon, they found that he was dead, and that a person named Chiacato was governing the kingdom, during the minority of the son of the late monarch. On informing the regent of their business, he desired them to carry the young queen to Casan, which was the name of the prince, who was then on the frontiers of Persia, with an army of sixty thousand men, guarding certain passes on the borders of the kingdom against the attacks of their enemies. Having executed this order, Nicolo, Maffei and Marco returned to the palace of Chiacato, and remained there nine months.

Magnificent Letters Patent.

At the end of this time, they bade farewell to Chiacato, who gave them four tablets of gold, each a cubit long, and five fingers broad, and weighing three or four marks. On them were engraved the following words: "In the power of the eternal

God, the name of the Great Khan shall be honoured and praised for many years, and whosoever disobeyeth, shall be put to death, and all his goods confiscated." Besides this preamble, they commanded that all due honour should be shown to the three ambassadors of the Khan, and whatever service they needed should be performed in every country and district, subject to his authority as to himself in person; that all necessary relays of horses and escorts, and their expenses, and every thing needful, should be supplied to them freely and gratuitously. All these orders were duly obeyed, so that at times they travelled with an escort of two hundred horse for their protection. During their journey, they were informed that the great Emperor of the Tartars, Kublai Khan, was dead. They considered that this absolved them of all obligation to perform the promise which they had made to him to return to his court. So they continued their journey to Trebizond, on the south side of the Black Sea, from which city they proceeded by way of Constantinople and Negropont to Venice, where they arrived safely, and with immense wealth, in the year 1295.

MARCO POLO.

Arrival at Venice.

On their arrival at their own house in the street of St. Chrysostom, in Venice, they found themselves entirely forgotten by all their old acquaintances and countrymen. Even their relations were unable to recognize them in consequence of their long absence. They had been away twenty-five years, and besides being much altered by age, they had

MARCO POLO.

almost forgotten their own language, and resembled Tartars in their dress and manners. They were finally compelled to make use of some extraordinary expedients to satisfy their family and countrymen of their identity, and to recover the respect which was their due, by a public acknowledgment of their name, family, and rank. For this purpose, according to Ramusio, they invited all their relations and connections to a magnificent entertainment, at which all three of them appeared clothed in rich habits of crimson-coloured Eastern satin. After their guests arrived they threw off these splendid garments, and before sitting down to the table, gave them to their attendants, still appearing magnificently robed in crimson damask. When the last course came on the table, they cast off these robes, as they had done the first, and bestowed them in the same manner upon the servants; they themselves still appearing gorgeously bedecked with crimson velvet.

When the dinner was over and all the servants had withdrawn, Marco Polo produced to the company the coats of Tartarian cloth or felt, which they had ordinarily worn during their travels, and ripping them open, took out an incredible quantity of valuable gems; among these were some that were recognized by those who were present at the entertainment, as having belonged to the family, and thus the three travellers proved themselves incontestibly to be members of the Polo family, and the identical persons they represented themselves to be. Very probably their relations were more ready to acknowledge them, when they saw their magnificence and wealth, than when they appeared before them in the rough attire of weatherbeaten travellers.

Marco taken prisoner by the Genoese.

Such is the account of these celebrated travels handed down to the present day. Their intrinsic merit, and the importance which they had in the eyes of the early discoverers of America, has led to this somewhat extended notice of them. Of these adventurous men, some further information yet remains. About three years after their return, hostilities were commenced between the republics of Venice and Genoa. The Genoese Admiral Lampa Doria, came to the island of Curzola, with a fleet of seventy gallies, to oppose whom, the Venetians fitted out a large naval force, under the command of Andrea Dandolo, under whom Marco Polo held the command of a galley. The Venetians were totally defeated in a general engagement, with the loss of their Admiral and eighty-five ships, and Marco Polo was unfortunate enough to be taken prisoner by the Genoese.

He was confined in prison at Genoa about a year, until the termination of the war between the rival states released him. While there, many of the young Genoese nobility are said to have resorted to his cell to listen to the recital of his wonderful travels and surprising adventures; and it is said that they prevailed upon him to send to Venice for the notes which he had drawn up during his peregrinations, by means of which his travels were written out in Latin, according to his dictation. From the original Latin they were translated into Italian, and from this again abridgments were afterwards made in Latin, and scattered over Europe. Some authors are, however, of the opinion that they were originally written in Italian, and it is said that a manuscript copy of the work in the writing of his scribe Rustigielo was long preserved, in the possession of the Soranza family, at Venice. Whether it now exists, or has ever been published, is unknown.

Marriages of the Polo family.

At the time of the captivity of Marco, his father and uncle were greatly alarmed for his safety, and fearing that in case of his death they should have no descendants to whom they would care to bequeath their vast wealth, it was agreed between them that Nicolo, his father, should marry again, which he did speedily. On his return from his confinement, therefore, Marco found his father with three children, the fruit of his second marriage. Maffei Polo, the uncle of Marco, became a magistrate of Venice, and lived for some time in much respect among his countrymen. Marco seems to have taken no offence at his father's second union, but married himself after his return from Genoa to Venice. He left two daughters, Moretta and Feantina, but had no male issue. He is said to have received among his countrymen the name of Marco Millioni, because he and his family had acquired a fortune of a million of ducats in the East.

He died, as he had lived, universally beloved and respected; for, with all his advantages of birth and fortune, he was humble and beneficent, and employed his great riches, and the interest he possessed in the state, only to do good.

MARCO POLO.

Effects of the travels of the Polos.

The best method of conveying to the mind of the reader a conception of the enthusiasm which his travels excited in Europe, is to make one or two extracts from the work itself. The splendid descriptions of the immense wealth of the countries he visited, inflamed the minds of adventurers of all countries, and the prospect of converting to the Christian faith so powerful a potentate as he represented the Grand Khan to be, was so replete with advantages to the eyes of all the religious enthusiasts of the age, that many priests volunteered to go as missionaries to his distant dominions. For a time these schemes were the favourite popular theme, but they languished at last from the difficulty of accomplishing them, and were not again revived, until after the lapse of two centuries they again attracted general attention, in connection with the speculations afloat concerning a new route to India. Mr. Irving says that these accounts offered "too speculative and romantic an enterprise not to catch the vivid imagination of Columbus. In all his voyages he will be found to be continually seeking after the territories of the Grand Khan; and even after his last expedition, when nearly worn out by age, hardships, and infirmities, he offered, in a letter to the Spanish monarchs, written from a bed

MARCO POLO.

of sickness, to conduct any missionary to the territories of the Tartar Emperor who would undertake his conversion." "It was this confident expectation of soon arriving at these countries, and realizing the accounts of the Venetian, that induced him to hold forth those promises of immediate wealth to the sovereigns which caused so much disappointment, and brought upon him the frequent reproach of exciting false hopes, and indulging in wilful exaggeration."[1] Americus, as has been seen, entertained the same ideas, but with more moderation, and anticipated more difficulty in carrying them out. The selections from the writings of Polo which will be presented to the reader are his descriptions of the magnificent city of Quinsai, and of the much-sought-for island of Cipango.

EXTRACTS FROM MARCO POLO'S DESCRIPTION OF QUINSAI.

At the end of three days' journey we came to Quinsai or Guinsai, its name signifying the city of heaven, to denote its excellence over all the other cities of the earth, in which there are so much riches and so many pleasures and enjoyments, that a person might conceive himself in Paradise. In this great city, I, Marco, have often been, and have considered it with diligent attention, observing its whole state and circumstances, and setting down

[1] Irving, vol. ii. p. 904—906.

MARCO POLO.

the same in my memorials, of which I shall here give a brief abstract.

Great exten and public buildings of the city.

By common report, this city is an hundred miles in circuit.[1] The streets and lanes are very long and wide, and it has many large market-places. On one side of the city there is a clear lake of fresh water, and on the other there is a great river which enters the city in many places, and carries away all the filth into the lake, whence it continues its course into the ocean. This abundant course of running water causes a healthful circulation of pure air, and gives commodious passage in many directions, both by land and water, through the numerous canals, as by means of these and the causeways by which they are bordered, carts and barks have free intercourse for the carriage of merchandise and provisions. It is said that there are twelve thousand bridges, great and small, in this city, and those over the principal canals are so high that a vessel without her masts may go through underneath, while chariots and horses pass above. On the other side of the city there is a large canal, forty miles long, which encloses it on that side, being deep and full of water, made by the ancient kings, both to receive the overflowings of the river and to fortify the city, and the earth which was dug out of this canal, is laid on the inside as a

[1] These miles are the Chinese measures called Li, of which 200 compose a degree of latitude. Calculating thus, the city would be 34 miles in circumference. The word is used by Marco in the same sense throughout the extracts.

MARCO POLO.

rampart of defence. There are ten great market-places, which are square, and half a mile in each side. The principal street is forty paces broad, having a canal in the middle with many bridges, and every four miles there is a market-place two miles in circuit. There is also one large canal behind the great street and the market-places, on the opposite bank of which there are many storehouses of stone, where the merchants from India and other places lay up their commodities, being at hand and commodious for the markets. In each of these markets the people from the country, to the number of forty or fifty thousand, meet three days in every week, bringing beasts, game, fowls, and in short every thing that can be desired for subsistence, in profusion; and so cheap that two geese or four ducks may be bought for a Venetian groat. Then follow the butcher markets, in which beef, mutton, veal, kid and lamb, are sold to the great and rich, as the poor eat of all kinds of offal and unclean beasts without scruple; all sorts of herbs and fruits are to be had continually, among which are huge pears, weighing ten pounds each, white within, and very fragrant, with yellow and white peaches of very delicate flavour. Grapes do not grow in this country, but are brought from other places. They likewise import very good wine; but that is not in so much esteem as with us, the people being content with their own beverage, prepared from rice and spices. Every day there are brought up from the ocean, which is at

MARCO POLO.

the distance of twenty-five miles, such vast quantities of fish besides those which are caught in the lake, that one would conceive they could never be consumed, yet, in a few hours, all is gone. All these market-places are encompassed by high houses, underneath which are shops for all kinds of artificers, and all kinds of merchandise, such as spices, pearls and jewels, and in some the rice wine is sold. Many streets cross each other leading into these markets; in some of which there are many cold baths, accommodated with attendants of both sexes, who are used to this employment from their infancy. In the same bagnios, there are chambers for hot baths, for such strangers as are not accustomed to bathe in cold water. The inhabitants bathe every day, and always wash before eating.

Judicial officers.

In other streets reside the physicians and the astrologers, who also teach reading and writing, with many other arts. On opposite sides of the squares are two large edifices, where officers appointed by his majesty promptly decide any differences that arise between the foreign merchants and the inhabitants. They are bound also to take care that the guards be duly stationed on the neighbouring bridges, and in case of neglect, to inflict a discretionary punishment on the delinquent.

On each side of the principal street, mentioned as reaching across the whole city, are large houses and mansions with gardens; near to which are the abodes and shops of the working artisans. At all

MARCO POLO.

hours you observe such multitudes of people passing backwards and forwards on their various avocations, that it might seem impossible to supply them with food. A different judgment will, however, be formed, when every market-day the squares are seen crowded with people, and covered with provisions brought in for sale by carts and boats. To give some idea of the quantity of meat, wine, spices, and other articles brought for the consumption of the people of Quinsai, I shall instance the single article of pepper. I, Marco Polo, was informed by an officer employed in the customs, that the daily amount was forty-three loads, each weighing 243 pounds.

Private residences and domestic habits.

The houses of the citizens are well built, and richly adorned with carving, in which, as well as in painting and ornamental buildings, they take great delight, and lavish enormous sums. Their natural disposition is pacific, and the example of their former unwarlike kings has accustomed them to live in tranquillity. They keep no arms in their houses, and are unacquainted with their use. Their mercantile transactions are conducted in a manner perfectly upright and honourable. They also behave in a friendly manner to each other, so that the inhabitants of the same neighbourhood appear like one family. In their domestic relations, they show no jealousy or suspicion of their wives, but treat them with great respect. Any one would be held as infamous that should address indecent expressions to married women. They behave with cordiality to strangers who visit the city for commercial purposes, hospitably entertain them, and afford their best assistance in their business. On the other hand, they hate the very sight of soldiers, even the guards of the Great Khan; recollecting, that by their means they have been deprived of the government of their native sovereigns.

Lake in the neighbourhood of the city.

On the lake above mentioned are a number of pleasure-barges, capable of holding from ten to twenty persons, being from fifteen to twenty paces long, with a broad level floor, and moving steadily through the water. Those who delight in this amusement, and propose to enjoy it, either with their ladies or companions, engage one of these barges, which they find always in the very best order, with seats, tables, and every thing necessary for an entertainment. The boatmen sit on a flat upper deck, and with long poles reaching to the bottom of the lake, not more than two fathoms deep, push along the vessels to any desired spot. These cabins are painted in various colours, and with many figures; the exterior is similarly adorned. On each side are windows, which can at pleasure be kept open or shut, when the company seated at table may delight their eyes with the varied beauty of the passing scenes. Indeed the gratification derived from these water-excursions exceeds any that can be enjoyed on land; for as the lake extends all along the city, you discover, while standing in the boat, at a certain distance from the shore, all its grandeur and beauty, palaces, temples, convents, and gardens, while lofty trees reach down to the water's edge. At the same time are seen other boats continually passing, similarly filled with parties of pleasure. Generally, indeed, the inhabitants, when they have finished the labours of the day, or closed their mercantile transactions, think only of seeking amusement with their wives or mistresses, either in these barges or driving about the city in carriages. The main street already mentioned is paved with stone and brick to the width of ten paces on each side, the interval being filled up with small gravel, and having arched drains to carry off the water into the canals, so that it is always kept dry. On this road the carriages are constantly driving. They are long, covered at top, have curtains and cushions of silk, and can hold six persons. Citizens of both sexes, desirous of this amusement, hire them for that purpose, and you see them at every hour moving about in vast numbers. In many cases the people visit gardens, where they are introduced by the managers of the place into shady arbours, and remain till the time of returning home.

Palace of the king, and his great luxury.

The palace already mentioned had a wall with a passage dividing the exterior court from an inner one, which formed a kind of cloister, supporting a portico that surrounded it, and led to various royal apartments. Hence you entered a covered passage or corridor, six paces wide, and so long as to reach to the margin of the lake. On each side were corresponding entrances to ten courts, also resembling cloisters with porticos, and each having fifty private rooms, with gardens attached,—the residence of a thousand young females, whom the king maintained in his service. In the company either of his queen or of a party of those ladies he used to seek amusement on the lake, visiting the idol-temples on its banks. The other two portions of this seraglio were laid out in groves, pieces of water, beautiful orchards, and enclosures for animals suited for the chase, as antelopes, deer, stags, hares, and rabbits. Here, too, the king amused himself,—his damsels accompanying him in carriages or on horseback. No man was allowed to be of the party, but the females were skilled in the art of coursing and pursuing the animals. When fatigued they retired into the groves on the margin of the lake, and, quitting their dresses, rushed into the water, when they swam sportively in different directions,—the king remaining a spectator of the exhibition. Sometimes he had his repast provided beneath the dense foliage of one of these groves, and was there waited upon by the damsels. Thus he spent his time in this enervating society, profoundly ignorant of martial affairs; hence the Grand Khan, as already mentioned, was enabled to deprive him of his splendid possessions, and drive him with ignominy from his throne. All these particulars were related to me by a rich merchant of Quinsai, who was then very old; and having been a confidential servant of King Facfur, was acquainted with every circumstance of his life. He knew the palace in its former splendour, and desired me to come and take a view of it. Being then the residence of the Khan's viceroy, the colonnades were preserved entire, but the chambers had been allowed to go to ruin,—only their foundations remaining visible. The walls, too, including the parks and gardens, had been left to decay, and no longer contained any trees or animals.

Revenue of the Khan.

I will now tell you of the large revenue which the Khan draws from this city, and the territory under its jurisdiction, which is the ninth part of the province of Manji. The salt of that country yields to him in the year eighty tomans of gold, and each toman is 70,000 saiks, which amount to 5,600,000, and each saik is worth more than a gold florin; and is not this most great and wonderful! In that country, too, there grows more sugar than in the whole world besides, and it yields a very large revenue; I will not state it particularly, but remark that, taking all spices together, they pay 3⅓ per cent., which is levied too on all other merchandise. Large taxes are also derived from wine, rice, coal, and from the twelve arts, which, as already mentioned, have each twelve thousand stations. On every thing a duty is imposed: and on silk especially, and on other articles, is paid ten per cent. But I, Marco Polo, tell you, because I have often heard the account of it, that the revenue on all these commodities amounts every year to 210 tomans, or 14,700,000 saiks, and that is the most enormous amount of money that ever was heard of, and yet is paid by only the ninth part of the province of Manji. Now let us depart from this city of Quinsai, and go to another called Tampin-gui.

MARCO POLO.

THE ISLAND OF CIPANGO.

THIS is a very large island, fifteen hundred miles from the continent. The people are fair, handsome, and of agreeable manners. They are idolaters, and live quite separate, entirely independent of all other nations. Gold is very abundant, and no man being allowed to export it, while no merchant goes thence to the mainland, the people accumulate a vast amount. But I will give you a wonderful account of a very large palace, all covered with that metal, as our churches are with lead. The pavement of the chamber, the halls, windows, and every other part, have it laid on two inches thick, so that the riches of this palace are incalculable. Here are also red pearls, large, and of equal value with the white, with many other precious stones. Kublai, on hearing of this amazing wealth, desired to conquer the island, and sent two of his barons with a very large fleet containing warriors, both horsemen and on foot. One was named Abatan, the other Vonsanicin, both wise and valiant. They sailed from Zai-tun and Quinsai, reached the isle, landed, and took possession of the plain and of a number of houses; but they had been unable to take any city or castle, when a sad misadventure occurred. A mutual jealousy arose amongst them, which prevented their acting in any concert. One day when the north wind blew very strong, the troops expressed to each other apprehensions, that if they remained, all the vessels would be wrecked. The whole then went on board and set sail. When they had proceeded about four miles, they found another small isle, on which, the storm being violent, a number sought refuge. Others could not reach it, many of whom suffered shipwreck and perished; but some were preserved, and sailed for their native country. Those who had landed, 30,000 in number, looked on themselves as dead men, seeing no means of ever escaping; and their anger and grief were increased, when they beheld the other ships making their way homeward.

The sovereign and people of the large isle rejoiced greatly when they saw the host thus scattered and many of them cast upon the islet. As soon as the sea calmed, they assembled a great number of ships, sailed thither and landed, hoping to capture all those refugees. But when the latter saw that their enemies had disembarked, leaving the vessels unguarded, they skilfully retreated to another quarter, and continued moving about till they reached the ships, and went on board without any opposition. They then sailed direct for the principal island, hoisting its own standards and ensigns. On seeing these, the people believed their

MARCO POLO.

own countrymen had returned, and allowed them to enter the city. The Tartars, finding it defended only by old men, soon drove them out, retaining the women as slaves. When the king and his warriors saw themselves thus deceived, and their city captured, they were like to die of grief; but they assembled other ships, and invested it so closely as to prevent all communication. The invaders maintained it seven months, and planned day and night how they might convey tidings to their master of their present condition; but finding this impossible, they agreed with the besiegers to surrender, securing only their lives. This took place in the year 1269. The Great Khan, however, ordered one of the commanders of this host to lose his head, and the other to be sent to the isle where he had caused the loss of so many men, and there put to death. I have to relate also a very wonderful thing, that these two barons took a number of persons in a castle of Cipango, and because they had refused to surrender, ordered all their heads to be cut off; but there were eight on whom they could not execute this sentence, because these wore consecrated stones in the arm between the skin and the flesh, which so enchanted them, that they could not die by steel. They were therefore beaten to death with clubs, and the stones, being extracted, were held very precious. But I must leave this matter and go on with the narrative.

Paper Money—Immense Wealth of the Great Khan.

With regard to the money of Kambalu, the Great Khan may be called a perfect alchymist, for he makes it himself. He orders people to collect the bark of a certain tree, whose leaves are eaten by the worms that spin silk. The thin rind between the bark and the interior wood is taken, and from it cards are formed like those of paper, all black. He then causes them to be cut into pieces, and each is declared worth respectively half a livre, a whole one, a silver grosso of Venice, and so on to the value of ten bezants. All these cards are stamped with his seal, and so many are fabricated, that they would buy all the treasuries in the world. He makes all his payments in them, and circulates them through the kingdoms and provinces over which he holds dominion; and none dares to refuse them under pain of death. All the nations under his sway receive and pay this money for their merchandise, gold, silver, precious stones, and whatever they transport, buy, or sell. The merchants often bring to him goods worth 400,000 bezants, and he pays them all in these cards, which they willingly accept, because they can make purchases with them throughout the whole empire. He frequently commands those who have gold, silver, cloths of silk and gold, or other precious commodities, to bring them to him. Then he calls twelve men skilful in these matters, and commands them

MARCO POLO.

to look at the articles, and fix their price. Whatever they name is paid in these cards, which the merchant cordially receives. In this manner the great sire possesses all the gold, silver, pearls, and precious stones in his dominions. When any of the cards are torn or spoiled, the owner carries them to the place whence they were issued, and receives fresh ones, with a deduction of 3 per cent. If a man wishes gold or silver to make plate, girdles, or other ornaments, he goes to the office, carrying a sufficient number of cards, and gives them in payment for the quantity which he requires. This is the reason why the Khan has more treasure than any other lord in the world; nay, all the princes in the world together have not an equal amount.

The Care and Bounty of the Monarch towards his Subjects.

He sends his messengers through all his kingdoms and provinces, to know if any of his subjects have had their crops injured through bad weather or any other disaster; and if such injury has happened, he does not exact from them any tribute for that season or year; nay, he gives them corn out of his own stores to subsist upon, and to sow their fields. This he does in summer; in winter he inquires if there has been a mortality among the cattle, and in that case grants similar exemption and aid. When there is a great abundance of grain, he causes magazines to be formed, to contain wheat, rice, millet, or barley, and care to be taken that it be not lost or spoiled; then when a scarcity occurs, this grain is drawn forth, and sold for a third or fourth of the current price. Thus there cannot be any severe famine; for he does it through all his dominions; he bestows also great charity on many poor families in Kambalu; and when he hears of individuals who have not food to eat, he causes grain to be given to them. Bread is not refused at the court throughout the whole year to any who come to beg for it; and on this account he is adored as a god by his people. His majesty provides them also with raiment out of his tithes of wool, silk, and hemp. These materials he causes to be woven into different sorts of cloth, in a house erected for that purpose, where every artisan is obliged to work one day in the week for his service. Garments made of the stuffs thus manufactured are given to destitute families for their winter and summer dresses. A dress is also prepared for his armies; and in every city a quantity of woollen cloth is woven, being defrayed from the tithes there levied. It must be observed, that the Tartars, according to their original customs, when they had not yet adopted the religion of the idolaters, never bestowed alms; but when applied to by any necessitous person, repelled him with reproachful expressions, saying,—begone with your complaints of a bad season, God has sent it to you, and had he loved you, as he evidently loves me, you would have similarly prospered. But since some of the wise men among the idolaters, especially the baksi, have represented to his majesty, that to provide for the poor is a good work and highly grateful to their deities, he has bestowed charity in the manner now described, so that, at his court, none are denied food who come to ask for it. He has also so arranged that in all the highways by which messengers, merchants, and other persons travel, trees are planted at short distances on both sides of the road, and are so tall that they can be seen from a great distance. They serve thus both to show the way and afford a grateful shade. This is done whenever the nature of the soil admits of plantation; but when the route lies through sandy deserts or over rocky mountains, he has ordered stones to be set up, or columns erected, to guide the traveller. Officers of rank are appointed, whose duty it is to take care that these matters be properly arranged, and the roads kept constantly in good order. Besides other motives, the Great Khan is influenced by the declaration of his soothsayers and astrologers, that those who plant trees receive long life as their reward.

V.

FELLOW-VOYAGERS OF AMERICUS.

ALONZO DE OJEDA AND JUAN DE LA COSA.[1]

OJEDA.

A BRIEF notice of the early career of the first of these navigators has been given previously in this volume. His subsequent exploits are quite interesting. It has already been seen from the account of Americus, who was his fellow-voyager in 1499, that he could have realized but a very trifling profit from his share in that expedition. In fact, he acquired nothing but renown as a bold and skilful fol lower of the seas. Many were the tales which were circulated of his prowess and intrepidity, and his popularity with the people, ever moved to enthusiasm by daring exploits, seconded by the powerful interest of his patron, the Bishop Fonseca, led him prosperously onward to royal favour. Soon after

[1] This illustration of the lives of Ojeda and De la Cosa is abridged mainly from the work of Mr. Irving, entitled the Lives of the Companions of Columbus. It was originally intended to have translated such portions of the "Viages Menores" of Navarréte as referred to the subject, but the full accounts of Mr. Irving, who, as he says in his Preface, has consulted this work, as well as many other valuable works and documents of reference, presented so complete an array of material that it was determined to abandon the original intention for the present plan.

FELLOW-VOYAGERS OF AMERICUS.

his return, he received a grant of six leagues of land in Hispaniola, and permission to fit out vessels for a further prosecution of discoveries on the coast of the mainland. He was prohibited from interfering with the traffic on the coast of Paria, within certain limits, but was granted a right to trade in all other parts, on condition of paying one-fifth of the profits of his voyage to the king. He was authorized to colonize Coquibacoa, and as an inducement was to receive half the revenue of the new colony, unless it exceeded 300,000 maravedis, in which case the surplus was to go to the crown.

Juan de Vergara and Garcia de Campos.

With such brilliant prospects before him, Ojeda found no difficulty in finding partners and assistance in his undertaking. Juan de Vergara and Garcia de Campos joined in his enterprise, making a partnership agreement for the term of two years. They fitted out four ships, the Santa Maria de la Antigua, the Santa Maria de la Granada, the caravel Magdalena, and the caravel Santa Ana. His partners each commanded one of the first-named vessels, his nephew, Pedro, the third, and Hernando de Guevara the fourth; the whole fleet being controlled by Ojeda himself.

The expedition set sail in 1502, and after procuring the usual supply of provisions at the Canaries, crossed the ocean in safety, and touched the shores of the New World on the coast of Cumana. This was the native name of the country, but Ojeda called it Val-fermoso, on account of its beauty and fertility. While supplying the immediate necessities of his vessels on this coast, Ojeda adopted an expedient savouring more of policy than justice. Knowing that he should want many utensils and articles of common use in his new colony, he determined to procure them from the natives of Cumana, rather than enrage the Indians in the neighbourhood of his proposed settlement. Their pillage was successful, but was the occasion of much bloodshed. Notwithstanding the orders of Ojeda to his men, to do as little damage as possible, the poor Indians suffered severely, their cabins were burnt, and several of their women carried into captivity, or only returned to them on the payment of a ransom. To the honour of Ojeda, it is said that he took nothing of the spoil but a hammock.

Settlement at Bahia Honda.

After a while the fleet proceeded to Coquibacoa, but finding the country in the neighbourhood extremely sterile, they went on further to a bay which Ojeda called Santa Cruz, and is the present Bahia Honda, where it was determined to form a settlement. They found in this place a Spaniard, who had been left by Bastides, a voyager who had visited those parts about a year previously. He had since been living peaceably with the Indians, and had acquired their language. The natives at first attempted to oppose the landing of Spaniards, but were soon overawed by the display of force which Ojeda made, and came forward to greet them with presents. The adventurers immediately commenced building their fortress, and storing in it their goods and provisions. All the

OJEDA IN IRONS.

They had hardly put out to sea before a fierce quarrel arose between Talavera and himself, with regard to their respective rights of command, which ended in his being seized by the freebooter's crew and loaded with irons.
(SEE P. 388.)

gold which they acquired by barter or plunder, was deposited in a safe box, under two keys, one of which was kept by the royal officer who accompanied the expedition, and the other by Ocampo.

FELLOW-VOYAGERS OF AMERICUS

Quarrels of Ojeda and his partners.

All the gold, however, which they were enabled to collect did not supply them with provisions, which grew day by day more scarce, notwithstanding the energetic efforts of the foraging parties continually despatched by the commander to ransack the country. The people murmured at their deprivations and sufferings, and above all a fear arose among them that they would lose their means of departure, in consequence of their ships having been attacked by a species of worm, which bored holes in the planks, and caused them to leak greatly. As is ever the case, discontent produced recrimination and quarrels, and the factions of the petty colony rose at last to such a height, that his partners at length entrapped Ojeda on board of one of the caravels, seized him, and put him in irons. They gave out that he had gone farther than his license from the sovereigns allowed, that he was a defaulter, for whom they would be liable as sureties, and that they were determined to take him to Spain for trial.

Ojeda made one or two attempts to compromise with his partners without success, and at last they sailed in the beginning of September, carrying away with them the whole colony, and the strong box, which was the main cause of all their disputes. When they arrived at the western coast of Hispaniola, their captive governor made a desperate attempt to escape from his confinement. The vessels were lying at anchor, about a stone's throw from the shore, when, relying upon his activity and skill as a swimmer, he slipped quietly over the side into the water, in the night-time, and made for the shore. But though his arms were left free, his feet were chained, and finding that the weight of his shackles was sinking him, he was compelled to cry for help, and, half drowned, was again put into confinement on board.

Legal process against Ojeda.

When they arrived St. Domingo, a long lawsuit took place before the Chief Judge of the island, who found Ojeda guilty, in spite of his protestations that his partners were the persons in fault. The decision pronounced him a defaulter, stripped him of all his effects, and brought him heavily in debt to the government. For a time he was looked upon as a ruined man, and though, subsequently, on an appeal by Ojeda to the royal council, the case was reconsidered, the decision reversed, and an order issued for the restoration of his property, yet the expenses of the lawsuit, in which he was engaged for nearly a year, consumed all his small fortune, and left him a bankrupt, though triumphant, litigant.

This judicial contest was decided in 1503, and for some years after that period no record appears concerning the movements of Ojeda, excepting one, which, without particularizing, mentions that he made another voyage to the vicinity of Coquibacoa in 1505. In 1508 he is found again in Hispaniola. With the roving and restless habits of the mariner, he seems to have united the common fault of sailors of all countries, a reckless and profuse extravagance, which led him to squander his resources, and kept him always in a state of poverty, although it did not weaken his love of daring enterprise.

FELLOW-VOYAGERS OF AMERICUS.

The gold mines of Veragua.

About this time the cupidity of King Ferdinand was attracted by the gold mines of the coast of Veragua, and projects were set on foot to establish colonies in that direction. Indisposed to increase the power of Columbus and his family, the wary monarch looked about for some one to appoint to the command of these colonies, and among others, Ojeda was thought of for the post. Although possessing, in the Bishop Fonseca, a strong friend at court, he was, unfortunately, too far absent and too poor to urge his claims, and had it not been for his lucky meeting with Juan de la Cosa, he would probably never have obtained the appointment.

Juan de la Cosa.

Juan de la Cosa was even at the time when he accompanied Americus on his second voyage, in the capacity of pilot, a veteran in maritime affairs. He had previously sailed with Columbus, and, as Navarrête says, somewhat sneeringly, "in the opinion of others as well as of himself," was thought not to be inferior to Columbus in his knowledge of navigation.[1] Peter Martyr relates, that the Spaniards esteemed the maps which were drawn by

[1] Navarrête, tom. iii. p. 4.

FELLOW-VOYAGERS OF AMERICUS.

him, and by another pilot named Andres Morales, as the best in the world, and that they were "thought to be more cunning in that part of cosmography which teacheth the description and measuring of the sea, than any others."[1] Soon after his return from the New World, in 1500, in the month of October in that year, he was solicited by Rodrigo de Bastides, to accompany him, in two caravels which he had fitted out, to search for gold and pearls. Bastides was a notary, and knew nothing of navigation, but confided the whole management of the navigation to Juan de la Cosa, who extended his fame for sound discretion and able seamanship.

Voyage of Bastides.

This voyage was extremely successful, and they had collected an immense amount of gold and pearls, when their good fortune was checked by an unlooked-for event. They found that their vessels were eaten through in many places by the destructive worms which abound in the Torrid Zone, and leaked so badly that they could scarcely be kept afloat long enough to enable them to reach Hispaniola. There they repaired their craft and put to sea, with the intention of returning to Cadiz, but were once more controlled by evil fortune, and driven back again by a succession of storms. The leaks broke out afresh, and after landing the most portable part of their rich cargo, the vessels foundered before they could get out the remainder. Bastides also lost the arms and ammunition saved

1 P. Martyr. Decade ii c. 10.

from the wrecks, being compelled to destroy them, lest they should fall into the hands of the Indians.

FELLOW-VOYAGERS OF AMERICUS.

The crew were divided into three parties, two of which were headed by Bastides and De la Cosa, and started for St. Domingo by three different routes. Bobadilla, at that time Governor of San Domingo, heard of their approach, and ordering them to be arrested on the charge of pursuing an illicit traffic with the Indians, sent them to Spain. He was tried there and acquitted, and so lucrative had the voyage proved, that he was enabled to pay a handsome sum to the crown, besides reserving a large fortune for himself. In reward for his services, the sovereigns granted him an annual revenue for life, to be drawn from the province of Uraba, which he had discovered, and an equal pension was assigned to De la Cosa, with the office of Alguazil Mayor of the same territory to which he was appointed.

It is probable that the veteran pilot remained at home for some time after his return from this voyage, enjoying his well-earned fortune, for it has been seen that he was ordered to attend the court in company with Americus, soon after the return of King Ferdinand from his journey to Naples, Soon after that time, he went to Hispaniola.

Connection of De la Cosa with Ojeda.

The history of the veteran was from this time till his death intimately connected with that of Ojeda. He had managed to acquire by his fortunate voyage with Bastides, and in the course of his other ramblings, considerable property, and having

FELLOW-VOYAGERS OF AMERICUS.

a high opinion of the talents and energy of Ojeda, with all the openheartedness of a sailor, he placed all his means at the disposal of his less fortunate friend. It was concerted between them that Cosa should proceed to Spain to promote his appointment by suit at court, and though opposed by a powerful rival, Don Diego de Nicuessa, he was successful, at least in part. King Ferdinand, with his usual shrewdness, favoured both the candidates, and dividing that part of the continent which lies along the Isthmus of Darien into two governments, he gave the eastern portion, extending to Cape De la Vela, to Ojeda, and the western, including Veragua, and extending to Cape Gracias a Dios, to Nicuessa. Each of them was bound to erect two forts in their respective districts, and were allowed the product of the mines they should discover, after a certain deduction for the crown.

Juan de la Cosa received the appointment of Lieutenant under Ojeda, and immediately fitted out a fleet of a ship and two brigantines, in which he embarked with about two hundred men. The armament of Nicuessa was much more powerful, owing to his greater command of means. These rival expeditions arrived at San Domingo at the same time. Ojeda welcomed his lieutenant with joy, and though somewhat mortified at the smallness of his force compared with that of Nicuessa, he soon found means, in the purses of his friends on the island, to recruit and increase his forces.

Bitter feud between Ojeda and Nicuessa.

During their stay, a feud arose between the rival

Governors. The bone of contention was the Island of Jamaica, which had been assigned undivided to both of them as a place to procure supplies for their respective colonies. Both of them claimed also the province of Darien as within their dominions. Ojeda, who was a better fighter than reasoner, proposed to settle their dispute by a personal combat, but the more prudent Nicuessa, smiling at the heat of his rival, insisted upon a deposit of five thousand Castillanos on each side, to be the prize of the conqueror, which he knew the purse of Ojeda would be too poor to furnish, though his pride was too great to acknowledge it. Juan de la Cosa, however, interposed to prevent any violence. The influence which the veteran had over the impetuous spirit of his commander is interesting. He seems to have stood by him as a Mentor, and warmly attached to one whom he knew to be faithful and devoted, and of courage beyond question, Ojeda suffered himself to be controlled in his rash impulses. The dispute was settled by the establishment of the river Darien as the boundary of the two governments, a most salutary compromise, owing entirely to the good judgment of the veteran pilot. The difference respecting Jamaica was settled by Don Diego Columbus himself, who took possession of it in the right of his father.

On the 10th of November, 1509, Ojeda set sail from St. Domingo. His force consisted of two ships, two brigantines, and three hundred men, among whom was the celebrated Pizarro, after-

Departure from San Domingo, 15th Nov., 1509.

FELLOW-VOYAGERS OF AMERICUS.

wards the conqueror of Peru. Cortez likewise intended to have sailed in the fleet, but was prevented by sickness. The voyage was short, for the experienced De la Cosa knew well the navigation. He knew too the warlike and treacherous character of the natives, and endeavoured to persuade Ojeda to commence a settlement in the Gulf of Uraba, where the people were less ferocious, and did not use poisoned arrows. Ojeda, however, would not alter his plans, and it is thought he had no objection to the prospect of a skirmish with the natives, for in that way he hoped to capture slaves enough to pay off his debts in Hispaniola. He landed, therefore, with the largest part of his force, and with a number of friars, who accompanied him as missionaries to convert the Indians, and his faithful lieutenant, unable to keep him out of danger, stood by to second him. He advanced towards the savages, who were drawn up on the shore, and ordered the friars to read aloud a certain manifesto, which had recently been prepared by divines and juristo in Spain, to be used in such emergencies, and which is sufficiently curious to merit being copied in full. It reads as follows:

Proclamation of Ojeda to the Indians.

"I, Alonzo de Ojeda, servant of the high and mighty kings of Castile and Leon, civilizers of barbarous nations, their messenger and captain, notify and make known to you, in the best way I can, that God our Lord, one and eternal, created the heavens and the earth, and one man and one woman, from whom you, and we, and all the people of the earth

FELLOW-VOYAGERS OF AMERICUS.

were and are descendants, procreated, and all those who shall come after us; but the vast number of generations which have proceeded from them, in the course of more than five thousand years that have elapsed since the creation of the world, made it necessary that some of the human race should disperse in one direction and some in another, and that they should divide themselves into many kingdoms and provinces, as they could not sustain and preserve themselves in one alone. All these people were given in charge, by God our Lord, to one person, named Saint Peter, who was thus made lord and superior of all the people of the earth, and head of the whole human lineage, whom all should obey, wherever they might live, and whatever might be their law, sect or belief; he gave him also the whole world for his service and jurisdiction, and though he desired that he should establish his chair in Rome, as a place most convenient for governing the world, yet he permitted that he might establish his chair in any other part of the world, and judge and govern all the nations, Christians, Moors, Jews, Gentiles, and whatever other sect or belief might be. This person was denominated Pope, that is to say, admirable, supreme, father and guardian, because he is father and governor of all mankind. This holy father was obeyed and honoured as lord, king, and superior of the universe by those who lived in his time, and, in like manner, have been obeyed and honoured by all those who have been elected to the Pontificate,

FELLOW-VOYAGERS OF AMERICUS.

and thus it has continued unto the present day, and will continue until the end of the world.

One of these Pontiffs of whom I have spoken, as lord of the world, made a donation of these islands and continents, of the ocean, sea, and all that they contain, to the Catholic kings of Castile, who, at that time, were Ferdinand and Isabella of glorious memory, and to their successors, our sovereigns, according to the tenor of certain papers drawn up for the purpose (which you may see if you desire). Thus his majesty is king and sovereign of these islands and continents by virtue of the said donation; and as king and sovereign, certain islands, and almost all to whom this has been notified, have received his majesty, and have obeyed and served, and do actually serve him. And, moreover, like good subjects, and with good-will, and without any resistance or delay, the moment they were informed of the foregoing, they obeyed all the religious men sent among them to preach and teach our Holy Faith; and these of their free and cheerful will, without any condition or reward, became Christians, and continue so to be. And his majesty received them kindly and benignantly, and ordered that they should be treated like his other subjects and vassals: you, also, are required and obliged to do the same. Therefore, in the best manner I can, I pray and entreat you, that you consider well what I have said, and that you take whatever time is reasonable to understand and deliberate upon it, and that you recognize the church for sovereign and superior of the universal world, and the supreme Pontiff, called Pope, in her name, and his majesty in his place, as superior and sovereign king of the islands and Terra Firma, by virtue of the said donation; and that you consent that these religious fathers declare and preach to you the foregoing; and if you shall so do, you will do well; and will do that to which you are bounden and obliged; and his majesty, and I in his name, will receive you with all due love and charity, and will leave you, your wives and children, free from servitude, that you may freely do with these and with yourselves whatever you please, and think proper, as have done the inhabitants of the other islands. And besides this, his majesty will give you many privileges and exemptions, and grant you many favours. If you do not do this, or wickedly and intentionally delay to do so, I certify to you, that, by the aid of God, I will powerfully invade and make war upon you in all parts and modes that I can, and will subdue you to the yoke and obedience of the church and of his majesty: and I will take your wives and children and make slaves of them, and sell them as such, and dispose of them as his majesty may command; and I will take your effects and will do you all the harm and injury in my power, as vassals who will not obey or receive their sovereign, and who resist and oppose him. And I protest that the deaths and disasters which may in this manner be occasioned, will be the fault of yourselves and not of

FELLOW-VOYAGERS OF AMERICUS.

his majesty, nor of me, nor of these cavaliers who accompany me. And of what I here tell you and require of you, I call upon the notary here present to give me his signed testimonial."

When the friars had finished reading this manifesto, Ojeda endeavoured to entice the Indians by signs of friendship and presents, which he exhibited. But they had suffered too much from the cruelties of other adventurers to be won by kind measures, and in answer to his advances, brandished their spears and prepared to fight.

De la Cosa tries to dissuade Ojeda from settling in this part of the country.

Juan de la Cosa again renewed his entreaties to Ojeda to abandon the country, but his choler was now so much roused, that he would not listen to reason, and, forgetful of the poisoned arrows of the natives, he uttered a short prayer to the Virgin, in whose protection he blindly confided, and buckling on his armour, charged furiously upon them. The old pilot could not sit still and see the fray, but rushed forward as gallantly as if it had been of his own seeking. The Indians soon dispersed, leaving a number killed and wounded on the field, and several were made prisoners in the course of the pursuit, which Ojeda followed for three or four miles, into the interior, in spite of the remonstrances of his Mentor. Still De la Cosa kept up with him, and joined in all the hair-brained risks which he ran, though continually remonstrating against his useless temerity.

At length they were stopped by a stronghold of the enemy. With his old war-cry of "Santiago,"

FELLOW-VOYAGERS OF AMERICUS.

Ojeda led his men to a furious assault. Eight of the bravest of the Indian warriors threw themselves into a hut, whence they discharged such showers of arrows, that for a time the hardiest of the assailants were kept at bay. The reproaches of Ojeda reanimate them, and an old Castilian soldier, stung by his cry of "Shame," fell pierced through the heart by an arrow, on the threshold of the door which he vainly attempted to force. At last, fire was applied to the hut, which in an instant was in a blaze, and the eight warriors perished in the flames.

Death of Juan de la Cosa.

Then they yielded, and seventy captives were sent back to the ships. Still the pursuit was continued; another village was reached, which was found deserted. The Indians had fled to the mountains with their women and children, and all their effects. Thinking themselves secure, by this time, in the terror of the natives, the Spaniards dispersed themselves over the country in search of booty, in small parties. Taking advantage of this incaution, the Indians again attacked them. They fought resolutely, but unavailingly, and were borne down by overwhelming numbers. On the first alarm, Ojeda collected a few soldiers, and defended himself behind a stockade which he erected. Juan de la Cosa, hearing of his commander's danger, rushed to his assistance. Before the gate of the enclosure, the brave pilot kept the savages at bay until most of his followers were killed and he himself severely wounded. Then Ojeda dashed among the Indians like a tiger, dealing his blows on every side. La Cosa was too feeble to second him, and took refuge in a cabin, where he defended himself till all but one of his men were slain; then sinking to the ground, and feeling that his death was drawing nigh, he said to his surviving companion, "Brother, since God has protected thee from harm, sally out and fly, and if ever thou shouldest see Alonzo de Ojeda, tell him of my fate."

Character of De la Cosa.

"Thus," says the eloquent historian, in words which it is impossible to abridge, "thus fell the hardy Juan de la Cosa; nor can we refrain from pausing to pay a passing tribute to his memory. He was acknowledged by his contemporaries to be one of the ablest of those gallant Spanish navigators who first explored the way to the New World. But it is by the honest and kindly qualities of his heart that his memory is most endeared to us; it is, above all, by that loyalty in friendship displayed in this his last and fatal expedition. Warmed by his attachment for a more youthful and hotheaded adventurer, we see this wary veteran of the seas forgetting his usual prudence and the lessons of his experience, and embarking, heart and hand, purse and person, in the wild enterprises of his favourite. We behold him watching over him as a parent, remonstrating with him as a counsellor, but fighting by him as a partisan; following him without hesitation into known and needless danger, to certain death itself, and showing no other solicitude in his dying moments but to be remembered by his friend.

The history of these Spanish discoveries abound in noble and generous traits of character, but few have charmed us more than this instance of loyalty to the last gasp, in the death of the staunch Juan de la Cosa. The Spaniard who escaped to tell the story of his end was the only survivor of seventy that had followed Ojeda in this rash and headlong inroad."

FELLOW-VOYAGERS OF AMERICUS.

Great anxiety on board the ships, and escape of Ojeda.

While these events were taking place on shore, those who remained on board their ships suffered the greatest anxiety for the fate of their comrades. Some days, elapsed and no news of them reached the vessels. Detached parties were sent a short distance into the woods in search of them, and boats were manned and proceeded to examine the shores in the hope of seeing something of their lost comrades. They did not dare, however, to go far inland, for they constantly heard the war-whoop and shouts of their savage foes ringing through the forest. One day, as they were about giving up in despair, they saw the body of a man in Spanish attire lying in a thicket of mangrove trees, and half concealed by the undergrowth of shrubs. The roots of the mangrove rise and intertwine with each other above the water in which they grow; and extended on these roots, with his buckler on and his sword in his hand, but so weakened by hunger and fatigue that he was unable to speak, the Spaniards found Alonzo de Ojeda. He was chilled with the damps of his hiding-place, but they soon kindled a fire, and, by degrees, he recovered sufficiently to tell them his sad story.

He had effected his purpose of cutting his way through the Indians, and almost in utter despair at the loss of so many brave followers, he had wandered about alone, scarcely knowing whither he was going, and had at last sunk down to die, where his remaining followers fortunately found him. All considered his escape miraculous, and when it was found that he was not wounded, although the marks of over three hundred arrows were on his buckler, their astonishment was redoubled, and Ojeda himself attributed it to another interposition of the Virgin in his favour. But the Indians were not destined to enjoy their triumph long. While his companions were busily engaged in administering to the wants of their commander, the ships of Nicuessa appeared in the offing. Ojeda, remembering his recent quarrel with the rival governor, feared that he would take advantage of his misfortunes, but his apprehensions were groundless. With the true spirit of a Spanish Hidalgo, he received Ojeda with open arms, expressed himself willing to forget all their differences, and placed himself and his men under the orders of Ojeda, to assist him in dealing a blow of vengeance upon his savage enemies.

Ojeda, with the aid of Nicuessa, prepares for another attack.

Again inspirited by this noble conduct, Ojeda prepared at once for the attack. The two governors, no longer rivals, landed with four hundred men, and set off with promptness for the Indian village in the night. They surrounded it before the natives were alarmed, for they thought that they had slain all the Spaniards, and were reposing in perfect security. Their sleep was broken first by the assault of the exasperated Spaniards, who soon set their dwellings in a blaze, and spared neither women nor children in the fury of their attack. The slaughter was great, and the vengeance complete, and leaving the smoking ashes of the ruined village, the Spaniards returned to their ships.

FELLOW-VOYAGERS OF AMERICUS

While searching in all directions for booty, of which they found a large amount, they discovered the body of the unfortunate Juan de la Cosa. It was tied to a tree, and swollen and discoloured in a shocking manner by the baneful poison of the arrows by which he was killed. Bitterly did Ojeda repent that he had not followed the advice of his trusty lieutenant, and in sadness and mourning he prepared too tardily to adopt his plans.

Settlement in the Gulf of Uraba.

Having determined to leave at once a place which had been so disastrous to him, Ojeda set sail once more with his disheartened followers, and after having made two or three vain attempts to discover the River Darien, steered for the Gulf of Uraba, on the eastern shore of which he fixed upon a place to build his fortress. With his usual energy, every thing that was needful was soon landed from the ships; houses were built, and his embryo capital, which he called San Sebastian, was protected by a strong wooden stockade and fortress. Feeling the weakness of his force, he lost no time in despatching a messenger to his friend,

FELLOW-VOYAGERS OF AMERICUS.

the Bachelor Enciso, whom he had engaged in his undertaking in Hispaniola, urging him to send forward his recruits and supplies with expedition. Again and again before their expected reinforcement could have arrived, were they attacked by the natives, and at last, when their provisions began to fail, and they were compelled to forage among the villages, in search, not of gold, but of food, the discouraged Spaniards were entirely routed, and pursued with yells to the very gates of their fortress. Some died in agony from their wounds, others perished with famine, and death came to be looked upon among them as a relief from horror and misery, to be welcomed rather than shunned.

Ojeda wounded.

Ojeda was thought by the Indians to possess a charmed life, for as yet they had never been able even to wound him. They determined, however, to test the fact, and having previously prepared four of their best marksmen, they led him into an ambush where these men could take sure aim at him. Three of their arrows glanced harmlessly from his buckler; the fourth pierced his thigh. Fearing from certain symptoms that it was poisoned, Ojeda ordered his surgeon to apply to the wound red-hot irons, to burn out the venom. The surgeon refused, and only yielded when Ojeda made a solemn vow that he would have him hanged if he did not comply. He endured this painful operation without a groan, and the wound was healed; the cold poison, says the good Bishop Las Casas, being consumed by the vivid fire.

FELLOW-VOYAGERS OF AMERICUS.

Arrival of Talavera with scanty supplies.

In the midst of their sufferings, and while daily looking for the arrival of the ship of the Bachelor Enciso, a strange vessel made its appearance at San Sebastian. It turned out to be a Genoese vessel which had been seized by one Talavera, and a band of piratical desperadoes, who, hearing of the condiuon of Ojeda and his associates, felt sure of being gladly received into his service, their supplies of provisions and reinforcement of men being absolutely necessary to the beleaguered colony. The good father Charlevoix thought their arrival was a manifest interposition of Divine Providence in their favour, and whether that was the case or not, it undoubtedly saved them when on the very brink of destruction. Still it was only a temporary relief. The ship of Enciso did not arrive, and in a short time, famine again raged in all its horrors, notwithstanding the scrupulous care with which Ojeda doled out to each of his suffering comrades his scanty allowance of food. Discontent and factions came with hunger, till finally Ojeda was compelled to enter into an agreement with his mutinous colonists, which had the effect of quieting them for a time. The agreement was that he himself should proceed to Hispaniola in quest of supplies, and that if at the end of forty days, during which they were to endure as well as they could the privations of San Sebastian, no relief or tidings of him should reach them, they were to be at liberty to abandon the colony, and return to Hispaniola in the brigantines. The government of the colony was, in the meantime, to be left in the hands of Pizarro, as his lieutenant, until the coming of the Bachelor Enciso.

Departure of Ojeda, and his shipwreck.

Having concluded this convention, Ojeda embarked in the ship of the piratical leader. It was an unlucky moment when he consented to take this course. They had hardly put out to sea before a fierce quarrel arose between Talavera and himself, with regard to their respective rights of command, which ended in his being seized by the freebooter's crew and loaded with irons. In vain did he revile them as recreants, pirates, and cowards, and offer to fight them all if they would give him a fair field on the deck, with his weapons in his hands, and attack him two at a time. They had heard too much of his skill and bravery not to fear him even with these odds, and he would probably have been carried in irons to Hispaniola, had not a violent gale ensued, which induced the pirates to set him free in order to have the benefit of his skill as a pilot. With all his efforts, however, against storms and currents, he was unable to carry the vessel into her destined port. After being tost about by the tempest for several days, he was reduced to the alternative of running her on shore on the southern side of Cuba, to prevent her from foundering at sea.

After the wreck of their vessel the pirates found themselves in a worse situation than they were in before they had captured her. With the undefinable yearning after the haunts of society, which civ-

FELLOW VOYAGERS OF AMERICUS.

ilized men always feel, they were anxious to reach Hispaniola, although they knew that dungeons and chains awaited them. Their only course was to travel on foot to the eastern extremity of the island, and there seek some means of transportation, and, valuable as the aid of Ojeda had been to them at sea, they soon found that the resources of his mind were of equal importance to them on shore. He gradually gained the ascendancy over them, and assumed the command, although they still regarded him with feelings of hostility; displaying thus the power which a master-spirit always exercises in the hour of difficulty and danger.

Sufferings of the Spaniards in Cuba.

Cuba, not at that time colonized, had become the refuge of many of the unfortunate inhabitants of Hayti who had fled from the tasks and whips of their masters, and found temporary security in the forests of the neighbouring island. Their accounts had inflamed the minds of many of the tribes who inhabited the villages, so that the march of the Spaniards was continually opposed both by the runaways and by the natives themselves. Ojeda at first easily repulsed their attacks, but finding that his men grew weaker daily, he resolved, for the remainder of the journey, to avoid as much as possible the villages, and accordingly led his men into the thickest of the forests, and by the broad savannahs, which stretched along the seashore. While thus avoiding one evil, he met with another, almost if not quite as great. The plains which the Spaniards entered at first, appeared covered with

FELLOW-VOYAGERS OF AMERICUS.

high grass and rank vegetation, which, though it rendered their progress slow, was but a trifling matter to what was in reserve for them. The ground gradually became moist under their feet, and finally ended in an immense morass, or salt marsh, where the water reached to their knees. Still they pressed forward, continually encouraged by Ojeda, who had no idea of the task he was undertaking. The marsh extended for upwards of thirty leagues, and the farther they proceeded, the deeper became the mire, until at last it seemed to them interminable, and they were ready to give up in despair. Numerous rivers and creeks intersected this fatal plain, which they had to cross, and many who could not swim were drowned. The only way in which they could sleep, was by climbing among the twisted roots of the mangrove trees, which grew in the water. Their provisions were almost exhausted, and their sufferings from thirst were extreme, when, having been eight days upon their journey, Ojeda determined to struggle forward with a few of the least weary of the men. He encouraged those whom he left behind to persevere, and taking from his knapsack a small picture of the Virgin, which the Bishop Fonseca had given him, and which he always carried about his person, he knelt before it, and made a solemn vow that he would erect a chapel for the service of his patroness in the first Indian village at which he might arrive.

Well did the venerable Bishop Las Casas say,

"the sufferings of the Spaniards in the New World, in their search for gold, were more cruel and severe than ever nation in the world endured; but those experienced by Ojeda and his men have surpassed all others." They were thirty days in crossing this immense and horrible swamp. Out of seventy men who entered it, only thirty-five evei emerged from it, and when Ojeda, with a few of the most vigorous of his advanced party, at last reached a spot where the land was firm and dry, their joy was unutterable, yet their weakness only permitted them to go a short distance to an Indian village ere they dropped down completely exhausted.

FELLOW VOYAGERS OF AMERICUS.

This village was ruled by a cacique named Cuyebâs. His tribe gathered around the Spaniards with wonder, but as soon as their story was told, vied with each other in acts of humanity to the suffering strangers. They bore them to their houses, and furnished them with food and drink, and the chief sent a large party into the morass with orders to bring out those remaining behind on their shoulders, if they were unable to walk. How noble an example they offered to their Christian guests—an example of humanity, indeed, which would have reflected honour upon the most civilized race.

Ojeda builds a chapel in fulfilment of his vow.

Ojeda, as soon as he had recovered from his sufferings, prepared faithfully to perform his vow. He built a small chapel in the village, and erected an altar, over which he suspended his much-valu picture of the Virgin. He next explained to the benevolent cacique, and many of the inhabitants, the main points of the Catholic faith, and more particularly the history of the Virgin Mother. However little they understood the doctrines which he endeavoured to teach them, they conceived a high respect for the picture which he left. They ever kept the little chapel cleanly swept, and decorated with votive offerings and flowers, and when Las Casas subsequently visited the place, he performed mass at its altar, and baptized under its roof the children of the humane and innocent natives.

Sends a message to Esquibel, in Jamaica.

This duty having been duly performed, Ojeda and his party proceeded on their journey. The inhabitants of this part of the coast received them everywhere kindly, and they continued their way to the province of Macaca, where Columbus had previously been well received, and where they also were hospitably entertained. This province was at the Cape de la Cruz, the nearest point on the coast to the neighbouring Island of Jamaica. Here they found a canoe, and one of their men, by name Pedro de Ordas, undertook the dangerous task of carrying a message across to the Governor Esquibel. The distance of twenty leagues was safely accomplished by the brave mariner in his frail bark, and as soon as the message was delivered a caravel was despatched by the governor to the assistance of the unfortunate discoverer and his com panions.

FELLOW-VOYAGERS OF AMERICUS.

It seems to have been the fate of Ojeda to be placed in mortifying positions with respect to his enemies. This very Esquibel, who now received him, with the greatest kindness, into his own house, he had, with foolish bravado, threatened to decapitate, when leaving San Domingo, in all the flush and glory of commanding a new expedition. He was no longer in a position even to assert the rights with which he conceived that Esquibel had interfered, and his warm heart was deeply touched by the generous conduct of his adversary. He remained several days with Esquibel, and when he set sail once more for San Domingo, parted from him in the best friendship.

News of the Bachelor Enciso.

On the arrival of Ojeda at this island the first enquiry that he made was for the Bachelor Enciso. He learned that he had sailed long before with supplies for the colony, but that no tidings had been heard from him. Anxious for the safety of his colony, and fearing that his partner had perished in the same storm in which he himself had been wrecked, he attempted to organize a new armament. But the prestige of success which had hitherto attended him was wanting. His disasters were well known, and in every one's mouth, and though when figuring as the commander of a new fleet, when his previous exploits were the popular theme, he found no lack of friends or followers, yet then all looked coldly upon him, and bankrupt in hope and fortune, his schemes, once so highly extolled, were pronounced wild and visionary. He was unsuccessful in all his endeavours, and never again left the Island of Hispaniola.

Last days of Ojeda.

It is sad to contemplate the ruin of a man possessed of so many gallant and noble qualities as those which distinguished Ojeda. He appears to have lingered some time at San Domingo, his health broken by hardship, and his proud spirit by poverty and neglect. Las Casas gives an affecting picture of his last moments. He died in such extreme want that he did not leave money sufficient to pay for his funeral expenses, and so deep was his humility, that he begged that he might be buried beneath the gateway of the monastery of San Francisco, as an expiation of his former pride, "in order that all who entered might tread upon his grave."

"Never," says Charlevoix, speaking of Ojeda, "was a man more suited for a coup de main, or to achieve and suffer great things under the direction of another; no one had a heart more lofty, or an ambition more aspiring; no one ever took less heed of fortune, or showed greater firmness of soul, or found more resources in his own courage; but no one was less calculated to be commander-in-chief of a great enterprise. Good management and good fortune forever failed him."

VI.

DOCUMENTS RELATING TO AMERICUS VESPUCIUS:

PRESENTED IN THE COLLECTION OF NAVARRÉTE.

DOCUMENTS OF NAVARRÉTE.

THE industry and research of Don Martin Fernandez de Navarréte have rescued from the Spanish archives of Simancas and Seville many notices and documents relating to Americus, which, at first, it seemed desirable to translate for this work. A subsequent consideration of them, and the large space they would necessarily occupy, if given *in extenso*, has led to the substitution of an abstract of their contents. They are arranged by that author in fifteen sections.

Numbers I. and II., dated respectively on the 10th and 15th of July, 1494, consist of a royal decree and letter respecting certain payments and proceedings of Juan Berardi, the agent in preparing the expeditions of Columbus.

Number III., dated April 11th, 1505, contains a royal decree, addressed to Alonzo de Morales, the treasurer of the queen, commanding him to pay Americus the sum of 12,000 maravedis.

Number IV., dated April 24th, 1505, is a royal letter of naturalization, in favour of Americus, for the kingdoms of Castile and Leon.

DOCUMENTS OF NAVARRÊTE.

Number V., dated August 23d, 1506, is a letter from the King Philip to the officers of the Board of Trade at Seville, inquiring what was necessary or important to facilitate the quick despatch of the fleet destined for the Spice Islands.

Number VI. is a certificate of the keeper of the archives of the Indies, at Seville, given to Señor Navarrête, of various notices relative to Americus, which are to be found in certain accounts there preserved. These consist of various accounts rendered by him, and of his receipts for money paid.

Number VII., dated March 22d, 1508, contains a royal decree, granting to Americus the salary of 50,000 maravedis, as chief pilot of the kingdom.

Number VIII. is another decree of the same date, making an increase of 25,000 maravedis to his salary.

Number IX. contains a royal declaration, setting forth at great length the duties and responsibilities of the new office of chief pilot, which is addressed to Americus in the name of the Queen Joanna.

Number X. is a continuation of the accounts which were commenced in number VI., and extending to the date of the death of Americus in 1512. This number contains, among other notices, one of a payment of 10,937 maravedis to the canon Manuel Catano, of Seville, as the executor of the will of Americus, that amount being the balance due of his salary at the time of his death.

Number XI. is a royal decree, granting a pension for life, of 10,000 maravedis per annum, to the widow of Americus, Maria Cerozo. This is dated May 22d, 1512.

DOCUMENTS OF NAVARRÉTE.

Number XII. contains the royal appointment of Juan Vespucci to the office of pilot, with a salary of 20,000 maravedis per annum.

Number XIII. contains a letter from the king to the Bishop Fonseca, requesting that he would inquire into the fitness of Andres de San Martin to succeed Americus in the office of chief pilot.

Number XIV. contains another decree respecting the pension of the widow of Americus, fixing it as a charge upon the salary of the chief pilot; the office at that time being held by Sebastian Cabot, who had succeeded Juan Diaz de Solis, the successor of Americus.

M. de Humboldt remarks on the letter of Santaren.

Number XV. is a long letter from the Viscount of Santaren, respecting the voyages of Americus made in the service of Portugal. This letter, dated the 15th of July, 1826, is in answer to one addressed to Señhor de Santaren, by Navarrēte, and contains some remarkable statements respecting the absence of any documentary evidence of the two last voyages of Americus. The writer was at the time Chief Master of the Archives of Portugal, and caused, as he says, diligent inquiry to be made for any documents relating to Americus in the Torre do Tombo, the receptacle of an immense quantity of manuscripts and accounts relative to the Indies, from the date of the discovery. In relation to this fact, the learned Humboldt remarks: "It is very strange, that notwithstanding the researches en-

DOCUMENTS OF NAVARRETE.

tered into by the Viscount de Santaren, at that time Chief Keeper of the Archives for the Kingdom of Portugal, and since then minister of foreign affairs, the name of Vespucius was not once met with in the documents of the Torre do Tombo." This omission is the more remarkable, as the King Emanuel, by whose command Vespucius performed his two expeditions in 1501 and 1503, took particular pains to preserve in remembrance the events of his reign. "How can it be explained," says the Viscount de Santaren, in his letter of 25th of July, 1826, "that this monarch, who often went in person to attend to the registration of documents drawn from the library of Alphonso V., forgot to record the books and diary which Vespucius pretends to have sent to him? How can it be conceived that the learned keeper of the archives, Damian de Goes, who employed so much time in matters relating to voyages and maritime discoveries, who communicated constantly with Ramusio, and who travelled himself over Italy, knew nothing of expeditions, made at a period only forty-five years before his own time?" "These objections," proceeds Humboldt, "have doubtless much weight, but negative evidence, such as the want of documents, cannot decide definitely the question as to the authenticity of the Portuguese voyages of Americus. He says himself, in his relation of his third voyage, that the king, much rejoiced at his arrival, made him warm proposals to start with a eet of three ships for the discovery of new lands.

He was not, from the commencement of the voyage, the commander of the expedition, but only a person whose nautical skill might be available, skill which was appreciated too late in Spain, in 1505. I can prove besides, by a passage of Peter Martyr, who was intimately connected with the nephew of Americus, that he was protected and in the pay of the Portuguese government. *Americus Vespucius Florentinum auspiciis et stipendio Portugalensium ultra lineam æquinoctialem adnavigavit.* His second Decade, which contains this striking passage, was written two years after the death of Americus, namely, in 1514."

DOCUMENTS OF NAVARRÉTE.

M. de Humboldt instances other proofs in favour of his position, among them the official evidence of Sebastian Cabot, and other celebrated pilots, relative to the true position of the line of demarcation between Spain and Portugal, which Munoz found in the archives of the Board of Trade at Seville. He goes on to remark, that many other events which produced a lively sensation in Europe at about the same time, left no traces in the public documents of the day, and cites by way of example the triumphant entry of Columbus into Barcelona, and his reception by the Catholic monarchs in a hall magnificently adorned. This is a circumstance well established by many historians of credit, yet no documents exist in the archives of Spain going to prove the fact.

So much space would not have been devoted to this letter, had it not been for the purpose of show-

DOCUMENTS OF NAVARRÉTE.

ing the effect of long-continued prejudice against Americus, and contrasting it with the result of a candid examination. Such an examination was made by M. De Humboldt in relation to these two voyages, and though, in the course of his work, some points of difference exist with the statements of this volume, yet he has evidently considered the subject with a desire to arrive at the truth, and a determination to divest himself, as far as possible, from all previous prejudices.

VII.

LETTER OF M. RANKE TO M. DE HUMBOLDT,

RESPECTING THE CORRESPONDENCE OF AMERICUS WITH SODERINI AND DE' MEDICI.[1]

LETTER OF M. RANKE.

IT seems to me by no means doubtful, that the member of the family of Medici, to whom some of the letters of Vespucius are addressed, is Lorenzo di Pier Francesco de' Medici, who was horn in 1463, and died in 1503. His identity is proved, not only by the arguments adduced by Bandini, but especially by the German work printed in 1505, which you have found in the library at Dresden, and in which the name of Lorenzo di Pier Francesco appears on the first page. This personage belonged to the younger branch of the Medici, which took no part in the power exercised by the elder branch. When, after the decease of Lorenzo the Magnificent, in 1492, Piero de' Medici took the reins of government in Florence, he separated himself from his cousins of the cadet branch, who, however, were as wealthy as the elder branch. A rivalry was the consequence of some differences

[1] Translated from a note to the Histoire de la Géographie du Nouveau Continent of M. de Humboldt.

LETTER OF M. RANKE.

which arose between them, combined with the weakness of the character of the new chief. The opposition of the cadet branch especially manifested itself at the time of the invasion of Charles VIII., when Piero de' Medici allied himself with the King of Naples, whilst his cousins entered into negotiations with France, and received the ambassadors of that power. When the victories and successes of Charles VII. excited great discontent among the people of Florence, the cadet branch of the family, and especially Lorenzo di Pier Francesco, favoured these movements.

Modern history offers numerous examples of these discords among the members of reigning families. The partisans of Pier Francesco adopted the name of Popolani.

The Soderini family.

The family of Soderini had long been reckoned among the adherents of the party of the elder branch of the Medici. Among the Florentine citizens, there was not one who had rendered more signal services to the father and grandfather of Piero de' Medici, than Tomaso Soderini, but Piero de' Medici forgot these services. The children of Tomaso, Paolo Antonio, Francesco, and Piero, found themselves neglected and treated with disdain. On this account they soon made common cause with the younger branch of the Medici, were involved in the revolution of the 9th of November, 1494, which expelled the elder branch, and took an active part in the republican régime, which was the result of these popular movements. It is true

LETTER OF M. RANKE.

that afterwards there were some slight differences between the Soderini and the Popolani, the younger branch of the Medici. It is certain that Lorenzo di Pier Francesco did not see with pleasure, in 1502, the nomination of Piero Soderini, son of Tomaso, as Gonfaloniēre of Florence; but, on the whole, the Soderini and the Medici of the cadet branch were united in their political interests.

Political connections of the Vespucci family.

Moreover, it can be proved that the Vespucci belonged to the republican party of Florence. Guido Antonio Vespucci, of whom Bandini speaks, was intimately connected with the movements of this party. He sat, immediately after the expulsion of Piero de' Medici, in 1494, among the twenty *accopiatori* of the first magistrate, conjointly with Lorenzo di Pier Francesco. He was afterwards Gonfaloniēre even, or supreme chief. The political connection of the Vespucci with the younger branch of the Medici, is further confirmed by a letter that Piero Vespucci wrote, in 1494, from Pistoia to Lorenzo de' Medici. This Lorenzo is very probably Lorenzo di Pier Francesco, the same to whom Americus addressed some of his letters during a long absence from Italy.

Nothing can be more natural than this connection of the navigator with the republican party in Florence. Even Francesco Lotti, whom Americus mentions in the relation of his second voyage, and by whom he sent to Lorenzo di Pier Francesco a chart of the world, was, in 1529, member of an administration entirely inimical to the Medici of the

LETTER OF M. RANKE.

elder branch. There was nothing singular in the title of *Magnifico*, given occasionally by Americus to Lorenzo di Pier Francesco. One might thus gratify the cadet branch, on account of its importance in the State, and because it had always, and by general consent, been accorded to the elder branch. Lorenzo di Pier Francesco died in 1503, but if we examine with care the end of the letter which Americus addressed to him, giving an account of his third expedition, we find nothing which would lead to the supposition, that this letter was written subsequent to the fourth expedition, that which terminated in June, 1504. I think that you have perfectly solved this chronological difficulty, which puzzled Bandini.

VIII.

THE VESPUCCI FAMILY.

THE VESPUCCI FAMILY.

The Genealogical Tree accompanying this portion of the work was engraved from a facsimile of that contained in the Reale Deputazione Sopra il Regolamento della Nobilita di Toscana. Many of these records of families are preserved in this establishment, some of them beautifully embellished with miniatures, in many cases the only preserved likenesses of the persons they represent. An account of the present members of the Vespucci family is extracted from "The Artist, Merchant and Statesman." The letters in which it appears were not originally written for publication, and some alterations and omissions have been made.

Florence, February —, 1845.

DEAR ——,

When I see you again, I shall have a long story to tell you of the descendants of Americus Vespucius. I will give you a part of it now.

It had always been a matter of wonder to me, that of all the Americans who had visited Florence, and written about its great men, no one should have said anything about the Discoverer's descend-

THE VESPUCCI FAMILY.

ants. Indeed, so entirely have we been cut off from all information on the subject, I must confess it was with the greatest astonishment I heard the other day, that there is one son and several daughters, lineal descendants of Vespucius, now living at Florence, in poverty, unnoticed and unknown.

I was making some inquiries at a *rēunion* of literary men, a few evenings ago, about the Vespucci family, and a gentleman who knows them well promised to introduce me to them the following day. He was a connexion of the family of Carlo Botta, the author of the History of our War of Independence. There is a man, too, of whom I shall say something at another time.

The next day this gentleman called round at the appointed hour, and we walked to the house together. "Is it not strange," said he, as we left the hotel, "that the descendants of the man who discovered your Continent, and who lived in the palaces of Princes and Kings, should now be obliged to become servants to get their daily bread. The sisters (with the exception of Ellena, who is living in America) are dependent on their daily earnings for their daily bread, and the brother, a well educated, noble young fellow, is employed by the Grand Duke's government in the office of finances, on a salary of $60 a year! They have all come together this morning, from the different scenes of their occupations, to meet the first American who has ever sought their acquaintance. What a strange meeting! A traveller from the distant con

THE VESPUCCI FAMILY.

tinent Vespucius discovered, coming, more than three centuries after his death, to his birth-place, to search out his descendants, who are living helpless, and dependent, on the very spot where their ancestor was a companion of princes, and lived on his own paternal estate!" We talked on, and we walked on, till we reached the house where the family had assembled. It was the house of a friend, perhaps of a connexion of the family.

Here we found them gathered. Two sisters and a brother, the young Cavaliere Amerigo Vespucci, with his youthful wife. Two sisters were absent —one beloved, who is teaching her own beautiful tongue in Paris, independent while her strength lasts—another in America, where, by her dissolute life and barefaced deceptions, she has blasted the prospects of her family, perhaps for ever! I have sometimes known the luxury of feeling the warm grasp of a hand shrivelled with hunger, as I entered the damp cellar of a worn-out, cast-aside English operative, to leave a mite, and speak a word of consolation, but I have never been where my presence seemed to excite so much gratitude. I had the evening before expressed a hope, that in spite of the bold fraud practised upon our government by an unworthy descendant of the Discoverer, some act of recognition of her innocent sisters might yet be passed by Congress, and they all still find a home for themselves, and their children, in the New World. These words had been borne to them, and they were the first gleam of hope that

THE VESPUCCI FAMILY.

had shot across their path for many years. Now when I entered they flocked around me and pressed my hand in silent gratitude, and I am not ashamed to say that we wept together. Before us hung a portrait of their ancestor, painted by Bronzino from life, which they had always preserved, and refused to part with at any price, even when they knew the pangs of extreme poverty. I felt strange emotions when I looked on that picture. The face of the bold Navigator was turned away from earth to the stars above him, and I could not but think he saw a New World there, and I blessed God that he did not behold the dark vale of misfortune his own descendants were to travel long after he was dead.

We sat down and talked about Vespucius, his fate and his fame.

" We hoped," they said to me, " that a frank and honourable appeal to the sympathies of your generous nation would have been responded to, with magnanimity. We did not feel that we had any *claim* to your bounty; we knew that all the world give Columbus the glory of the discovery of America. They say it is more than enough that Vespucius give his name to the American Continent. (He had nothing to do with this.) But still we rejoice that the application that was made was rejected. Injustice would have been done to all parties, by a grant, from which we should have received no advantage nor honour; and such strange conduct as our sister was guilty of, deserv-

THE VESPUCCI FAMILY.

ed no better reward. But we hope you will tell the facts to your Government, that no portion of the blame may fall on us. If the day shall ever come, that your Congress shall show any recognition of us, as the descendants of the Discoverer, whatever way they may select of doing it, it will fill us with gratitude. It would, indeed, be an inspiring hope, if we could believe it would ever be realized, that we should one day be able to provide ourselves with a home in the New World, and go and live there, and be buried at last in the soil our father was the first to step on. Do you think we should be kindly received among the Americans, after we have been so badly represented there?"

I could not but feel, when I saw the tears fall from the sisters' cheeks, how deeply, how cruelly they had been injured. Nor could I help breathing to them the hope that when all the facts should be known, to our people and our Congress, something for them would be done. The expression of this hope seemed to flash a gleam of joy and cheerfulness over their countenances; and when I remembered that our people are a generous people, I could not believe this hope would ever be clouded by disappointment.

They brought out a few relics of Vespucius. At last they unrolled their genealogical table, which showed a proud race. Their ancestry can be traced back clearly in one bright line, to the early ages, before Peter the Hermit went over Europe to arouse

THE VESPUCCI FAMILY.

its millions to march to the recovery of the Saviour's Tomb. In that line there were many illustrious men. Warriors, Ambassadors, Naval Heroes and Discoverers, Scholars, Artists, Poets and Magistrates, many of whom had formed alliances with the great and the noble of different countries. They had filled the highest stations in the old Republic of Florence, and left their impress upon their times. They had been the familiar companions of kings and princes, lived in their own palaces and been lords of their own estates. How were they now?

They are greatly attached to the Grand Duke; and they told me he has always shown them great kindness. They are indebted to his generosity for an annual pension, which was decreed by the Signory of Florence to the Discoverer ages ago, and which every successive sovereign has regarded. Such is the veneration still felt for the memory of that wonderful man who has shed so much glory over Tuscany. This pension is necessarily small, for the Grand Duke's revenue is inconsiderable; and a great number of poor and unfortunate individuals look to him for assistance. His aid is never denied, and the kind and delicate manner in which it is bestowed, makes it a thousand times more grateful. But I shall speak of the generous and paternal character of this noble Sovereign by and by.

It was a long visit—we talked till midnight—and when I came away, I could not but feel grateful that a casual, but kind word that fell from my lips the evening before, had secured for me the opportunity of shedding some light upon hearts that had so long been overcast with the deepest gloom.

THE VESPUCCI FAMILY.

A day or two after, I received a call from the learned and courteous Count Græberg de Hemso, Chamberlain and Librarian to the Grand Duke, with an invitation to be present the following evening at a presentation at court. These Drawing Rooms, which are held during Lent, are attended without parade; and I was glad of an opportunity of seeing a Prince who had, by his mild, paternal government, won the love of his own subjects—by his enlightened views of Art, Government, and Literature, the respect of all Europe—and by his kindness and attention to literary men, gained their admiration and esteem.

During the conversation (which I have no hesitation in relating, since he has often expressed the same feelings, and does not conceal them anywhere), he alluded kindly to the interest I had manifested in behalf of the Vespucci family which was the first intimation I had of his knowing what I had said or done. He said "he regretted most deeply the unfortunate circumstances which attended the application made to our Government in favour of the Vespucci," and he asked me if I "thought it would have succeeded if it had been properly made." I could not but express the fullest belief that it would.

"It is really a pity, then," said he, "that the indiscretion of one member of the family should

THE VESPUCCI FAMILY.

have placed it out of the power of your Government, to have done an act of generosity, which would have placed that unfortunate family under such lasting obligation. I regret it deeply, too, for another reason; for I lost so fine an opportunity of being myself placed under an obligation I should have been equally sensible of, to a great and free people, who are advancing more rapidly in the arts and sciences, and in all that constitutes true civilization, than any other nation in the world. You think a kind feeling will still prevail in America towards the Vespucci when the facts are known; and I must say I know of no act of a foreign Government, that could afford me so much satisfaction, as that your Congress should publicly recognize the claim of the descendants of our Great Tuscan to your kind remembrance."

The Grand Duke courteously told me, that although it did not become him to interfere in the matter, nor to do anything in his public capacity, "particularly," said he, "as no interchange of diplomatic courtesies exists between my Court and the President, which I regret, yet, if you can suggest any manner in which I can contribute to the consummation of your own views, it will afford me unmingled pleasure to do so." He had the kindness also to say, that at any time it would give him much satisfaction to receive any communication from me on the subject, or a visit from me at the Palace.

The Grand Duke has now gone down to the Maremma. Knowing it was my intention to leave

Tuscany soon, he obligingly sent me an invitation to visit him there, when he would have leisure to confer with me on the subject.

THE VESPUCCI FAMILY.

Believing this chit-chat about the Discoverer and the descendants of his family may interest you, I will tell you the rest as soon as the rest comes.

But now I am tired, and so are you.

Your true, — &c., &c.

Florence, ——, 1845.

DEAR ——,

Since my letter about the Vespucci Family, I have often met them, and they have won my heart completely. The sisters are highly esteemed for their purity, and beloved for their kind and amiable qualities. They are exceedingly intelligent and clever, and I find everybody likes them. The young Cavalier Amerigo is a heroic fellow, who works for his bread, and says some good luck will turn up for them all, one day or another. He, and indeed all of them, are anxious to come and live in this country. "Do you think," said the brother to me, this morning, "that I could get my living in America? I think I could learn to cut down your big trees, and build a log cabin."

A few mornings ago, I received a box, with a note. You may judge of my surprise, when I opened the letter, and found it contained a request, signed by the family, that, as I was the only American who had ever sought them out, it was the first

THE VESPUCCI FAMILY.

time they had ever had an opportunity of sending to America the portrait of their ancestor, and they begged I would accept the picture, as a token of their regard for myself and for the American People. I opened the box, and saw it contained the beautiful portrait of Vespucius, painted by Bronzino, his friend, during his life-time. What to do with the picture, required very little time for me to decide. I certainly would not accept such a gift for *myself*, for I could never make any proper return for so valuable a relic. Nor, if I could, would I rob the family of almost the last fragment of the Discoverer's wealth or treasures still left them. I sent it back, and went to them to make an explanation. They all seemed wounded that I had not accepted the picture, and they besought me to comply with their request; but I did not feel it would be right to do so.

The next day the portrait came back again, leaded and sealed by the officer of Customs, the exportation permission given, and the duty paid. Young Amerigo came in soon after, and begged me not to deny their request. "We would not sell it," said he, "but we wish to have it go to the New World, and you may do what you please with it there."

I took it on these conditions, and I shall carry it with me to Washington, to see if the Government will not purchase it for the Capitol. To us it will be invaluable. It is the best, and almost the only undoubted portrait of Vespucius, in the world. It has always been in the possession of the family, the letters of the family assure me, and I am told by many of the Florentines, it is not only authentic beyond a doubt, but one of the best portraits made during that early period. Powers was delighted when he saw it, and his first exclamation was—"Our government must have it for the Capitol, at any price." He thus speaks of it in a note, last evening. * * "Your picture of Americus Vespucius ought to belong to our government, and be placed in the Capitol. I think it is the original, from which the best engravings of the great man have all been taken. There are no artists of our day who paint such pictures. There are some, perhaps, who paint as well, but not in that style,—and for me, that would be proof enough of its authenticity, if there were wanting others of the most satisfactory kind. I have not seen young Americus," &c.[1]

THE VESPUCCI FAMILY.

I shall give Congress an opportunity of purchasing this invaluable portrait, the only one they will ever be able to get, and it will then be in my power to show the family that the American Congress are not unmindful of the children of the man who discovered the continent. Some fortunate accident may yet give us the portrait of Columbus in Spain; and then we shall have two works of art, simple, it is true, but worth more to our nation than any others in Europe. I do not know what our Gov-

[1] This note of Powers and other important proofs are deposited with the Librarian of Congress.

THE VESPUCCI FAMILY

ernment may ever be inclined to do for the Vespucci family. I hope some suitable recognition of them will be had. Some small tract of land, at least, it would not be improper to give them from the public domain; and it would be an act which would win the gratitude of the family for ever, and the admiration of all Europe. You may judge of the feelings of the Grand Duke by the following Letter I had the honour to receive a day or two ago from his Intimate Secretary, who wrote it at the dictation (I am informed) of the Sovereign himself. I give it to you literally.

HONOURABLE SIGNORE:

His Imperial and Royal Highness, the most Serene Arch Duke of Austria, Grand Duke of Tuscany, my August Sovereign, to whom, you, Honourable Signore, have expressed a belief, that the generous and powerful American Nation would be disposed to recognize with favour, by some act of liberality, the last children of Americus Vespucius; has charged me to assure you, in his Royal Name, that it would prove infinitely grateful to him and his Government, if ever there should be made so solemn a demonstration of gratitude and of munificence.

The name of that great man, venerated from one sea to the other, gathers in itself too grand a part of the glories of Tuscany, to make it possible that the family which has descended from him should ever be forgotten by us. They have long enjoyed beneficence and honours; and the young Amerigo, son of Cavalier Captain Cesare Vespucci, is now an *employé* in a Royal Department. He is the last offspring of the family of that illustrious Italian, who brought to the light of civilization that vast land which bears his name, and which is now advancing the proud mother of many noble and generous children.

THE VESPUCCI FAMILY.

I have the honour to subscribe myself, with sentiments of distinguished consideration, your most devoted and obedient servant,

CAVALIERE CARLO FELICI,

Intimate Secretary of the Cabinet of H. I. and R. H., the Grand Duke of Tuscany.

Sig'r C. Edwards Lester,
Consul of the United States of America at Genoa.

Florence, April 8, 1845.

This noble letter was attended by a permission from the Grand Duke to make any use of it I might judge would conduce to the interests of the Vespucci family. Such is the spirit of this Prince, who is, indeed, worthy of holding sway over the city where Lorenzo de' Medici lived to honour all that was noble in man's heart, or lofty in genius.

Your true—

This is not a suitable place to enter into any discussion of the propriety of granting the request contained in the following petition. It is now before the American Congress, where we hope it will

THE VESPUCCI FAMILY.

receive the attention it merits. But it is impossible to suppress a feeling of regret, that the injudicious conduct of any member of the family of the Navigator should have prejudiced the interests of all bearing the name of Vespucci. The petition will speak for itself. Regarded, as it must be, as evidence of the desire of the family to live in a land bearing the name of their ancestor, it is impossible to avoid expressing a hope that their moderate requests may be granted. The letter, which follows the petition, will explain the transmission of the portrait of Bronzino to this country. Both are translated from the original Italian.

TO THE GENEROUS AMERICAN CONGRESS.

Only one family exists which is in direct descent from that of the Florentine navigator, Americus Vespucius. It consists of the young Amerigo, with his wife and four sisters, Elena, Theresa, Eliza, and Ameriga, as appears by the genealogical tree, drawn during the lifetime of their father, the Captain Cesare Vespucci. Elena, possessing a disposition somewhat indocile and unmanageable, absented herself from her father's house and proceeded to London. Thence she crossed the ocean, and landed upon the shores of Brazil, at Rio Janeiro. From that city she proceeded to Washington, the capital of the United States. She presented certain petitions to the governments of both countries, using, and perhaps abusing, the glorious name of her ancestor. Her family are ignorant both of the tenor and of the result of these applications.

THE VESPUCCI FAMILY.

Amerigo and his sisters have resolved to make the following requests:

First. That the American Congress would grant to them and their descendants the right of citizenship.

Second. That the generous American people would give them a sufficient quantity of land, to enable them, by their own exertions, to maintain thereon, with respectability, the name of their Ancestor, of which they are so proud.

The remarkable political events which have of late years convulsed Europe, and destroyed the estates of so many ancient families, have also wrecked the fortunes of the Vespucci race. They are at present reduced to poverty, though they yet hope for better fortune, through the generosity of the great American people.

Signed, AMERIGO VESPUCCI.
ELIZA VESPUCCI.
TERESA VESPUCCI.

Letter to C. Edwards Lester, from Amerigo Vespucci.

I cannot allow you to leave Italy without manifesting the sentiments of profound gratitude which I entertain towards you. The courteous and kind manner in which you have treated us—almost as fellow-countrymen—will never leave my memory or my heart. Your last and greatest act of good-

THE VESPUCCI FAMILY.

ness, is the task you have been pleased to undertake for us, of conveying to the American Congress, the sentiments of my family, depressed by so many misfortunes and the commotions of late years. While I beg you to continue to give us your assistance in making known to Congress our desires and hopes, will you have the kindness to accept an ancient portrait of our glorious ancestor, taken from life, and which is the only memorial of him which remains to my unfortunate family? I trust you will look with pleasure upon the features of the man who gave his name to the vast and beautiful portion of the globe to which you have the good fortune to belong.

The Vespucci family wish you a pleasant voyage, and would express to you their profound gratitude and consideration.

Your humble servant,

AMERIGO VESPUCCI.

Florence, 18*th March*, 1845.

INDEX.

INDEX.

A.

B.

C.

D.

E.

F.

G.

H.

I.

J.

K.

L.

M.

N.

O.

P.

---

* The work contains, including the engravings, 462 p.p.

NOTE

TO

THE FOURTH EDITION.

THIS work, which has now passed to a Fourth edition, has been recently revised by Mr. LESTER, and it goes out with new claims to the confidence of the Public. The circumstances under which it first appeared, prevented it for some time from getting into general circulation. Nothing else could even temporarily have kept the book from wide popularity—for it contained within itself the most essential elements of success.

In "The Life and Voyages of Americus Vespucius," are given to us, for the first time in the English Language, the original writings of Vespucius himself. Here a signal service was rendered to History, and to American Literature. It seems hardly credible that those Journals of the Great Navigator should have so long escaped the notice of American Scholars. No little attention had been bestowed upon Columbus, and various biographies and records of that extraordinary man had appeared in England and America. One of our most popular authors, now owes much of his fame, to having given his readers so glowing and romantic an account of "The Voyages of Columbus," as we all acknowledge Mr. Irving's book to be. But it contained little that learned readers did not know before. It was but a graceful and fortunate effort, to familiarize the American mind, with what the pioneer pen of Navarrete—the great Spanish Historian—had, after indefatigable labor, already published to all Europe.

Mr. Lester's long residence in Italy, and the special favor with which he was treated by the Grand Duke of Tuscany, gave him extraordinary facilities for entering this new field of study and investigation. He collected nearly everything of value that is now supposed to exist, published or unpublished, on the subject of Americus Vespucius. No writer of any celebrity had preceded him in this new track; he had to make his investigations for himself; and while it has been acknowledged by the scholars, the journals, and the institutions of Europe, that the "Life and Voyages of Vespucius" was a valuable contribution to the historic knowledge of the world, the spirit of the work has been applauded for its impartiality, especially so far as Columbus is concerned. No attempt was made in this work, to set aside any claims of the great Genoese to the gratitude and admiration of mankind. But the attempt was made, and with acknowledged success, of rescuing the name of Vespucius from the odium which had been cast upon it, by the unjust accusations of his enemies. These accusations had remained unanswered for more than three centuries, when Mr. Lester began this work. He has demonstrated that Americus Vespucius, so far from having given his name to the continent, had no agency whatever in naming it; and that the Western World was not known by the title of America, until after Vespucius was dead.

To show how high an estimate has been placed on this work, the publisher is allowed to introduce a letter which has never before appeared, written under the instructions of the Grand Duke of Tuscany, by the learned Count Graberg de Hemso, who, for nearly forty years, occupied the honorable post of Grand Chamberlain and Chief Librarian to the Grand Duke of Tuscany. The Count had early entered with earnestness and enthusiasm into Mr. Lester's views on the subject of the preparation of this work, and had given him all the assistance that lay in his power. The original of this letter is in the possession of the publisher.

Florence, March 15*th*, 1847.

SIR:—With feelings of real pleasure I comply with the commands of his Imperial and Royal Highness the Archduke, Grand Duke, my August Master, in acknowledging the receipt of your learned and highly interesting "Life and Voyages of Americus Vespucius," and in assuring you that this valuable donation has been received with great pleasure, not only in consideration of the more than common talent and erudition displayed in the performance, but also of the very courteous manner in which you speak, particularly of His Highness, and in general of Italy and the Italians, who must, of course, feel alike grateful for the new and brilliant light you have spread over the authentical pedigree and biography of that famous Italian navigator.

The elegant volume, having been kept to this time in the Grand Duke's own Cabinet, has just now, by express order of His I. and R. Highness, been placed conspicuously in his splendid Palatine Library, and I have been commanded to offer you His Highness's warmest thanks for your polite and kind attention.

And having thus fulfilled my Royal Master's behests, and performed an agreeable duty, in communicating them to you, I, at present, add only, that, with the most perfect esteem and respect,

I have the honor to be, Sir,
Your obliged and faithful servant,
CT. JACOB GRABERG OF HEMSO.
Chamberlain and Chief Librarian
to H. I. and R. Highness.

To C. EDWARDS LESTER,
United States Consul, at Genoa.

It is not thought improper also, to introduce into this note, passages from some other sources, indicating the value of this volume, as a contribution to history, and as furnishing to American readers a vast deal more accurate, reliable, and interesting information about Americus Vespucius, than had ever been given before.

Cambridge, May 6th, 1850.

GENTLEMEN:—I have read with much interest "The Life and Voyages of Americus Vespucius," as containing a spirited sketch of the events connected with the early discoveries in America, and especially as presenting a translation of the original letters of Vespucius, and other materials of much historical value drawn from original sources. I look upon it as a work filling an important space in the early history of the New World, as conveying to American readers a mass of curious facts, which could be obtained only from various books difficult to be procured, and in foreign languages. Respectfully and truly yours,

JARED SPARKS.

The following, which is but one of numerous notices of this work in the leading journals of Europe, appeared in the "Espero," the chief literary authority of Genoa:

"We are glad to learn that a translation of this valuable historic work, written by Mr. Lester, who has for some years so ably and acceptably discharged the duties of the American Consulate in this city, is in course of preparation by experienced and accomplished hands. Our readers all know how much Italy has already been indebted to America for the illustration of some of the brightest passages in our history. Mr. Irving's book put us immediately into possession of all the authentic materials that had come to light, up to the period of its publication; and all Italy opened its heart to receive the 'Life and Voyages of Christopher Columbus.'

"The publication of Mr. Lester's 'Vespucius,' has placed us under a new obligation, because, although the work is not so voluminous as Mr. Irving's, it is far more original, and has thrown great light upon a subject that had not attracted among Italian writers the attention which it deserved. It is singular that, with the exception of Bandini, who wrote a small work on the subject, nothing really of much value had been published in Italy on the subject of 'Vespucius.' It was a new and inviting field for historic investigation, and it is a matter of profound astonishment, that our scholars should have allowed the writers of the Western World to get so far ahead of them in this interesting and splendid path of fame.

"During Mr. Lester's visits to Florence, in 1844–5, he was treated with great condescension and regard by His Imperial and Royal Highness, the Grand Duke of Tuscany, to whom Mr. Lester made known his intentions of writing 'The Life and Voyages of Americus Vespucius.' The sovereign became deeply interested in Mr. Lester's labors, and extended to him every facility in his power. The libraries were thrown open to him, and the learned Count Graberg de Hemso, the Grand Duke's librarian, devoted much of his time in assisting Mr. Lester in his investigations. Under such favorable auspices, Mr. Lester pushed his investigations on this subject far beyond any other writer; and it ended some three or four years afterwards, in giving us altogether the completest work on that subject which has ever appeared. He has been justly rewarded for his labors by tokens of respect from the Grand Duke—by being elected a member of the Imperial and Royal Valdarnese Academy, Del Poggio—and from His Holiness, Pius IX., he received a large silver medal as a token of appreciation. We are glad also to learn that our own gracious sovereign has, in the most flattering manner, made known to Mr. Lester his respect and esteem.

"We find occasion, in connection with these facts, to express our admiration for the wisdom which seems to guide the policy of the United States, in choosing for their foreign representatives men of talent and literary abilities. One man like Mr. Lester, holding an official post and using the facilities it gives him for literary and historical investigations, reflects enduring lustre upon the government which appoints him. We believe that Mr. Irving's 'Columbus,' was the result of his connexion with the United States Embassy at the Court of Madrid; while many other American representatives in foreign countries, have distinguished themselves by their contributions to literature.

"Although we have not space to make many extracts from this work, and much less to enter into a broad and minute analysis of its contents, yet the most superficial Italian reader will discover in what respects this work is especially valuable to us.

"1st. The book opens with a clear survey of the commercial state of the world, previous to the discovery of America. A brief but brilliant account is given of Italian manufactories—the advanced state of civilization in 1400—the effects of the conquest of the Eastern Empire—the invention of the compass and the astrolabe—the various expeditions that were sent out on voyages of discovery by the courts of Spain and Portugal, &c. The writer then approaches his immediate subject, the birth of Vespucius, which took place in 1451. He gives the origin of the Vespucci family—the offices of state which its distinguished members held, and then passes on in his rapid narration, with almost the compactness, and with more than the fire of Plutarch.

"2nd. Mr. Lester has succeeded in giving us an accurate but graceful translation of the letters of Americus Vespucius, written to the Gonfaloniere of the Republic of Florence, and the Princes of the House of the Medici. It is the first time they have ever been presented entire in the English language; and it is a curious and not a flattering fact, that even in the Italian language, we did not before possess any pure and entire transcripts of the original letters of Vespucius himself. These were all mixed up with foreign idioms and dialects.

"3d. The summing up of the writings and character of Vespucius, in the eighteenth chapter, is one of the ablest and most philosophical analyses we have for a long time seen. We give it to our readers entire.

"4th. Another item of value in this work, is in the second part, which is made up of collections from a great variety of quarters, which serve to illustrate the subject. Brief, but interesting accounts are given of the origin of many of the expeditions of that time, and the characters and histories of those to whom they were committed; while the book closes with the modern history of the Vespucci family—to whose living members Mr. L. is well known to have shown much kindness—thus completing a noble and enduring work.

"In thus paying this tribute to Mr. Lester, whose genius has illustrated one of our greatest historic names, we cannot withhold our admiration for the impartiality with which he has treated his subject, and the justice and even the magnanimity with which he has steered clear from the temptations that surrounded him on every side, of depreciating in some manner, the claims of Columbus to the discovery of America. Even here in Genoa, the birthplace of that immortal man, this has been a subject of remark; and although our readers are aware that Mr. Lester has achieved reputation by several other works that have been widely circulated in his own country and in Europe, yet he has claims now upon our lasting regard, more especially for the services he has rendered to the cause of Italian history."

EXTRACTS FROM NOTICES OF THE PRESS.

"The subject of this work is sufficient of itself to attract and interest every American. The man who gave name to this great western continent can never be forgotten. The volume before us is not the production of a few short days; it has occupied months of labor and research. Many old manuscripts in Italian, Spanish, and German, bearing on his life and voyages, have been examined; and all the large libraries in this country have been searched for collections relative to the great discoverer. It is written in that flowing and attractive style which characterizes all Mr. Lester's productions, and cannot fail to have an extensive circulation."—*Albany Spectator.*

"Mr. Lester has been engaged for years in gathering materials for this work. His residence and position as a representative of the American Government in Italy, near the birth-place of the great navigator, after whom this continent was named, gave him access to records, and facilities in collecting his data, of the utmost importance to the production of a complete and reliable history."—*Summit Beacon, Ohio.*

"This is a very interesting and instructive volume, especially to Americans, as it relates to the discovery and early history of this continent. The fourteen plates, illustrating various points in the history of the great navigator, add to the value of the work, and still more to its acceptableness to the common reader" —*New York Journal of Commerce.*

"Mr. Lester has made a most agreeable book in his life of this world-renowned navigator, and it is printed and illustrated in such a style as greatly to increase its attractions. The author resided some years in the land which gave birth to Americus, and he had abundant opportunity to obtain valuable material for the work, which he has now perfected, with the assistance of Mr. Andrew Foster of Boston, whose invaluable services are kindly acknowledged in the preface."—*New Haven Palladium.*

"This is a large, well-printed volume, devoted to the life of the great navigator, and to the incidents connected with the discovery of the New World. Mr. Lester's long residence in Italy, and his personal acquaintance with the living members of the Vespucci family, afforded him rare opportunities of obtaining information."—*New York Mirror.*

"In this elegantly printed volume, the compilers have preserved all the information accessible respecting this celebrated voyager. The documents, the history, incidents, and reflections here embodied are worthy of being examined, and the book itself will be a valuable acquisition."—*New York Christian Observer.*

"This is a worthy tribute to one of the great navigators, whose name and history will be for ever connected with the American continent. The work is well worthy of attention as a repository of much that is valuable, bearing on the early history of the New World. The publisher has evidently spared no pains to make the work, in its externals, attractive and worthy of the subject."—*New York Baptist Recorder.*

"The narrative has all the interest of the most exciting romance, with the merit of substantial truth, and is written in Lester's most brilliant style, with copious side and foot notes. This is a truly valuable book."—*Akron Standard, Ohio.*

"A large volume, elegantly bound and illustrated with fine engravings. This work fills up a void of too long duration in American literature, and while its presence will ornament, its absence will leave a library imperfect"—*The Alabamian.*

www.ingramcontent.com/pod-product-compliance
Lightning Source LLC
LaVergne TN
LVHW020938110826
845150LV00004B/901

* 9 7 8 1 4 2 5 5 5 1 6 1 2 *